LM 0341515 5
KU-288-876

# enjoying RACQUET SPORTS

Withdrawn from
Lambeth Libraries

Other titles in the Enjoying series
**ENJOYING GYMNASTICS**
**ENJOYING SOCCER**
**ENJOYING COMBAT SPORTS**

# enjoying RACQUET SPORTS

by the Diagram Group

NEW YORK & LONDON

**Library of Congress Cataloging in Publication Data**

Diagram Group.
Enjoying racquet sports.

Includes index.
1. Racket games.
I. Title.
GV990.D5 1978 796.34 77-14284
ISBN 0-448-22192-6

Copyright © 1978 Diagram Visual Information Ltd.
All rights reserved
Printed in England by Cox & Wyman Ltd., London, Fakenham & Reading

**IN THE UNITED STATES** PADDINGTON PRESS LTD.
Distributed by
GROSSET & DUNLAP

**IN THE UNITED KINGDOM** PADDINGTON PRESS LTD.

**IN CANADA** Distributed by
RANDOM HOUSE OF CANADA LTD.

**IN SOUTHERN AFRICA** Distributed by
ERNEST STANTON (PUBLISHERS) (PTY.) LTD.

**Written by** David Heidenstam
**Copy editor** Maureen Cartwright
**Assistant copy editor** Elizabeth Wilhide
**Art editor** Graham Rosewarne
**Artists** Henrietta Chapman, Stephen Clark, Robert Galvin, Susan Kinsey, Pavel Kostal, Janos Marffy, Kathleen McDougall, Graham Rosewarne
**Art assistant** Brian Hewson
**Research assistant** Kati Boland

**Consultants** David Gray (General Secretary, International Tennis Federation)
C.J. Landrey (Assistant Secretary, Badminton Association of England)
O.A. Cussen (Coaching Secretary, Badminton Association of England)
R.B. Hawkey (Chairman, Rules Committee, International Squash Rackets Federation)
D. Kingsley (Executive Director, US Squash Racquets Association)
Captain A.M. Potter Jr (former squash racquets coach, US Naval Academy)
United States Racquetball Association
Mike Zeitman (Assistant to the President, International Racquetball Association)
J.W. Nobbs (racquet manufacturer)
E.H. de Planche (USAF Athletic Director, RAF Mildenhall, UK)
Murray Geller (President, United States Paddle Tennis Association)
H. Roy Evans (President, International Table Tennis Federation)
Tony Brooks (Secretary-General, International Table Tennis Federation)
Alan Hydes (former English international table tennis player)
American Platform Tennis Association
Howard Hammer (President, American Paddleball Association)
R. Pitcher (National Paddleball Association)

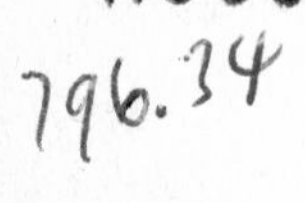
R66047
796.34

## Foreword

Racquet sports — once the pastime of monks and courtiers — now live in the days of fiberglass racquets, sports centers, and glass-walled courts. So they are both very old and very new. They have been played for centuries; yet the youngest sport in this book is under thirty years old. They are familiar to everyone; but only recently have people stopped thinking of them as slightly "snobbish." They are some of the first sports we think of, when we look for social exercise; but only now are they becoming some of the first that young athletes think of, when they look for a professional career.

This book looks at all the popular racquet games — together with their very close relatives, the "paddle" games (played with a solid paddle or "bat"). The skills sections introduce the techniques of play; the rules sections give a complete breakdown of all the playing rules (plus an outline of the rules that apply to tournament events, such as the powers of officials, time allowed for injury, etc). Each game also has a foreword on its character and history, while the description of the court and equipment includes advice on choosing your racquet or paddle and looking after it.

To use this book, begin with the "basics" in the introductory chapter, then turn to the sports that interest you. Read the skills sections especially carefully — every sentence is important. And when you come to play, start gently, and don't get discouraged. If you can, join a local club and get expert help. Remember these games — like all games — are meant to be fun! But also remember that good players make it look so easy only because they worked so hard at getting to be good.

We would like to thank all the players and coaches who have given us the benefit of their experience; and all the governing bodies of these sports, for working so closely with us. But finally, we must make two apologies. For simplicity, the text is written as if players were always right-handed — and always male. So if you are a woman, please forgive us; and if left- handed, please reverse the instructions as necessary.

**Picture Credits**

Tony Duffy – Allsports
Howard Hammer
The Mansell Collection
Eamonn McCabe – Photosport
Metropolitan Line
Arthur Shay
George Sullivan

# Contents

**tennis**
Almost everyone knows what tennis is. But if you had to describe the basic idea of it, you could call it a game in which the opponents face each other with a net between them, and hit a ball back and forth over it with racquets.

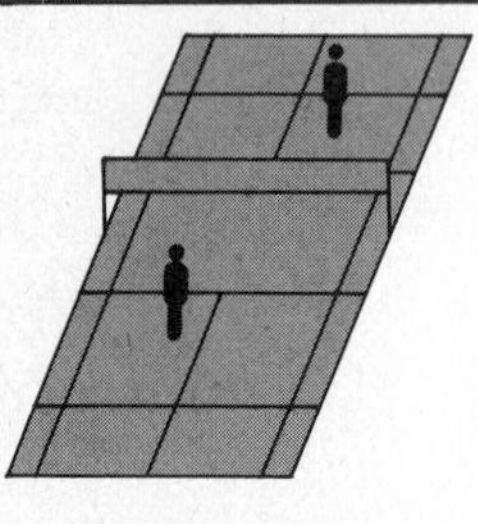

**badminton**
Badminton is like tennis in many ways, but it uses a higher net, and a shuttlecock instead of a ball. Each player tries to stop the shuttlecock touching the ground on his side of the net.

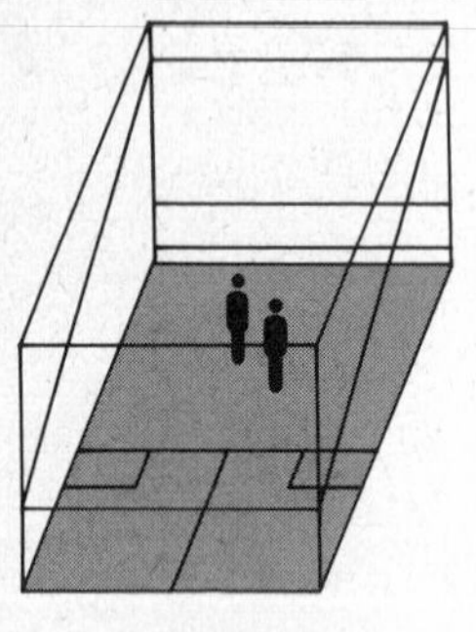

**squash**
Instead of having a net, squash uses a "walled court," in which opponents share the same space, face the same way, and keep hitting the ball back toward one wall. In fact, in squash the court is like a room, and the ball may be bounced off the other walls on its way to the target wall.

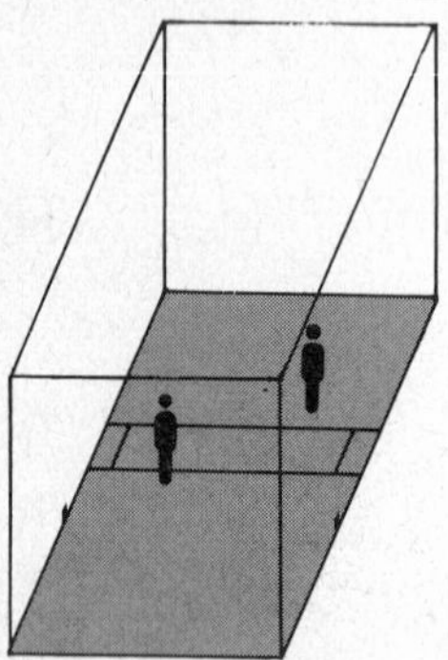

**racquetball**
This game is very like squash, but it uses a short-handled racquet. Also the walled court for racquetball is not always a complete room: some games are played on one-wall or three-wall courts.

**paddle tennis**
This introduces the paddle: a short-handled "bat," with a solid face in place of the stringing used on racquets. The game itself is just like tennis—only on a smaller scale.

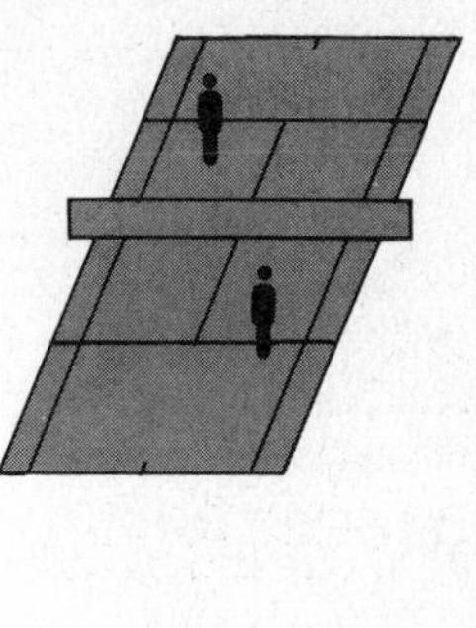

**table tennis**
Using paddles again for the ultimate miniaturization of tennis. Instead of a court 78 feet long, a 9-foot table is used (although the playing space around it has to be fairly large).

**platform tennis**
This paddle game is a kind of cross between net games and walled-court games. The opponents face each other, separated by a net, as in tennis. But they may also hit the ball after it has bounced off the "walls" of taut wire around the court.

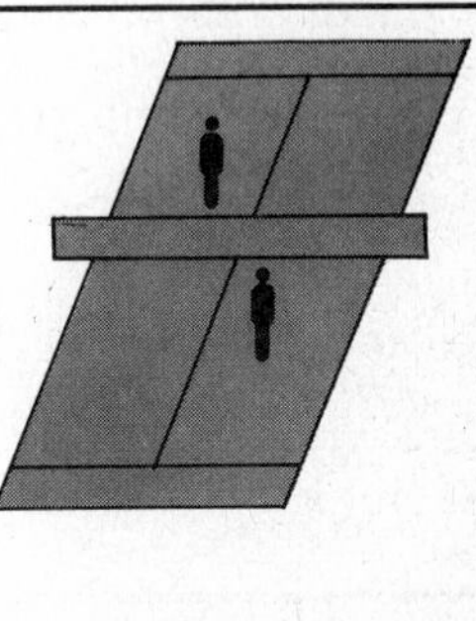

**paddleball**
Here paddles are used in a game of the true walled-court type—although, even more than in racquetball, the courts often have one or three walls, rather than four.

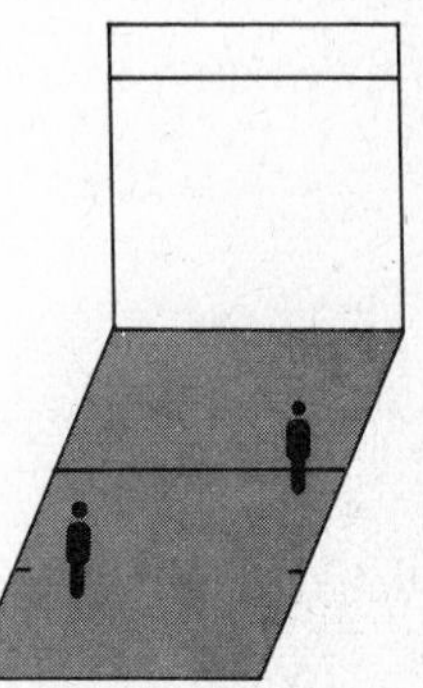

**racquets and paddles**
A true racquet is distinguished by the "stringing" across its face. A paddle (although called a "racquet" or a "bat" in the U.K.) has a solid head, sometimes pierced by holes. Note that the length of the handle is not a crucial difference: a racquetball racquet, for example, has a short handle.

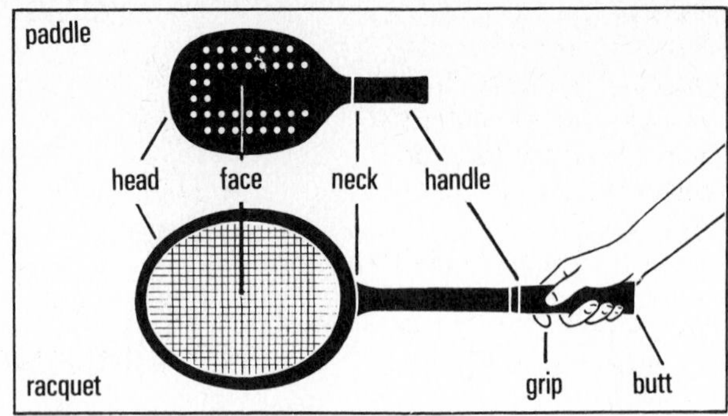


**forehand**
Whether you are right-handed or left-handed, when you hold a racquet or paddle one face of it lines up with the palm of your hand. This is called the "forehand" side, and if you hit the ball with this face of the racquet or paddle, it is called a forehand stroke.

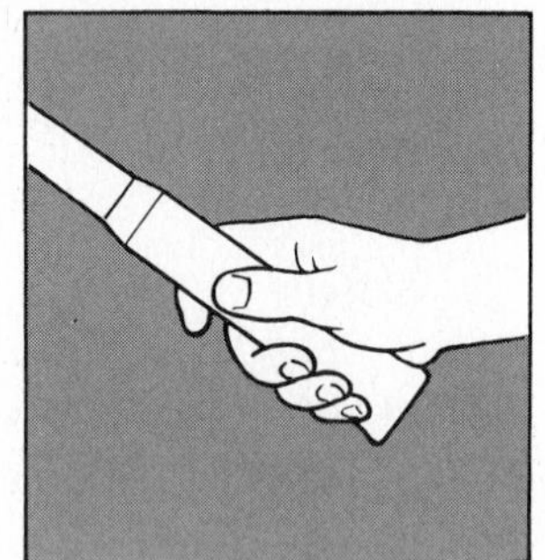

forehand

**backhand**
The other face is on the same side as the back of your hand. This is called the "backhand" side, and if you hit the ball with this face it is called a backhand stroke.

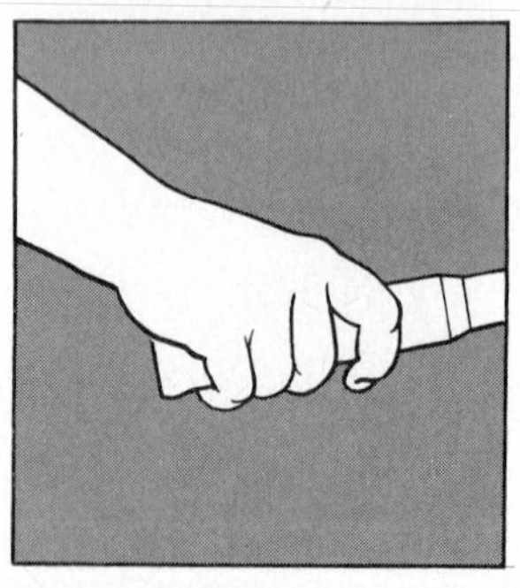

backhand

**forehand and backhand grips**
The grip is not only the part of the handle that you hold, but the way you hold it. Details are given under each sport; but note that usually a different grip has to be used for forehand and backhand strokes. (For the reason for this, see "forehand and backhand angles," p. 16.)

**length of grip**
Another way in which the grip can vary is in length – i.e., how far up the handle the hand is placed. In general, a short grip (**a**) gives more control to the stroke, while a long one (**b**) gives more power and flexibility.

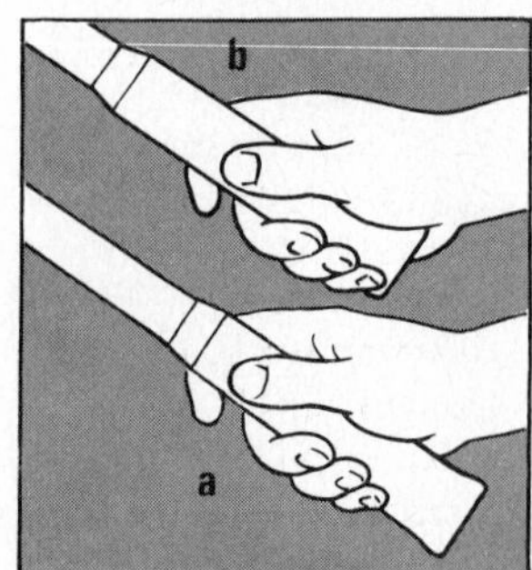

**the stroke**

A stroke is a movement of the racquet or paddle to hit the ball. Any stroke can be divided up into:
a point from which the racquet or paddle starts moving toward the ball – the "start" (**a**);
a point at which it strikes the ball – the "contact" (**b**);
and a point at which it ends up after hitting the ball – the "follow-through" (**c**).
In some strokes the racquet moves only a short distance from start to finish (**d**), in others a much greater distance (**e**).
Before the start of the stroke, there usually has to be a movement away from the ball, to get the racquet or paddle to position (**a**). This is called the "backswing" (**f**), and may also be long or short.

**timing**

Strokes also vary in when they hit the ball. If the player hits the ball before it has bounced on the ground, it is called a "volley" (**a**) (also known as "hitting the ball on the fly").
If he hits it just as it comes off the bounce, it is called a "half volley" (**b**).
If he hits it when it is rising from the bounce, it is called an "early" contact (**c**).
If he hits it when it is at the top of its bounce, it is called a "peak" contact (**d**).
If he hits it when it is falling from the top of its bounce, it is called a "late" contact (**e**).
If he hits it when it is about to bounce a second time, it is called a "very late" contact (**f**).

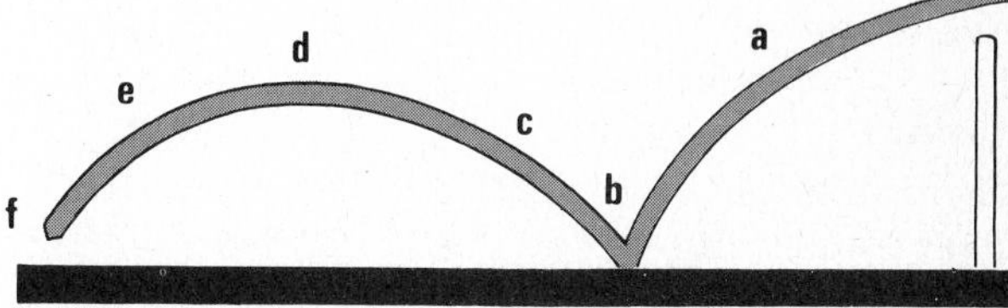


**timing in badminton**

In badminton, a shuttlecock is used instead of a ball, and it must be hit before it touches the ground. So strokes are simply divided into:
those that make contact when the shuttlecock is above net height (**a**);
those that make contact when the shuttlecock is lower than the top of the net (**b**);
and those that make contact when the shuttlecock has almost reached the ground (**c**).

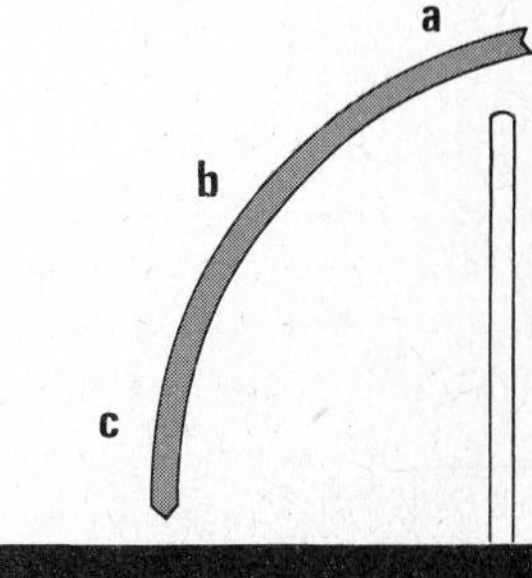

**shots – net games**
In a net game, there are four basic shots:
the drive, which travels parallel with the ground (**a**);
the lob, which goes high in the air (**b**);
the smash, which is hit downward from above head height (**c**);
and the drop shot, which falls close to the net (**d**).

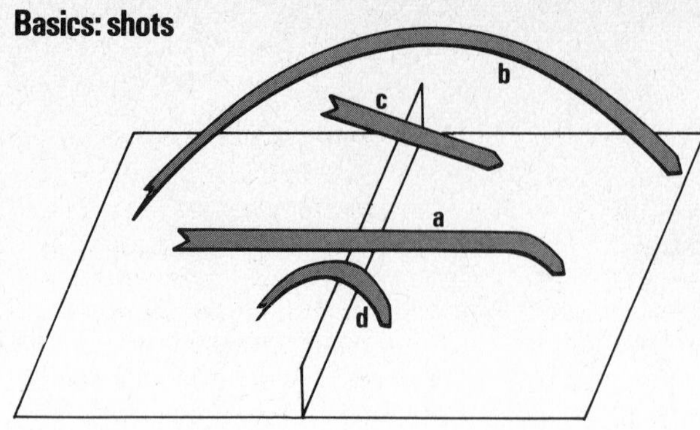


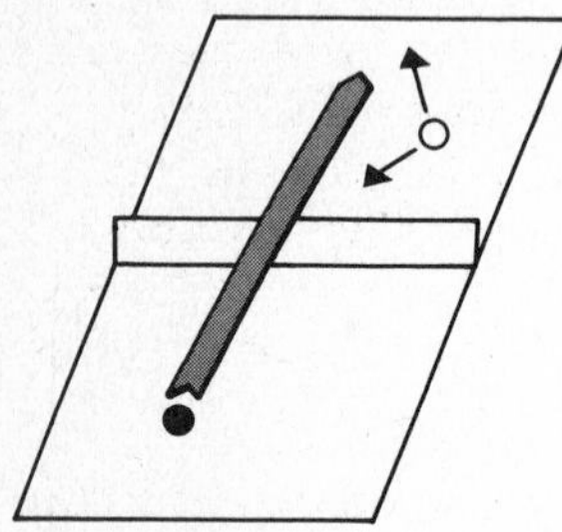

**the drive**
This is the fundamental shot in most games. Traveling low and fast, it forces your opponent to decide whether to come close to the net, to volley it, or to retreat to the base line to play it after it has bounced.

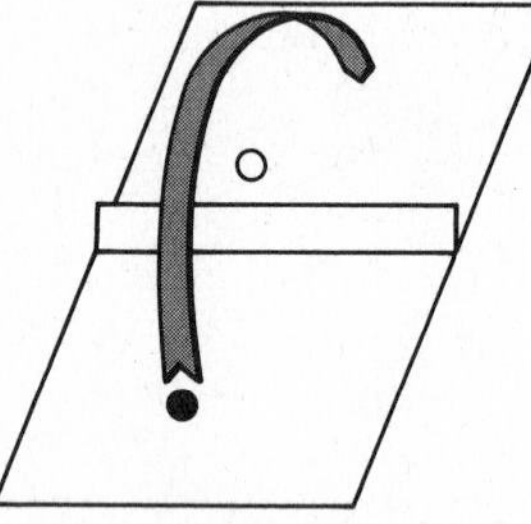

**the lob**
This is usually played so it goes over your opponent's head and bounces near the base line. Sometimes it is a defensive shot, used to gain time while you get back in a good position. At other times it is an attacking shot, played in the hope that your opponent will not get to it quickly enough to make a good return. (In badminton, the lob is called a "clear.")

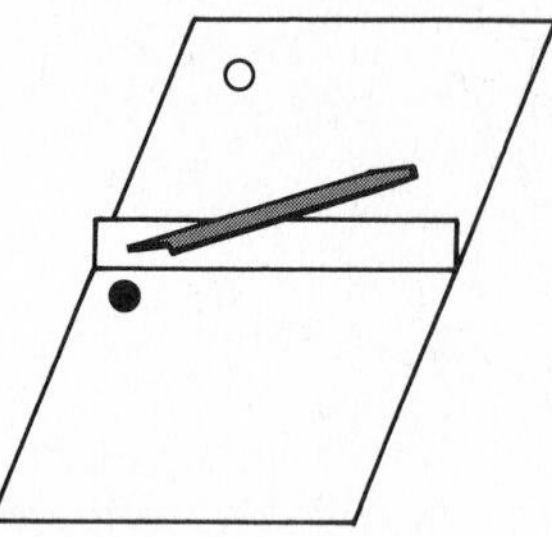

**the smash**
Also called the kill, this is the most aggressive shot of all – sending the ball with full force out of your opponent's reach, so he has no chance of returning it.

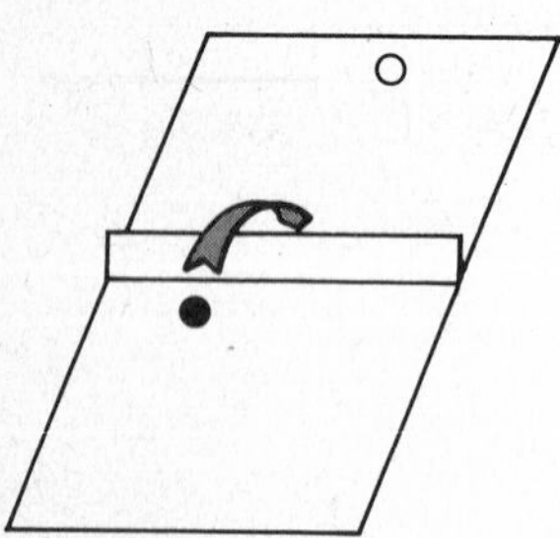

**the drop shot**
This is a delicate shot, used to catch your opponent away from the net. Again, it is meant to give your opponent no chance of a reply – for if he does get to it, he can often volley his return past you out of reach.

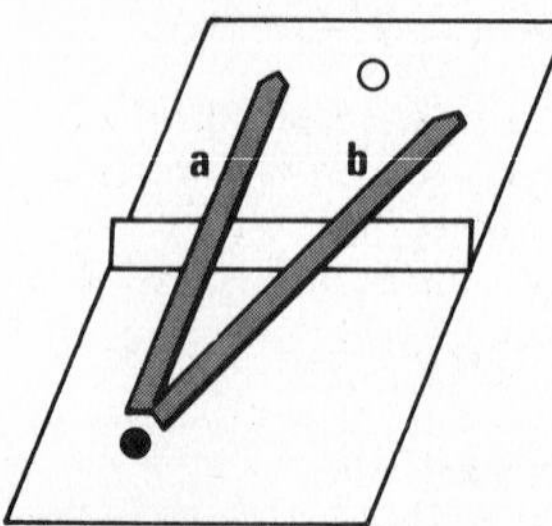


**angle of shot**
Any shot can be played either "down the line" (**a**) or "cross court" (**b**).

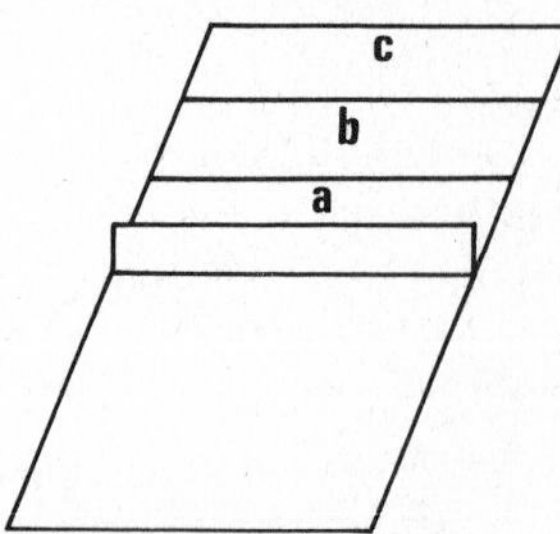


**depth**
Shots also vary in depth – i.e., the part of the court they are hit into; a shot can be hit to bounce in front court (**a**), center court (**b**), or back court (**c**). Shots to center court are easiest to make, but also give fewest problems to your opponent.

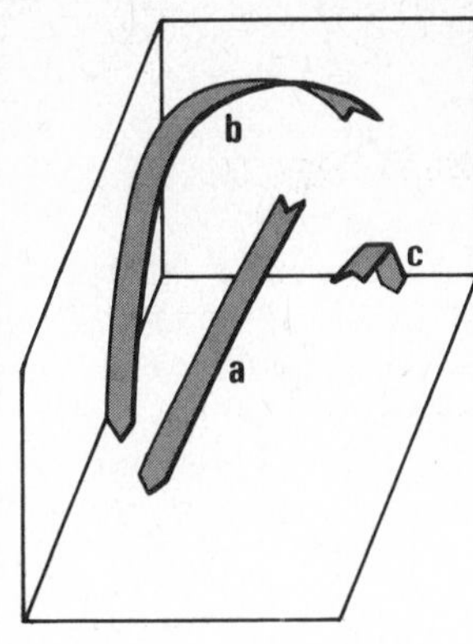


**shots – walled games**
Just as shots in net games can be classed by their path across the net, those in walled games can be classed by their path back from the front wall. They can come back into front court, center court, or back court. And those that travel fairly parallel to the floor can be called drives (**a**); those that arc high in the air, lobs (**b**); and those that "die" off the front wall, kills or drop shots, according to the force they were hit with (**c**).
But by itself this is not very useful, because most walled games are played in four-wall courts, where the ball bounces around from one wall to another before coming to rest. A shot going to the front wall can travel via the back wall and/or one or more side walls – and it can come back the same way to bounce in any part of the court. So the angle of a shot becomes a central issue. In fact the possible paths of a ball around the walls are limited only by how much bounce it has (which varies from one game to another). But it is quite useful to think of the five main types of shot given below.

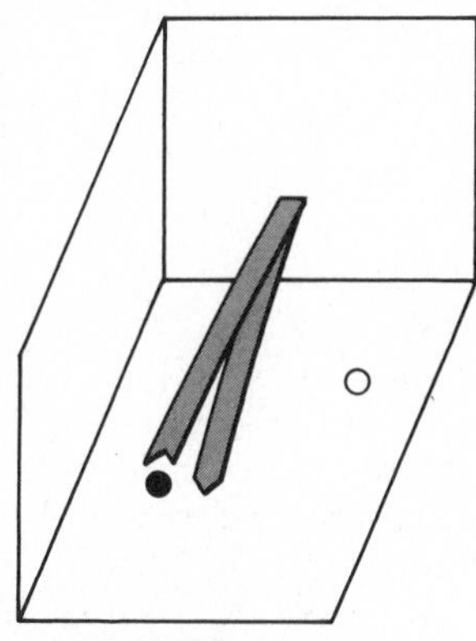

**straight shots**
These go to the front wall and come back along the same line. (A special type is the "alley" shot that skims along close against a side wall.)

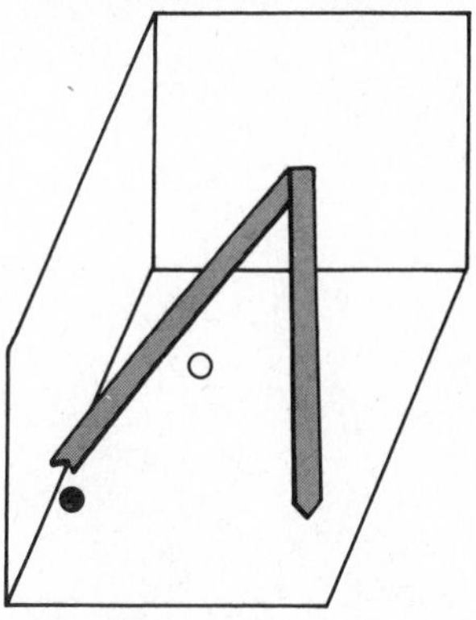

**cross-court shots**
These go to the front wall at an angle, and rebound into the other side of court. Like the straight shots, they include both lobs and drives.

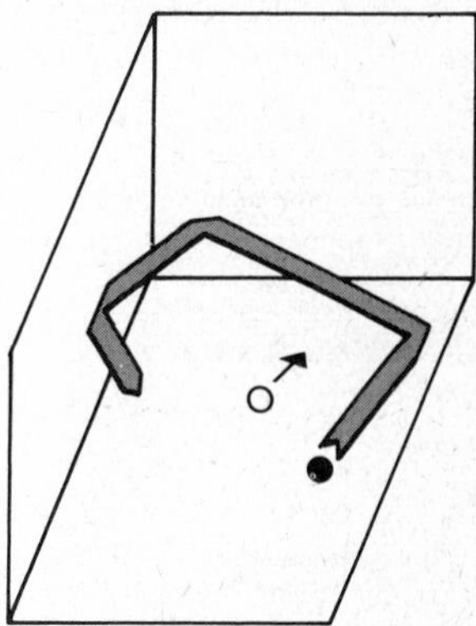

**ricochet shots**
These wrong-foot your opponent by going from one wall to another around the court.

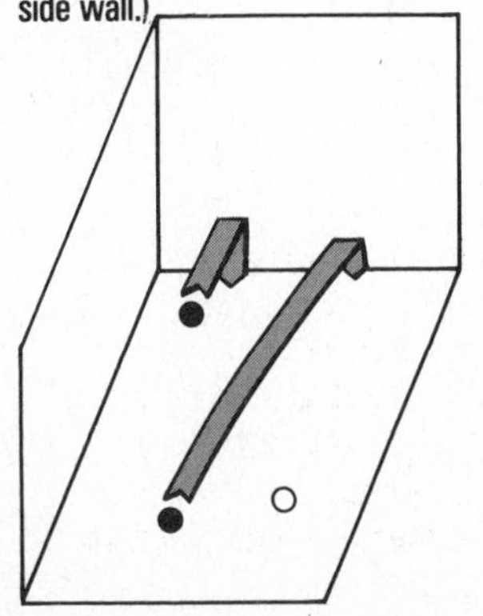

**kills and drop shots** (left)
These are shots that "die" close to the front wall – either because they bounce very low or very weakly against the front wall, or because they are highly angled when they hit it.

**back-wall shots** (right)
These are shots hit onto the back wall in a defensive attempt to get the ball back to the front wall.

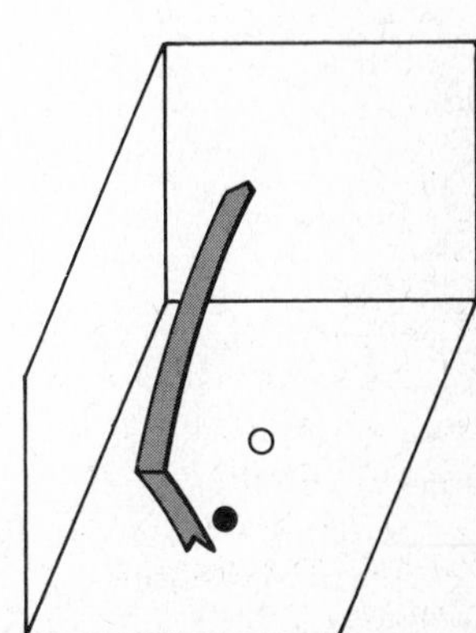

**pace**
The pace of play can change from shot to shot. This is the result of three things: how soon you hit the ball, how hard you hit it, and what type of shot you play. For example, it speeds up the pace if you volley the ball with a hard-hit drive or smash; it slows the pace if you take the ball late in its bounce, and hit a gentle lob.

**power, deception, precision**
Judge all your strokes on these three qualities. Effective power is shown by the speed given to the ball; deceptiveness, by how late in the stroke it is, before your opponent can tell what shot you hope to play; precision, by how near your shot comes to the one you hoped for. You do not always want maximum power; but you usually want maximum deception and precision, and often all three. The trouble is that they do not work together. In general, the more power you have, the less the precision; the more precision, the less the power; the more disguised the start of a stroke, the less the precision in the one finally played. You must choose which is most vital for the shot you want. But all benefit from the extra time given by anticipation, good footwork, and an early backswing.

**angle of face**
Proper control here is vital. Assuming there is no spin on the ball, then:
if the racquet or paddle face is vertical to the ball's path, it will hit the ball back along the same path (**a**);
if the face is "closed," it will hit the ball downward from that path (**b**);
if it is "open," it will hit it up (**c**).
But it is more useful to think of the angle of the face to the ground. For example, a vertical face sends a drive straight back (**d**). A closed one controls a high-bouncing ball (**e**). An open one can scoop a ball up off the ground (**f**). In this book, the "angle" of a racquet or paddle means its angle to the ground.

**forehand and backhand angles**
Hold your racquet or paddle out on your forehand, its face vertical (**a**); then swing it over to your backhand. Its face will have opened automatically (**b**). You have to turn your wrist to make it vertical again – and this reduces power and control. So most racquet sports use a different grip on the backhand – turning the racquet in the hand, to save turning the wrist (**c**).

**spin**

Three types of spin can be put on a ball: topspin (**a**), backspin (**b**), and sidespin (**c**). Some games use spin more than others; nevertheless the techniques and effects do not vary much. (In tennis, though, the effects are different: see p. 47.)

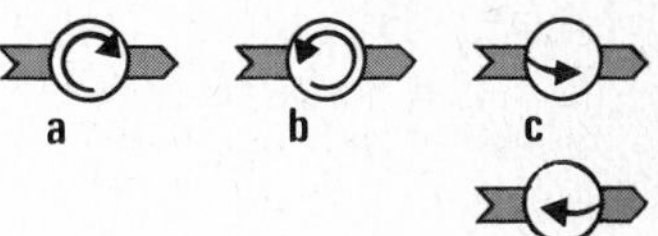


**topspin** (below)

This is put on the ball by an upward movement of the racquet or paddle.

The resulting shot "floats" in the air, with a longer, flatter path than normal, and then falls steeply to the ground.

When it bounces on the ground, it speeds up, shooting forward with a lower rebound than usual. When it hits a racquet or paddle, it rebounds higher than usual (and the same applies when it hits the wall of a walled court).

To control it, for a return that does not soar in the air, you must hit the ball with racquet/paddle face closed.

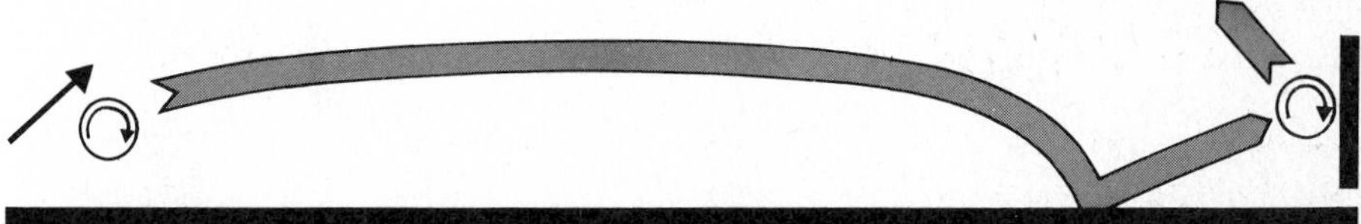

**backspin** (below)

Also called "chop" or "slice," this is put on the ball by a downward movement of the racquet or paddle.

The resulting shot arcs in the air, climbing and falling more steeply than usual.

When it bounces on the ground, it slows up – "dying," with a steeper and weaker rebound than usual. When it hits a racquet or paddle, it falls away lower than usual (and the same applies when it hits the wall of a walled court). To control it, for a return that lifts the ball enough to get it back, you must hit it with racquet/paddle face open.

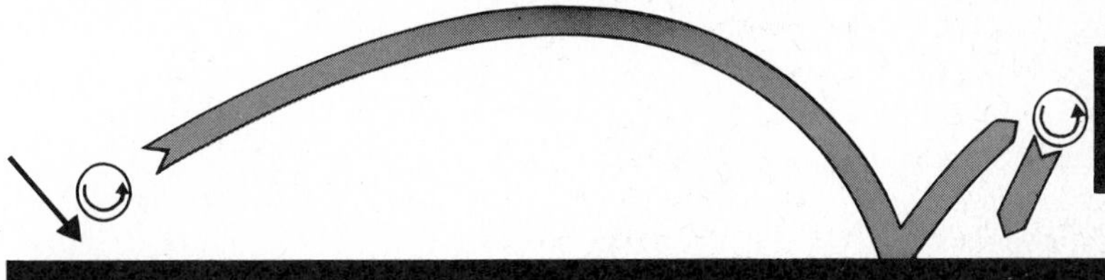

**sidespin** (below)

This is put on the ball by a sideways movement of the racquet or paddle.

The resulting shot moves sideways in the air, and shoots sideways when it bounces on the ground, on racquet or paddle, or on a wall.

To control it, for a return that gets the ball back along the path it came on, you must hit it with the racquet or paddle angled sideways against the force of the spin.

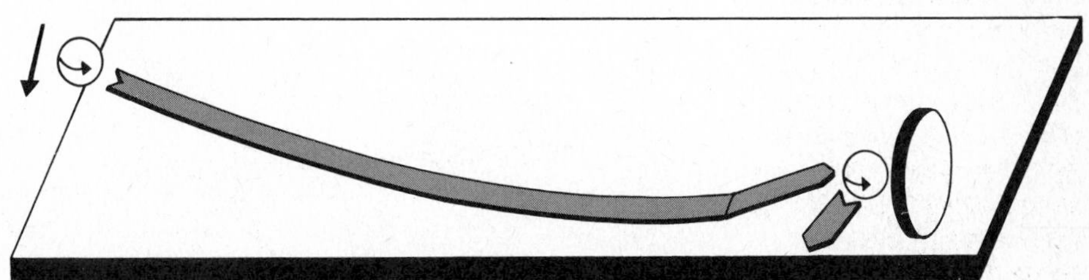

**ready stance**
This is the stance to wait in, until you know where to move for your next stroke. It varies a little from one game to another. But basically you should be alert and relaxed, with feet apart and flat on the ground, knees and hips flexed, weight forward on the balls of the feet, shoulders level and relaxed, and arms forward, with racquet or paddle head up.

**watching the ball**
This is a skill to be practiced like any other. Almost all beginners let their eyes wander to their opponent's face – or, in walled games, worse still, to the front wall, as they wait for the ball to appear against it. You should be aware of your opponent; but your concentration must always be on the flight of the ball, right up to the moment of impact.

**preparing the stroke**
A good player often seems to have all the time in the world for his strokes. This is simply due to anticipation, preparation, and footwork. Preparation should begin the moment you spot your next shot: pivot from the ready stance (**1**), so starting the backswing (**2**), which you finish as you move into position (**3**). This sequence is vital.

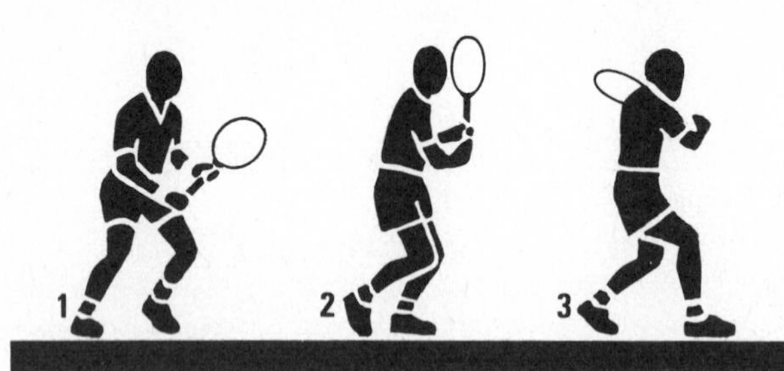


**footwork**
A long stride, pushing off from the ball of the rear foot, gives an efficient gliding run (**1**). The final step in, as you play the stroke, is usually with the leg opposite to the side on which the stroke is being played (i.e., with the left leg on a forehand stroke, the right on a backhand). So you may need a chassée movement just beforehand – that is, the rear leg only closing on the front one (**2**), before the same front leg moves forward again. On the final step in (**3**), the knees must generally bend, to get the body down to the ball. Other footwork includes: a sideways shuffle (**a**), for moving back while watching the ball; the badminton "fencer's lunge" (**b**); and (in racquetball, for example), the dive of desperation (**c**)!

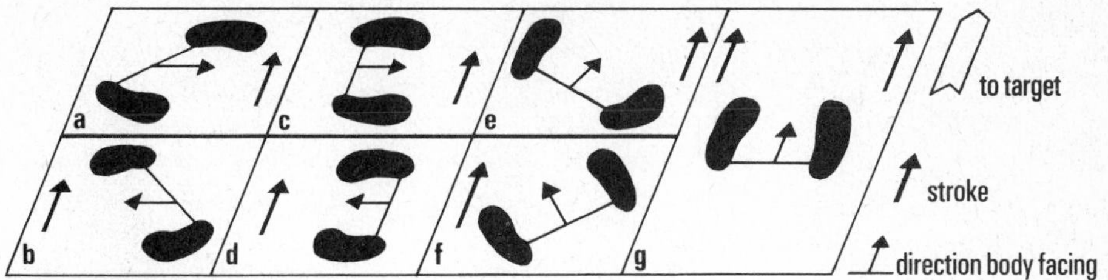


**stance on the stroke**

If, at the moment you play the ball, your opposite leg has crossed in front of you, this is called a "closed" stance (forehand, **a**; backhand, **b**). This is the usual stance for the stroke in most racquet sports. But sometimes a stroke is made from a "neutral" stance (**c** and **d**) or an "open" one (**e** and **f**). For some volleys, or for rushed strokes, a stance "straight on" to the target may be used (**g**).

**building up the stroke**

A stroke is not just an arm movement: it is arm movement, leg movement, weight movement, and body movement. These are the elements that must be studied separately, and then blended into a single fluid unit. The source of power in the stroke must be understood – it depends on the sport and the shot. It may just be a snap of the wrist (a). It may be a flick of hand and lower arm (**b**), or a stiff-armed swing from the shoulder (**c**). It may even be a full-blooded body movement to which the arm adds little. But the more powerful the stroke, the more likely it is that the whole of the body is involved in powering the ball (**d**).

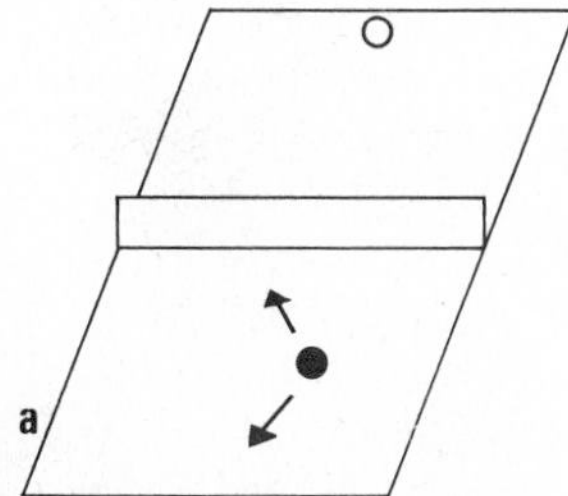


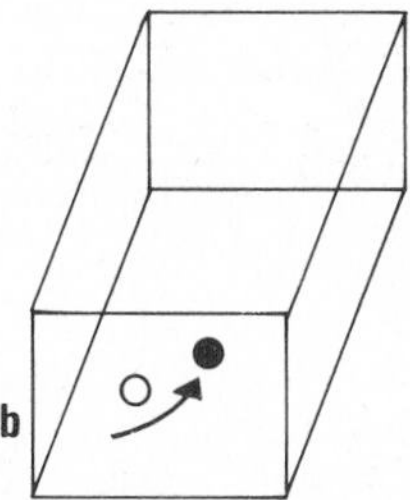


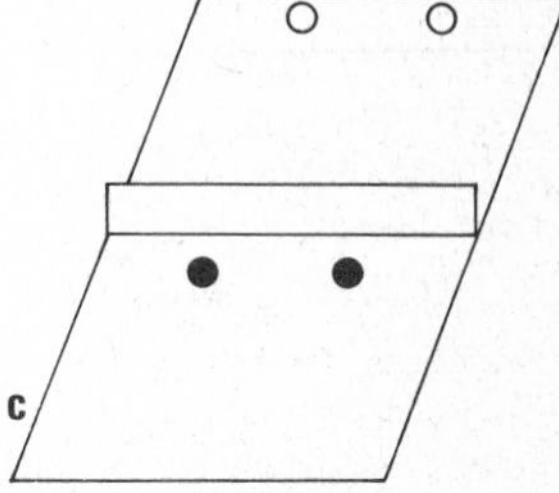


**after the stroke**

After each stroke, you must try to get a "base" position – one that will give you a good chance of reaching your opponent's next shot. In most net games, this means a difficult choice between going back to the center of the base line, and coming forward to the net (**a**). But in walled games your base is the center court position (**b**) – and you must get there without obstructing your opponent. In doubles games, partners divide the court between them in some way (**c**).

**mental skills**

Success demands mental skills as well as physical ones. If you were the mythical perfect player, you would:
never play badly through nervousness;
never lose concentration as a game progressed;
never give up when facing someone you thought was a better player;
never get distracted or upset by your bad luck and your opponent's good luck;
always take your time and relax;
always have a clear idea of the kind of game your opponent was playing;
always anticipate where your opponent's next shot would go;
always know what your own tactics should be;
always have the patience to keep to winning tactics – however unspectacular;
always have the courage to change losing tactics – however successful in the past;
and always expect to win, and never give up when the game looked as good as lost.

**reading a game**

Some of these mental skills can be practiced. For example, watching matches – preferably live – can be very good training in "reading" players' shots and styles of play. Watch how each player prefers to position himself; what shots he likes to make; where he likes to play them from; and where he likes to play them to. Also assess what his weaknesses are: which shots he avoids making, and which he fails to return. Finally, try to anticipate each stroke as the player backswings.

**tactics: positioning**

The rule here is to "play from strength": after each stroke, try to get back to a strong "base" position, where you are fairly sure to be able to intercept the next shot. This means, in most net games, that you must choose between going back to the base line or coming forward to the net. A center-court position is too easily "passed" by a drive you cannot reach. How you choose depends on what is happening and what you think will happen – but also on your skills and personality. Some players like to hit steady drives and lobs from the base line. Others, more aggressive and flamboyant, want to move in to volley at the net. (Note: badminton has its own positioning – see p. 62 – while in table tennis, of course, the problems are rather different.)
In walled games, in contrast, center court is your ideal "base." You move forward from it to attack, and also if your opponent is in front court with the ball, and you are afraid of a drop shot or kill. You move back from it only to retrieve a back court shot.
Finally, in all doubles games, matters are more complicated, since you are dividing the court with your partner. As he moves, you may have to move, to keep level with him, cover a weakness (his or your own), or fill a gap.

**tactics: shots**

The rule here is "play to weakness"; play the shot that will keep your opponent on the defensive. Go for an outright point winner only when the chance comes. In the meantime, choose the "percentage shot" – i.e., the one with the most margin for error (given the situation, and your skills). Send the ball away from your opponent, to move him out of position – or at least keep him in a defensive one. And play to his weaknesses, to force him into errors. If he is weak on the backhand, play to that side. If he likes to play from the back court, let your shots bounce up front. If he likes a slow pace, speed it up. If he is unfit, make him run. Even in the knock-up before the game, you can start to watch for skills and weaknesses and compare them with your own. Then play accordingly.
But if you play the same shots too often, your opponent starts to anticipate them. If you use the same tactics all the time, he can counter them. And if you play to the same weakness all the time, it may become a strength. So the second part of the "play to weakness" rule is the principle of surprise. You must be just unpredictable enough to keep your opponent guessing: suddenly playing the unexpected shot, angling it in an unforeseen direction, giving it fresh spin or pace. All this is helped by deception on the stroke – i.e., by backswing, footwork, and lead-in that look as if you were going to play a different shot.

### training

There is no need to train for a sport, to enjoy it. On the other hand, in racquet sports as in all sports, the top players are the ones who have built on their natural abilities by deliberate effort. There are two elements in this: physical condition, and the practice of skills. The first demands hard physical effort, the second intelligence, concentration, consistency, and perseverance.

### physical fitness

Success at racquet and paddle games depends on strength, speed, and stamina, as well as skill. But the sports alone are not enough to develop these properly; so if you want to progress you need the right kind of exercise. Running, jogging, circuit training, and calisthenics (i.e., push-ups, sit-ups, squat leg thrusts, etc.) are all useful. Weight lifting and isometric exercises are less likely to help.

### practice

a) To learn any stroke, begin with the footwork. Then add the body movement, and finally the swing of the arm. Build all these together before trying out the stroke with a ball. Always get expert advice if you can; otherwise it is as easy to build up bad habits as good ones.
b) You have to be disciplined to get the most out of practicing with a partner. It is no good simply knocking the ball back and forth at random.

### individual practice techniques

To practice when alone, try the following techniques. (It is best to practice one stroke diligently for about 10 minutes, before switching to another one.)
a) Make the stroke movements in front of a large mirror.
b) Get out on a court, and move from one point to another as if playing an imaginary ball. This integrates stroke and footwork. Progress to running, as if playing a match.
c) For net games, get a number of balls together, and practice from one end of the court, dropping each ball in front of you and hitting it down to the other end. Then go to the other end and hit them back. Bounce the ball to different heights to try out different strokes. Use boxes or tin cans as targets, to improve your aim. Practice serving in the same way – and you may find it helps if you start close to the net, and then gradually retreat toward the base line as you find you are getting every service into the service court.
d) Another good way of practicing for net games is to use a backboard or wall, with a net or target marked on it. The ball then returns to you, for you to play.
e) In walled games, of course, it is much easier. On court, the ball comes back to you, and you can play against yourself. Imagining targets on different parts of the front wall may also help.
f) Just to practice mobility, you can dot a number of balls around a court, and time how quickly you can pick them all up, reaching with one hand as if for a stroke. Keep changing your route so you have to turn different ways.

### partner practice techniques

a) If only one of you is learning the game – or one of you is taking a rest! – the non-player can call parts of the court for the player to run to. The player has to get there as fast as possible, and play a stroke against an imaginary ball; then get back to his base position before the next call. Different parts of the court can be given the names of colors, for example, so they can be called easily. Each "rally" of calls should last for about 10 strokes.
b) Alternatively, if you have a good supply of balls, your partner can "feed" you with them, so you can practice a specific stroke. He can start by throwing them from quite close to you; then move further away; then throw them in increasingly rapid succession; then begin to hit them to you with his own racquet or paddle.
c) The next stage is to hit a ball to and fro, with each of you trying one specific stroke. For example, one may hit cross-court drives, for the other to reply with drives down the line – this means both of you have to keep moving from one side of court to the other. Or one may hit lobs for the other to volley or retrieve. Try to be accurate and keep the rally going, not to win points.
d) The final stage, short of playing a match, is a "conditioned game," in which you have to practice something because that is the only way you may score points. For example, to practice deep drives, you could play a game in which each player lost the point every time he hit a shot into center court or front court. Or, to practice volleys, you could rule that a player lost the point if he let the ball bounce.

# Tennis

# Tennis

Tennis is the best known of all racquet games. It can be a gentle social pastime, or a sport needing the speed, concentration, and endurance of a first-class athlete. First steps in tennis are perhaps not as easy as in some other games: some skill is needed for real enjoyment. But once the skill is there, it is all the more satisfying.

Tennis as known today is just on 100 years old. In medieval times there were games in which a ball was hit back and forth over an obstacle — either out in the fields, or in walled courtyards in castles and monasteries. At first, the player's bare hand hit the ball; then gloves, wooden bats, and finally strung racquets were developed. But by the late 18th century the outdoor version had almost vanished, and the walled game — "royal (real) tennis" — was limited to a few of the very wealthy.

However, by the mid 19th century a few people were starting to experiment with outdoor tennis again, and in 1874 an Englishman, Major Wingfield, patented a game he called "Sphairistiké." With its hour-glass-shaped court, five-foot-high net, and diamond-shaped serving box, it bore little resemblance to the tennis we now know. But it did spark off great interest, and still more experimenting. Just three years later, the first "world amateur championships," at Wimbledon, established the game for which Wimbledon is still world-famous today.

# Court

Tennis is played on an open court divided in two by a net across the center. Opponents face each other across the net, and use their racquets to hit a ball back and forth over it.

**court**
The court is marked out as shown. Grass is now less common than other surfaces, which include asphalt, concrete, shale, clay, composition, and synthetic "carpets."

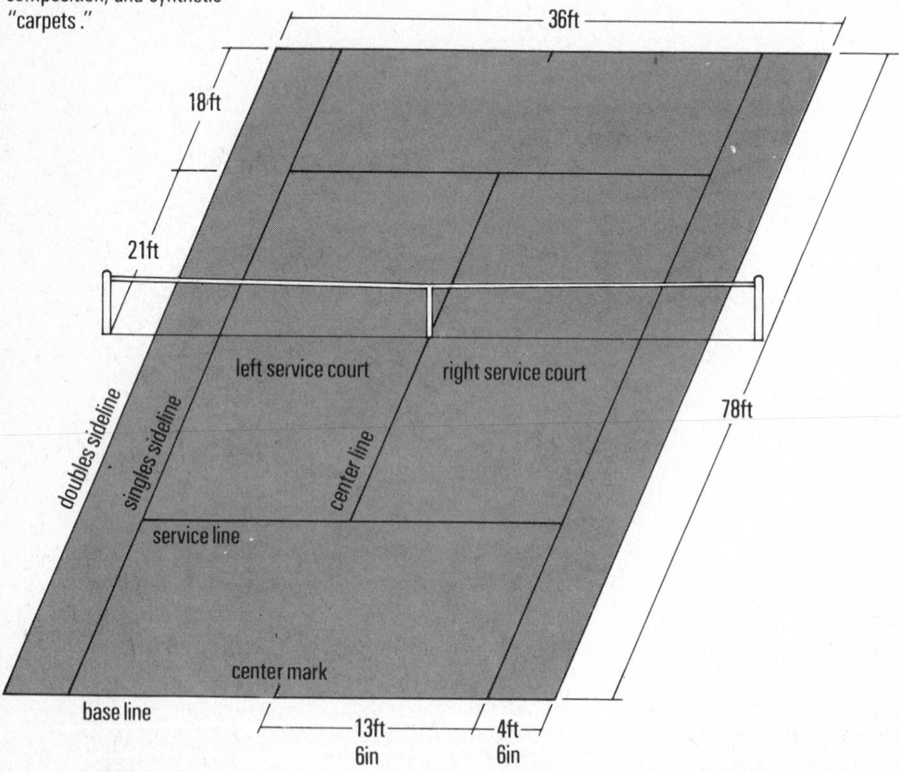

36ft
18ft
21ft
78ft
left service court
right service court
doubles sideline
singles sideline
center line
service line
center mark
base line
13ft 6in
4ft 6in

**singles and doubles**
Tennis can be played between two players (singles), or four players teamed in two pairs (doubles). In singles, the doubles alleys at each side do not count as part of the court.

singles
doubles

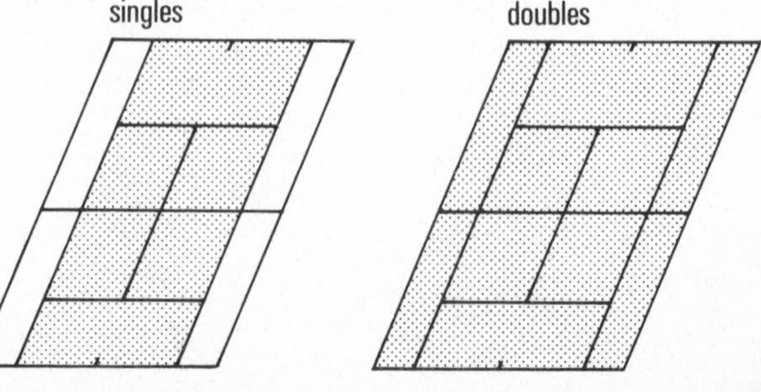

**net**

The net is suspended between two posts, from a cable covered by white tape. At its center it is kept taut by a vertical strap that should be fixed firmly to the ground.

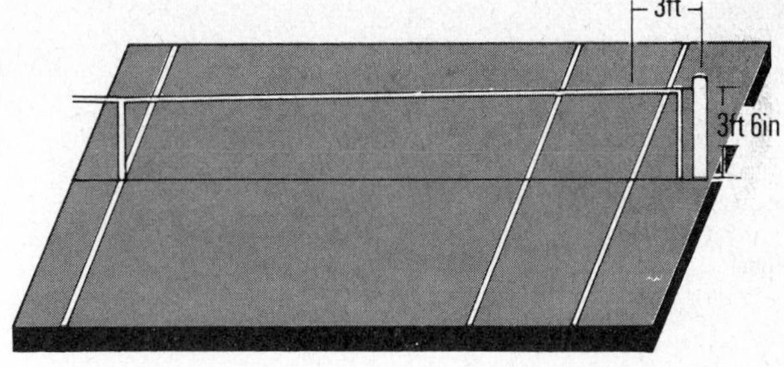


**adjusting the net**

The height of the net can be altered by turning a handle on one of the posts. For play, the height at the center of the net should be 3 feet. This height can be measured off by placing one racquet above another, as shown.

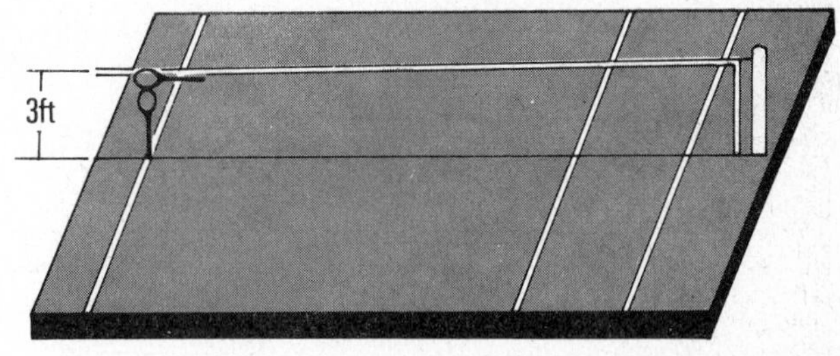


**singles sticks**

When the normal dual-purpose court is used for a singles match, the rules lay down that singles sticks ought to be used. These support the net at a point 3 feet outside the singles playing area. They also mark off the parts of the net that are not to count as part of the court. They are usually only used in tournament competition.

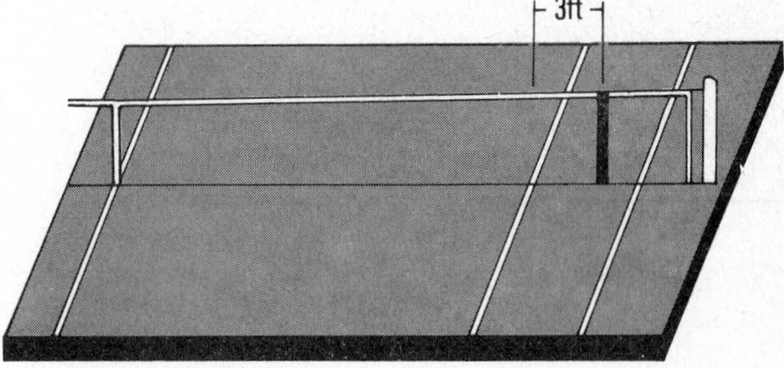

Tennis equipment is quite simple, but can vary widely in quality, so careful choice is necessary.

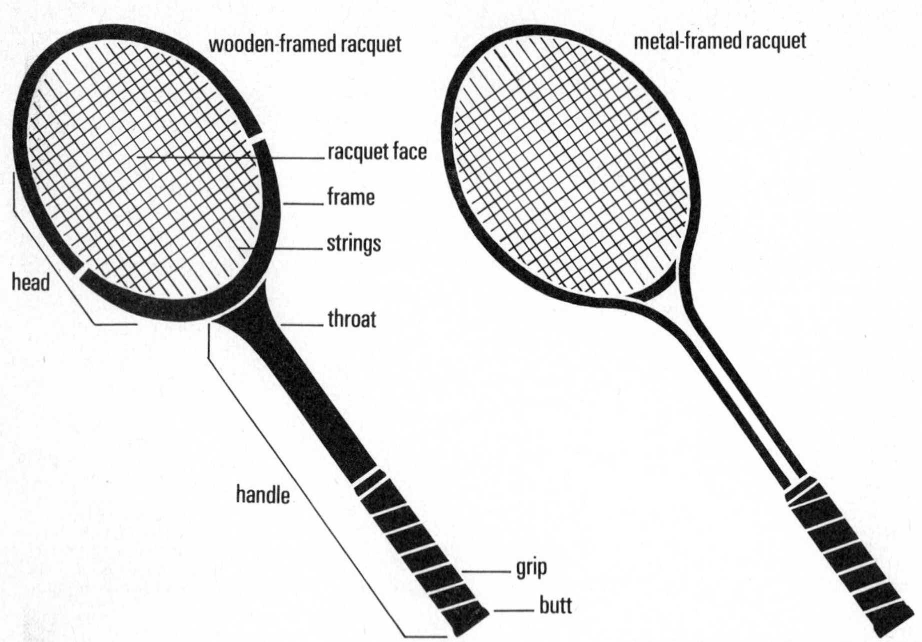


**racquet**

There are no official rules about the racquet, but in practice all tennis racquets look fairly similar. There are important differences, however: in materials used, weight, grip size, balance, and string tension.

a) frame. This is usually wood or metal. Wood is traditional. Some players think that metal gives more power but makes ball control harder.

b) strings. These are usually gut or nylon. Nylon is long-lasting and dampproof, but gut has more spring and is almost always used by top players.

c) weight. This can vary from 12½ ounces or less up to 14¾ ounces. A light racquet makes for quick movement, a heavier one for power.

d) grip size. This can vary from 4 to 5 inches around. A small size allows wrist flexibility and fast racquet movement, a larger one gives firmer ball control. (Grip material also varies.)

e) balance. A racquet may be head heavy, handle heavy, or evenly balanced. Again, a head-heavy racquet makes for power, a handle-heavy one for quick movement. Players who like to stay back near the base line often prefer a head-heavy racquet, while those who play a net game often choose an evenly balanced or handle-heavy one.

f) string tension. This varies from 50 to 60 pounds, for normal use, up to 70 pounds for the top-class player. High tension gives more power but makes ball control more difficult.

In general, a beginner should choose a wooden-framed, nylon-strung racquet, with normal tension and even balance, and (most important) with whatever weight and grip size he finds comfortable. Typical weights for men are 13¼ to 14½ ounces, for women 13 to 14¼ ounces. Children under 10 years should use a junior racquet, those over 10 a light adult one (down to 12 ounces). It is very important for a beginner not to use a racquet that is too heavy for him. On the other hand, one that is too light (or with too small a grip) will give poor ball control.

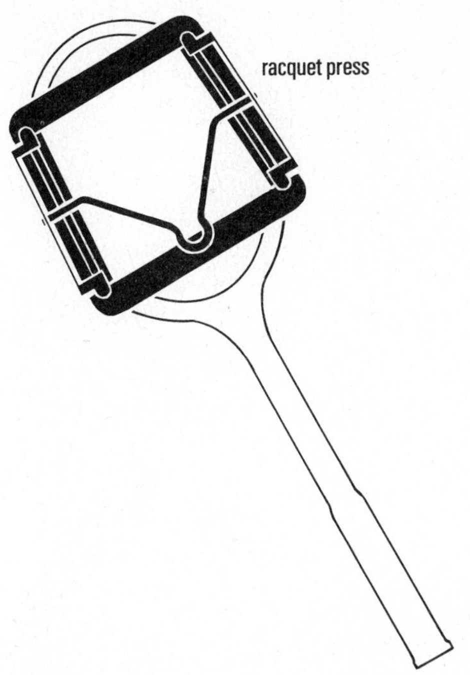


**care of racquet**

When not in use, a wooden racquet should be kept in a press, under even pressure; laid horizontally or hung from the throat; and kept away from cold, heat, and damp.

Outdoors, a gut-strung racquet should be carried in a waterproof case, and never used with damp balls. If such a racquet does get wet, dry it with a cloth, and rub the end of a wax candle over the strings to stop them drying out too quickly and snapping. A worn racquet can be revarnished.

**ball**

Tennis balls for official competition use must be white or yellow, weigh between 2 and 2¼ ounces, and bounce between 53 and 58 inches high when dropped 100 inches onto concrete. Balls that meet these requirements when packed are usually stamped as approved by the national governing body. (Those packed in airtight containers keep their characteristics longest.) Approved balls are expensive, but usually each has a good quality outer casing that plays well and wears slowly. Cheaper balls vary greatly in quality.

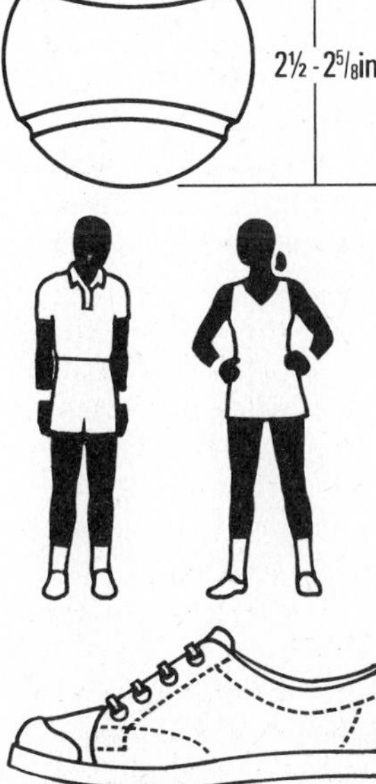


**dress**

Formal and competition wear is shirt and shorts for men, and skirt or shorts and blouse, or a dress, for women. A good material is one that absorbs perspiration, and washes and dries easily. The standard color is white, though most professional tournaments allow colored clothing. Other needs include:

socks–absorbent, and thick enough to protect the feet;

canvas sports shoes with rubber soles (sneakers) – preferably ones designed for tennis;

a sweater or track-suit top, to wear after play;

and if necessary, a hairband and/or wrist sweatbands. Again, shoes and socks are normally white though often with colored trimmings.

In this outline, the "sides" can be either singles players or doubles partnerships.

The aim in tennis is to win points. But for each point, the ball must be put into play. This is called the service. The player who puts the ball into play is called the server.

Once the ball is in play, the players hit it back and forth over the net (the rally) until one of them is unable to return it, and loses the point. For example, he may hit the ball so it goes into the net, or so it does not bounce in court on the other side; or he may not manage to hit it at all.

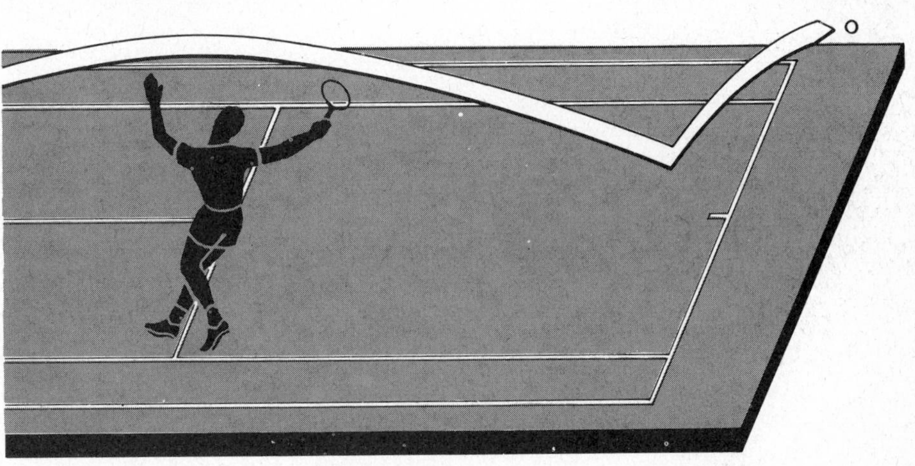

At the start of a tennis match, the sides spin for ends and service in the first game. As a result of this, one side chooses which end to play in the first game, and the other chooses whether to be server or receiver in that game.

A game is won by the first side to score four points – unless the sides reach three-all, in which case one must get two points ahead of the other to win the game. (Points in tennis are called in a special way, see p. 37.)
The service changes after each game. Ends generally change after every other game.

The first side to win six games wins the "set" – but, again, if the sides reach five games all, they must go on until one side gets two games ahead of the other.

When one set is won, the next set begins. Men's matches are played over three sets or five sets, women's or mixed matches over three sets. In all cases, the match ends as soon as one side has won a majority of the sets.

Putting the ball into play—the service—is a very important part of tennis, and special rules apply.

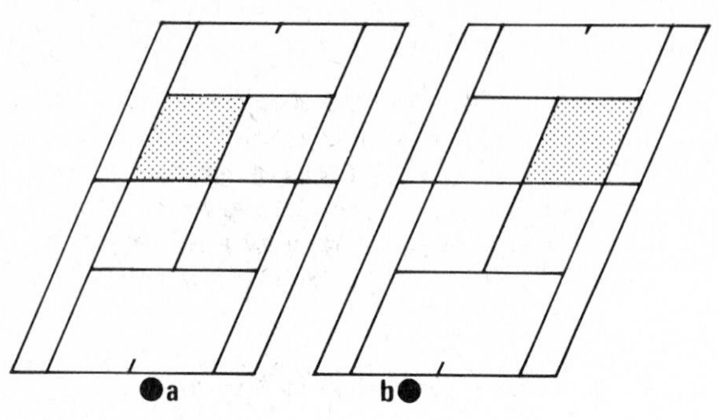


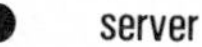

server

service court

**the service**
Basically, the service is a diagonal shot. The server stands behind his own base line, to one side of the center mark; and he hits the ball over the net into whichever service court is diagonally opposite.
For the first point of each game, he stands to the right of the center mark to serve (**a**). For the second, he stands to the left (**b**), for the third back to the right, and so on alternately.

**taking the service**
To serve, the server must throw the ball into the air, and hit it before it reaches the ground. There are no rules about how this should be done, but in fact tennis players serve overarm – hitting the ball when it is above their head.

**serving position**
The drawing shows the area that the server must stand in to serve: behind (not on) the base line, and between (not on) where the center mark and sideline would be if they continued behind the base line.

**during the service**
When the server is ready to throw the ball up, his feet must be at rest. Once he throws the ball, he may move his feet slightly; and he may even lean forward over the base line (or jump in the air) so that his body and feet are directly above the court surface. But, until he has hit the ball, he must not actually touch his feet down anywhere, except in the serving area already described; and he must not change his position in that area by walking or running. Once he has hit the ball, he may move as he likes.

**faults**

A service is not good if:
the server breaks any of the rules described;
or he tries to serve and misses the ball;
or the ball does not cross the net (**a**);
or it bounces before crossing the net (**b**);
or it does not first hit the ground in the correct service court (i.e., the one diagonally opposite) (**c**);
or it hits a post, or anything else outside the court, before bouncing in court (**d**).
(Note that throwing the ball up does not commit a server to serving. He may let it fall and try again. Only if he tries to hit the ball, does it count as an attempted service.
Also note that the lines that mark out a service court count as part of it.)
If a service is not good, it is called a "fault." The server then tries again to make a good service, into the same service court. If he fails again ("double fault"), he loses the point–even though his opponent has not even had to try to return the ball.
On the other hand, if a service is good, and the opponent cannot return it, then the server immediately wins the point.
Once the point is decided (whether by the service or by the play that follows it), the server then serves for the next point, from the other side of the center mark – unless it is the end of the game, in which case service passes to the opponent for the next game.

**let service**

If the ball touches the net, but still goes into the correct service court, it is called a "let" (**e**). This means that the service is taken again (so if it was the first attempt, the server still has two attempts to make a good service).
It is also a let if:
the ball touches the net, and then hits the receiver (or anything he is carrying);
or the server serves (or makes a fault) before the receiver is ready.
But if the receiver tries to return the service, he cannot claim that he was unready.

If the point is not won or lost on the service itself, then the opponents hit the ball back and forth over the net, until one of them fails to make a good return and so loses the point.

**basic return**
Basically, it is a good return if a player hits the ball so that it passes over the net and bounces in court on his opponent's side (**a**). It does not matter if the player was outside his own court when he hit the ball (**b**)—so long as he was on the right side of the net. And it does not matter if he had let the ball bounce on his own side before he hit it (**c**)—so long as it did not bounce on his side more than once. (In fact, a service must be allowed to bounce before it is returned.)

**playing with singles sticks**
If you are playing with singles sticks—see p. 27—then a return that has touched the posts, or the net or cord outside the sticks, is no longer good. But one that has only touched one of the singles sticks—or has passed outside the stick without touching anything—is good.

**playing at the net**
It is always a bad return if the player, or his clothes or racquet, touches the net, post, cord or metal cable, strap or band, or the ground in the opponent's court (**g**).
It is also a bad return if he hits the ball before it has crossed to his side of the net (**h**). But if the ball bounces on his side of the net, and then rebounds or is blown back over the net, the player may reach over to strike it (**i**) (provided that he does not touch the net, etc). A player's racquet may also pass over the net in a follow-through, after hitting the ball on his own side of the net.

It is still a good return if the ball lands on the lines that mark the edge of the opponent's court (**d**); these count as part of the court. A return is also good if the ball touches the net, posts, cord or metal cable, net strap or band (**e**)—provided that it passes over them and hits the ground in the opponent's court.

A ball may even be returned outside the post (**f**)—again, so long as it then first hits the ground within the opponent's court. This holds good whether it passes above or below the level of the top of the net, and whether or not it touches the post itself.

Finally, it is also a good return if a player still manages to return the ball after it has hit another ball lying in court.

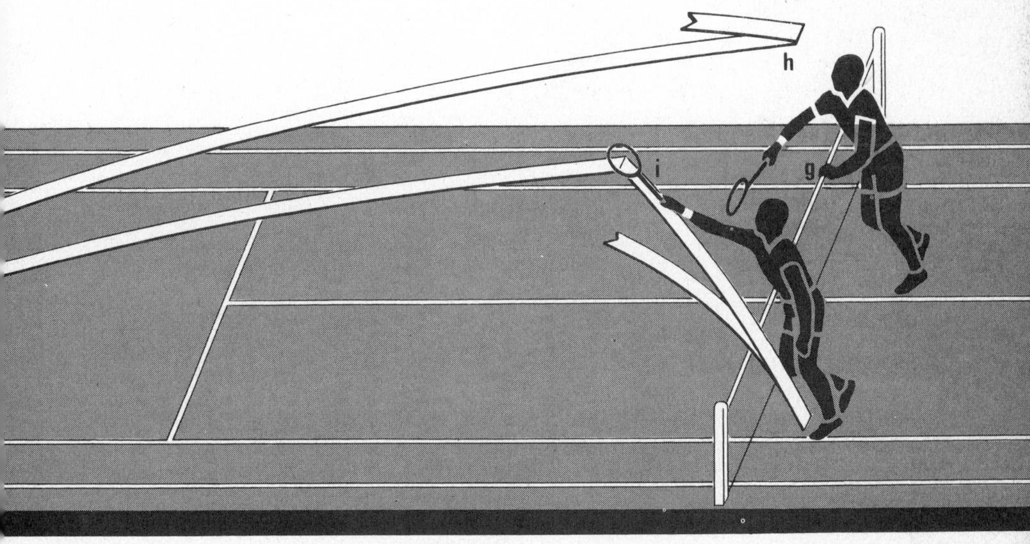

**losing the point**

A player loses the point if:
he does not return the ball before it has bounced twice on his side of the net (**a**);
or he hits the ball into the net (**b**);
or he hits the ball before it has crossed to his side of the net (**c**);
or he hits the ball more than once in trying to return it (**d**);
or he hits the ball over the net but not into the opponent's court (**e**);
or he hits the ball so that it only goes into the opponent's court after it has touched the ground (or an object) outside the court (**f**).
He also loses the point if:
the ball touches him or anything he is wearing or carrying, apart from his racquet or his hands (**g**);
or, while the ball is in play, he, or his racquet, or anything he is wearing or carrying, touches the net, posts, singles sticks, cord or metal cable, strap or band, or the ground within his opponent's court (**h**);
or the ball touches a permanent fixture outside the court before he hits it but after it has bounced in court on his side;
or he deliberately hinders an opponent (but the point is replayed if the hindrance was accidental).

**start of play**

The choice of service and ends for the first game is usually decided by one player spinning a racquet in the air and catching it, while the opponent calls "rough" or "smooth" (referring to whether the rough or smooth face of the racquet stringing will be facing upward). The winner of the call can choose to serve or receive in the first game (with the other player having choice of ends); or he can choose ends (in which case the other player chooses to be server or receiver). (Alternatively, the winner can ask the other player to make the first choice.)

**changing ends**

In each set, players change ends at the end of the first, third, fifth, and subsequent alternate games. They

The scoring system in tennis may seem confusing at first, but in fact it is quite simple.

also change ends at the end of a set, if the total number of games in that set was an odd number.

**scoring a game**
In each game, a player begins with no score, called "love." The first point he wins in the game gives him a total score of 15. The second brings the total to 30, the third to 40. After this, the next point wins him the game—unless his opponent has also reached 40, in which case one of them has to get a two-point lead to win (see "deuce," below).

**calling the scores**
Scores in a game are called out after each point, with the server's score first. So if the server has won two points, the receiver none, the score is called "30-love." If the players have each won the same number of points, then the score is called (for example) "30-all." But if both players have won three points, the score is not called "40-all," but "deuce."

**deuce**
After the call of deuce, the next point won by a player scores him the "advantage"—called "advantage Jones," for example, or, informally, "your (or my) advantage." Then if the same player wins the next point, he wins the game. But if he loses it, the score goes back to deuce. It does not matter how many times "deuce" is called, in a game. The game is not won until one of the players wins the next two points after the call.
(Note: in some professional tennis, "deuce" is not used; whoever wins the fourth point wins the game.)

**scoring the match**
After each game, the score in games is called: for example, "Jones leads by 5 games to 3 in the first set." Service changes between the players, they change ends if necessary, and the next game begins. The first player to win six games wins the set—unless the score reaches five games all, in which case play goes on until one player is two games ahead. After one set, the games of the next set begin, proceeding in the same way. A men's match over five sets is won by the first side to win three sets. A women's or mixed match, or a men's match over three sets, is won by the first side to win two sets.

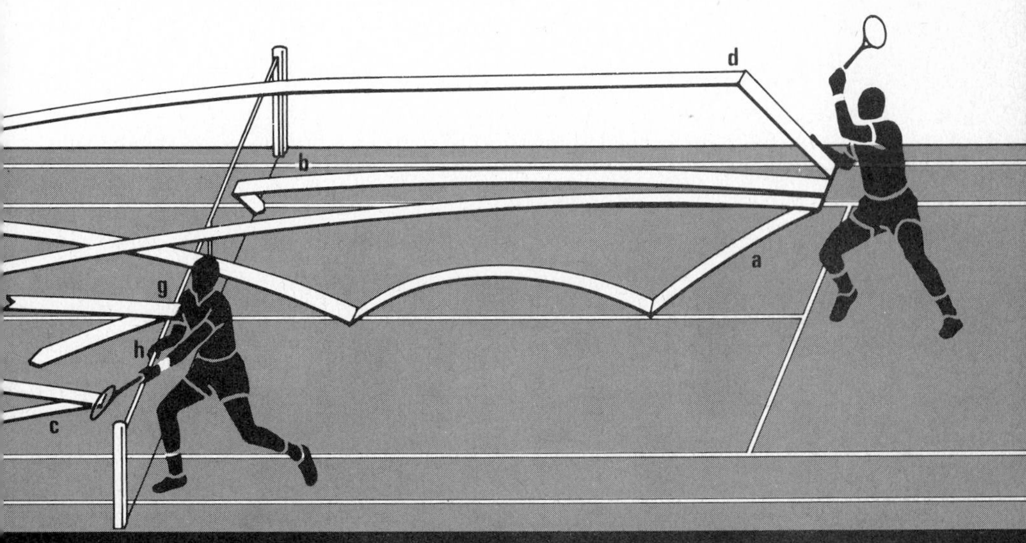

# Rules: doubles

The main rules differences in the doubles game are the wider playing area (see page 26), and the order of service.

**serving**

At the start of play, the choice of service and ends is decided in the usual way.

The pair about to serve in the first game (a and b) then decide which of them will serve for that game. They choose a, for example. When the first game is over, the opposing pair (x and y) decide which of them will serve for the second game. They choose x, for example.

In the third and fourth games, the other players serve: in the third, b; in the fourth, y.

In the next game, a serves again, and the same order is kept throughout the set.

At the beginning of the next set, each pair may decide to change its serving order.

First game

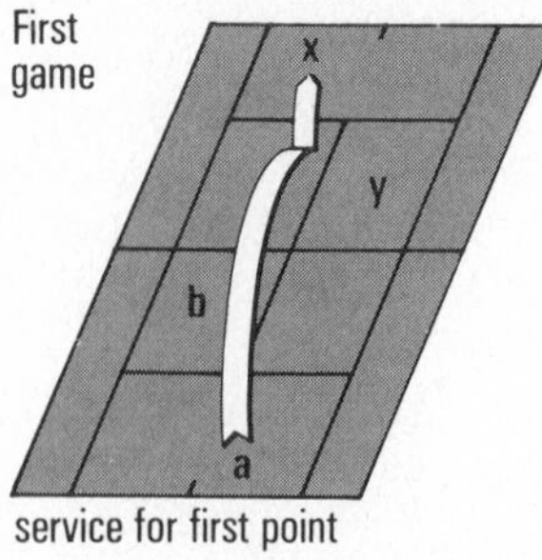

service for first point

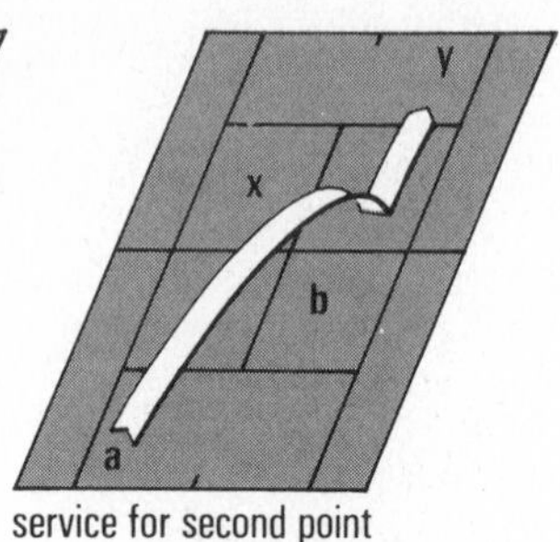

service for second point

Second game

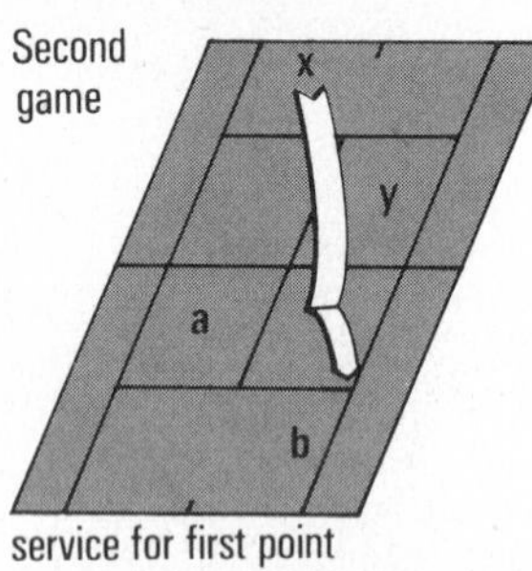

service for first point

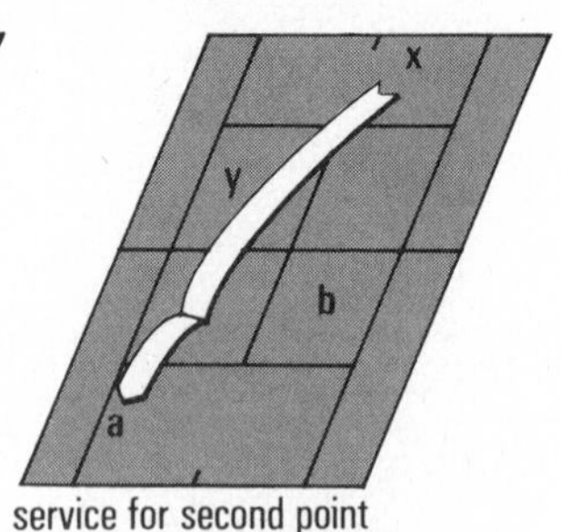

service for second point

**receiving**

The pair about to receive in the first game of a set (x and y) decide which of them will receive the service for the first point. They choose x, for example; y receives the service for the second point, x the service for the third, and so on. Thereafter, x receives all the first services in that set, when his pair are receiving.

Similarly, at the start of the second game, a and b choose which of them will receive the first services in that set, whenever they are receiving. They choose b, for example.

Third game

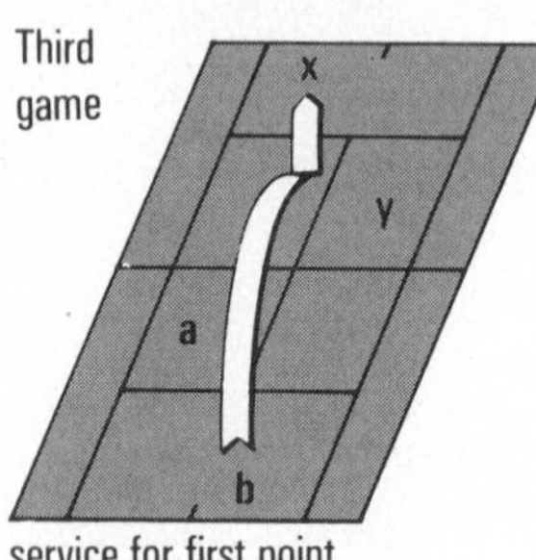

service for first point

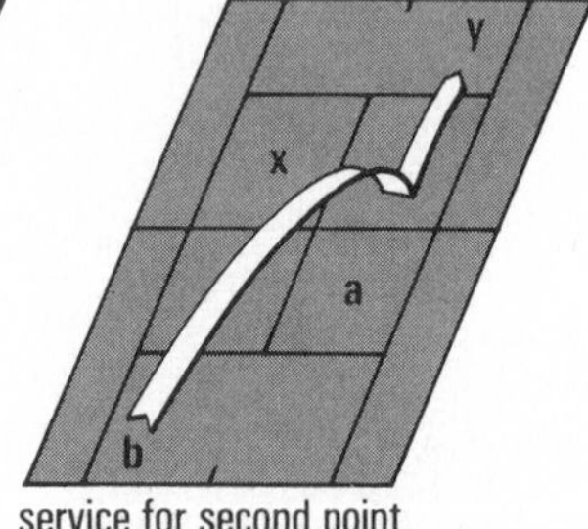

service for second point

**good and bad services**

In addition to the singles rules, a service is also a fault if the ball hits the server's partner (or anything he is wearing or carrying). But the service wins the point if the ball touches the receiver's partner (unless it is a let).

**playing the ball**

In a rally, of course, the ball must be hit first by a member of one pair, then by a member of the other pair. Members of the same pair cannot both hit the ball before returning it over the net.

But—except when receiving the service—it does not matter which member of a pair hits the ball.

Most international (and national) tournaments are held under the rules of the International Tennis Federation.

**events**
Men and women do not normally compete against each other in tournaments–except in the mixed doubles, where the pairs each consist of a man and a woman. So the usual categories of competition are: men's singles; men's doubles; women's singles; women's doubles; and mixed doubles.

**officials**
Tournament officials include:
umpire (**a**);
net-cord judge (**b**);
foot-fault judge (**c**);
and linesmen (**d**).
There may also be a referee, to whom appeal may be made on questions of tennis law.

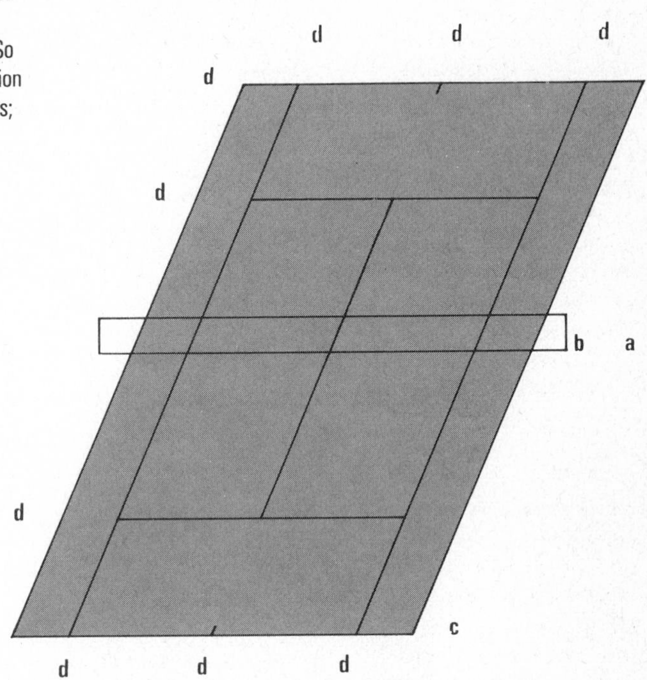


**duration**
Play in a tournament match is continuous, with a maximum of one minute between games. Play is not delayed to let a player recover his strength or get advice. However, a player is allowed up to 10 minutes' rest after the third set–or after the second set if women are taking part. (In equatorial countries, the allowance is 45 minutes.) Also, the umpire may suspend play if factors outside the players' control make it necessary.

**tie-break system**
To prevent long sets, most tournaments use a tie-break system when sides are 6-all or 8-all (though the final set of a match must usually be played out). In the ITF system, the first side to win seven points in the tie-break wins the set. But if the score reaches six points all, one side must get a two-point margin, to win.
The player whose turn it is to serve is server for the first point. Thereafter players serve for two points, before the service rotates.

Services are from alternate courts starting from the right. Players change ends after every six points and at the end of the tie-break. The side serving first in the tie-break receives in the first game of the next set.

**forehand grip**
The standard forehand grip is called the Eastern forehand. To find this, hold the racquet by the throat with your non-playing hand, so the racquet head is vertical to the ground (**a**). Place the palm of your playing hand flat against the strings (**b**), slide it down to the handle (**c**), and close fingers and thumb around the grip (**d**). This should give you the grip shown. The palm is against one side of the handle; the tips of the thumb and of three fingers lie flat against the other side. Note that the fingers are spread out, with the index finger forward as if on a trigger. Normal "length" is when the butt of the handle presses against the heel of the hand, as shown. The grip is light but firm.

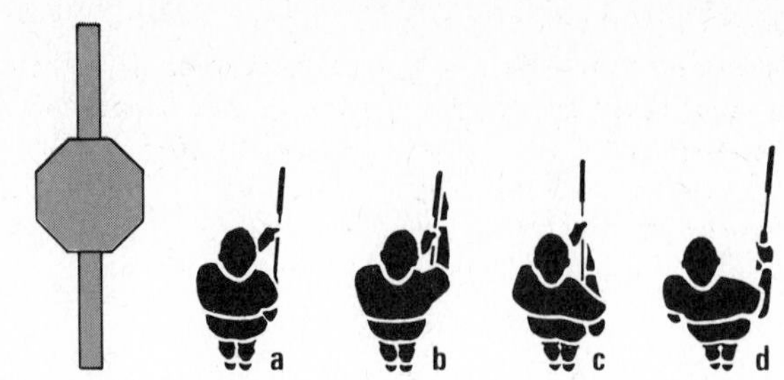


forehand grip

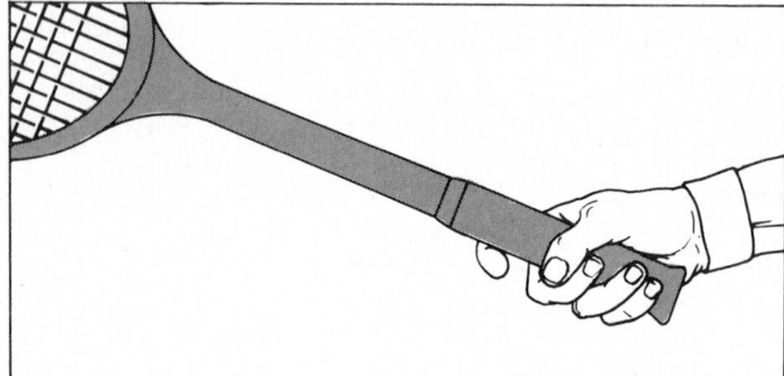

**backhand grip**
The standard backhand grip is called the Eastern backhand. To find it, hold the racquet by the throat with your non-playing hand so the left bevel of the grip is pointing up (**a**). Place the thumb of your playing hand flat and straight along the left bevel (**b**), and (without moving it) close your fingers around the grip (**c**). Then let the tip of the thumb shift down toward the tips of the fingers, and turn the racquet head to vertical (**d**). This gives the grip shown; note that the index finger and length are as for the forehand.

backhand grip

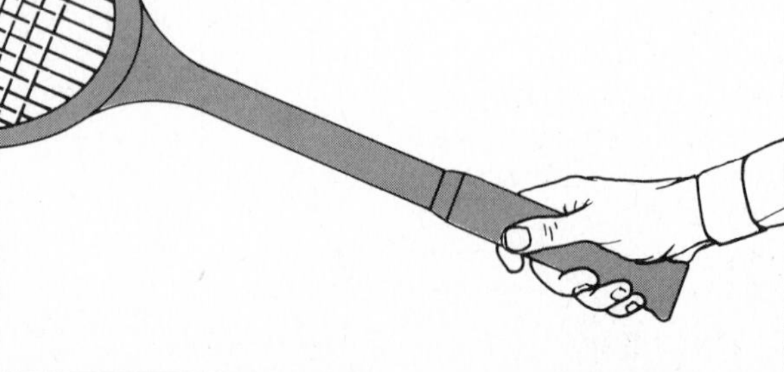

**changing grips**
Once both grips are familiar, change between them in play by twisting the racquet a quarter of a turn at the throat with the non-playing hand.

**ready stance**

An alert stance is vital. Face the net with feet apart. Knees and hips should be flexed slightly, so weight is forward on the balls of both feet (but keep the heels on the ground). Hold the racquet lightly in the forehand grip, pointing forward head up. Arms should be away from the body, with the fingers of the left hand steadying the throat of the racquet. Keep shoulders level and relaxed.

**receiving service**

There is no set position: it depends on the type and strength of service expected, and the receiver's skills. But the diagram shows possible receiving positions for a fast service (**a**) and for a slow service or a second service (**b**), and two possible positions for the receiver's partner in doubles (**c** and **d**).

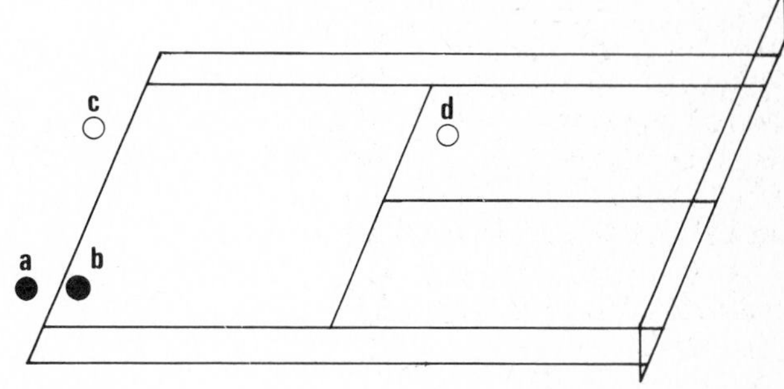


**playing positions**

In singles, after each stroke, you should get back to the center of the base line (**a**), or come forward toward the net (**b**, then **c**). Try to avoid staying in the area between base line and service line. In doubles, partners usually try to keep alongside each other; both back at the base line if necessary but if possible both up at the net.

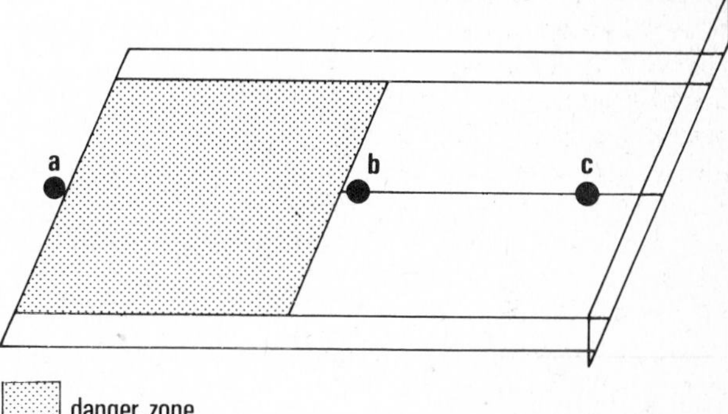


**positioning the ball**

The ideal places to which to play the ball are the six shaded squares shown in the diagram. These are the hardest points for your opponent to cover.

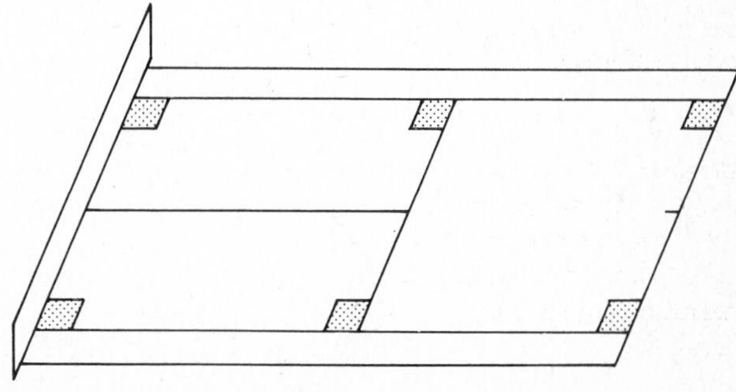

**drives**

The drive is the basic tennis stroke. It should feel as if the racquet is being swung through the ball – making contact, ideally, just after the peak of the bounce. Note, in both drives shown, how your body turns sideways on the backswing, and how the knees are bent to get down to the ball. But other details can vary, including footwork, backswing, and stance.

a) footwork. This has to suit the circumstances. Here the forehand happens to use a forward chassée (see p.18), while the backhand is being taken on a sideways run.

b) backswing. Both backhand and forehand are shown here with a high backswing. But on the forehand it is usually better for a beginner to take the racquet back at waist height.

c) stance. For a backhand drive this is usually " closed," as shown: i.e., the leg nearer the ball is well forward and parallel to the net. Forehands are often taken in the same way, especially on a sideways run; but they can also use a more open stance, as here.

**forehand drive**

Pivot out of the ready stance (**1**), letting go the racquet throat with your left hand. Begin the high backswing as you step forward (**2**). Get shoulders and hips sideways to the ball as the backswing is

**backhand drive**

Pivot out of the ready stance (**1**), using your left hand to help take the racquet back. Turn shoulders, arms, and racquet as a unit (**2**), as your left hand slides down to the racquet grip. Step forward, watching the ball over your right shoulder as the racquet starts to

**volleys**

Volleys can be used to angle a ball away, drop it back over the net, lob it over the opponent's head, or send it hard into his back court. They use very little backswing and only a short follow-through. On high (attacking) volleys, the racquet punches at the ball. On low (defensive) ones it is more of a blocking movement, with the racquet face open to lift the ball.

**forehand volley**

This forehand volley sequence also shows how a forehand stroke on the run can be made from a closed stance. Note how the body pivots, knees bend, and left arm helps with balance.

completed (**3**). Then bring the racquet down in a loop as you step into the stroke (**4**), and make contact with the ball by your front leg as your weight swings forward (**5**), bending your knees to get down to the ball. Follow through high with your knees still bent (**6**).

loop down (**3**); and meet the ball opposite your leading leg (**4**), with the racquet parallel to the ground, body sideways to the net, arm straight, and wrist locked. Let the swing of the stroke lift the ball clear of the net (**5**), and follow through high (**6**) with knees still bent and left arm helping balance.

**backhand volley**

Unlike the backhand drive, a backhand volley is often made from an open stance. Note how the left hand helps bring the racquet back, the wrist stays firm, and the weight leans into the ball.

**grips**

A beginner should use the normal forehand grip, but advanced players prefer the "chopper" grip shown. This is close to the normal backhand grip, but with the thumb wrapped around the handle – as if you were going to chop wood. (Note that the index finger is still extended forward.)

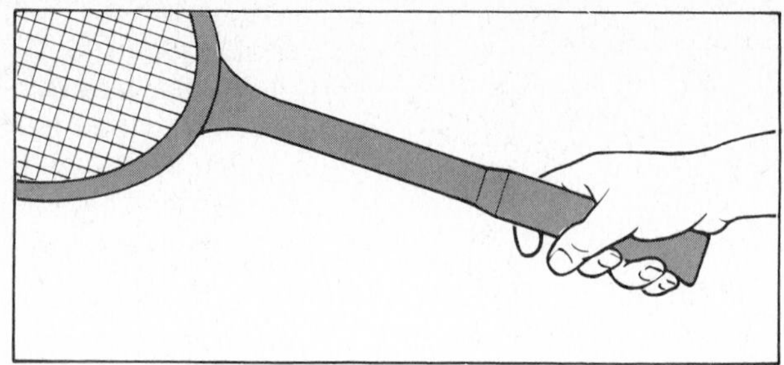

**positioning**

At the start of the service, always stand so that a line joining the toes of your feet points directly at the target (**a**). In singles, against a right-handed opponent (**b**), stand about 2 feet wide of the center mark to serve to the right-hand court, and 4 or 5 feet wide to serve to the left. Against a left-hander, reverse these distances (**c**). (In doubles, stand wider). These positions give good angles to the opponent's backhand, as shown. But also practice services to all the targets shown in **d**, and vary between these in play.

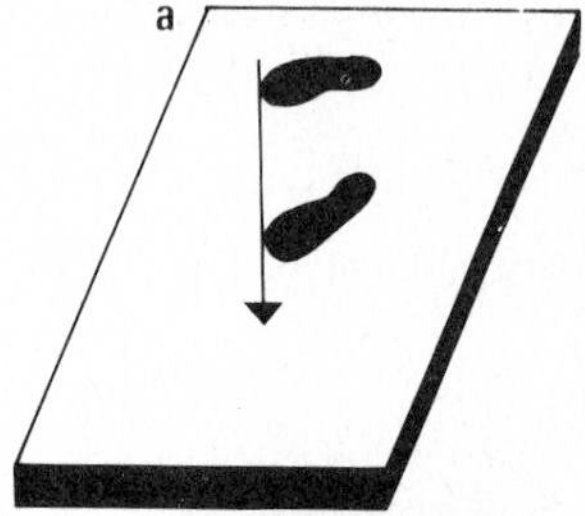


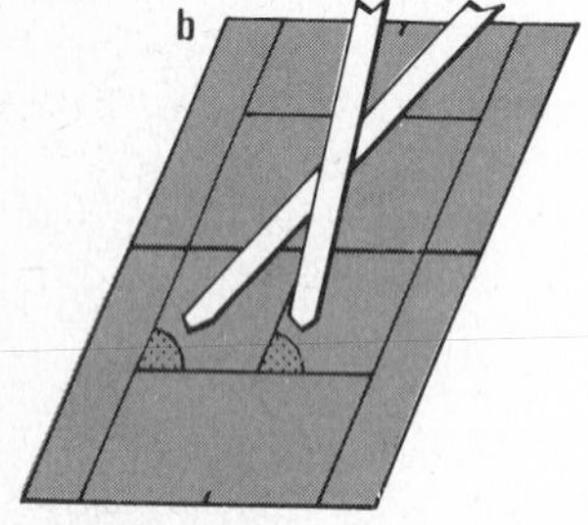


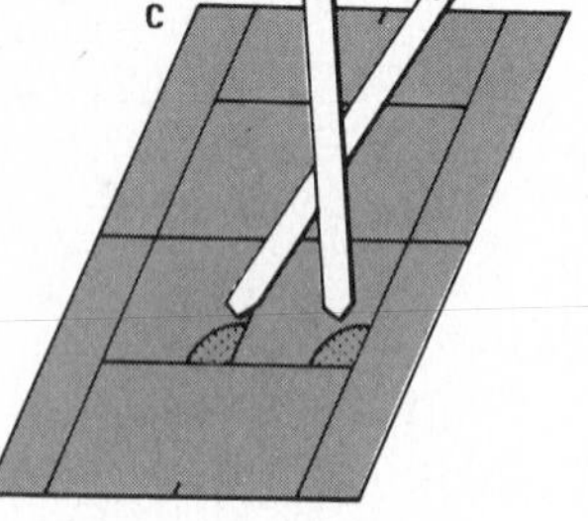


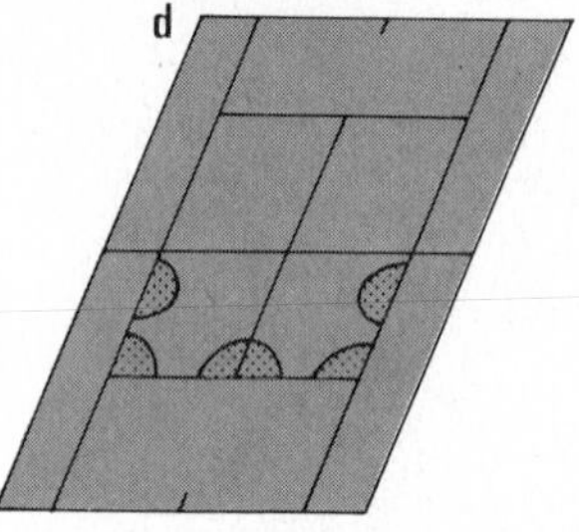


**service**

Start with weight forward, and racquet head pointing at the target (**1**). Then let both arms fall straight as your body weight starts to swing back (**2**). Bring your front arm up to place the ball, while the racquet swings back and up, and your body turns sideways (**3,4**). Your front arm should go on pointing at the ball after it has left your hand (**5**). The racquet swings behind your head, knees bend, and the body tilts back (**6**).

**beginner's service**
Start by standing as shown (**1**), racquet resting lightly against your left hand and pointing forward at the target. Then raise both hands together (**2**). The racquet comes back past your head as your body turns sideways, while your other hand "places" the ball. Gradually build on this, adding upward stretch, "backscratcher" loop, and then the full backswing.

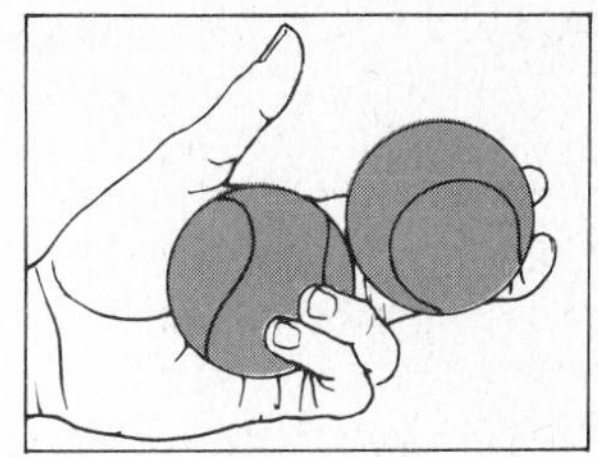

Use the grip shown to hold two balls in one hand if necessary; but many top players prefer to keep the spare ball in a pocket.

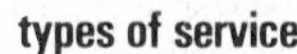

**types of service**
There are three main types:
the normal flat service, without spin (see "service," below);
the slice service, which has sidespin from right to left;
and the American twist, which mainly has topspin.
The last two both use the chopper grip. The twist is only for very advanced players, but the slice can be tried once the basic flat service is mastered. The ball is thrown up so it would fall to the right of the server, and struck a long glancing blow from left to right with the arm slightly bent.

As your body starts to move forward again, let the racquet drop into the "backscratcher" position (**7,8**); then throw it at the ball as you uncoil (**9**), making contact as your shoulders come parallel to the net (**10**). Finally your weight carries you forward into the court, as the follow-through brings the racquet right across your body (**11,12**).

**lob**

This is played with normal grip, footwork, and backswing (**1**), but the racquet swings lower so it is rising as it meets the ball (**2**), and continues for a high follow-through (**3**). Use an open racquet angle for the impact. For a defensive shot that gains time, hit the ball sharply up; for an attacking shot, hit lower less powerfully, and add topspin.

**smash**

Use the forehand or chopper grip. Get in position, sideways on, directly under the falling ball, with your left arm pointing up at it (**1**). Lean back, taking your racquet back over your shoulder into the backscratcher position (**2**). Then throw the racquet at the ball, letting your weight come forward and shoulders turn for the impact, and follow through (**3**).

**half volley**

When forced to take the ball off the bounce, get sideways to the net (**1**) and well down to the ball, so you are almost touching the ground with your trailing knee. From a short backswing, meet the ball just as it comes off the ground (**2**), using a slightly open racquet face and a rising swing. Follow through in the direction you are aiming the shot (**3**).

**drop shot**

Disguise is important here: use normal grip and backswing (**1**). The stroke is also as usual up to the moment of impact, when the wrist turns to slide the racquet under the ball (**2**), for a firm but gentle pushing and lifting action. The follow-through must be level and must follow the flight of the ball (**3**). Some players add backspin.

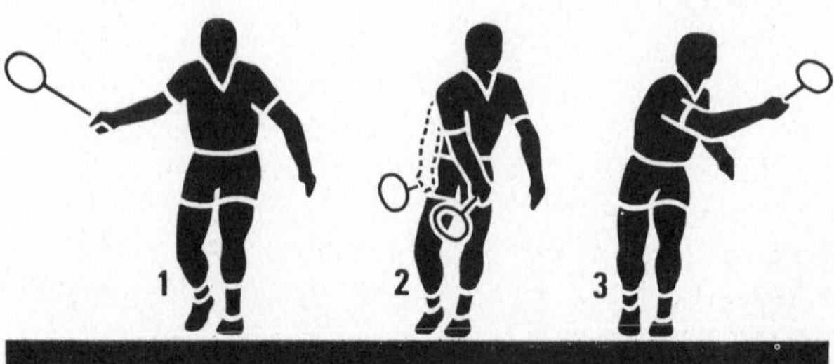

**spin**

Although it should not be tried by beginners, spin – mainly topspin – is once again a feature of top-class tennis. The techniques used to apply it are fairly typical of racquet sports in general (see p. 17). Compared with the stroke for a "flat hit" without spin (**a**), the topspin stroke (**b**) swings low to meet the ball with a rising motion; and after impact the wrist turns to roll the racquet face up and over the ball. The stroke for backspin (**c**) meets the ball with a falling motion, and a slightly open racquet angle; and after impact the wrist turns to slide the racquet under the ball. But because of the way the fluffy nap of a tennis ball meets the air, the effect of spin is rather different from other racquet sports. Compared to a drive without spin (**a**), a topspin drive dips in the air – so it can be aimed higher or hit harder, and still bounce in court (**b**). On bouncing, it kicks up, rebounding high and forward. Backspin, on the other hand, makes the ball rise in flight – adding depth to a shot aimed low, and gaining time by holding it in the air longer (**c**). On the bounce it stays low and short. Sidespin is also sometimes used.

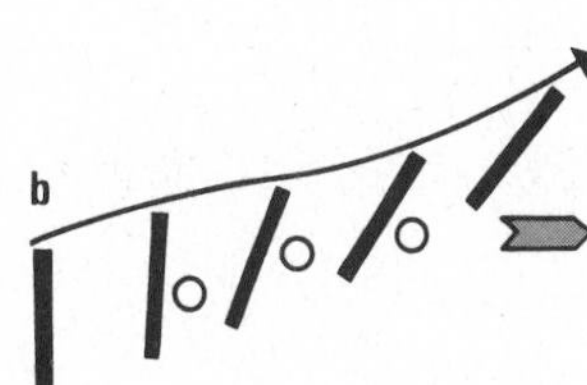


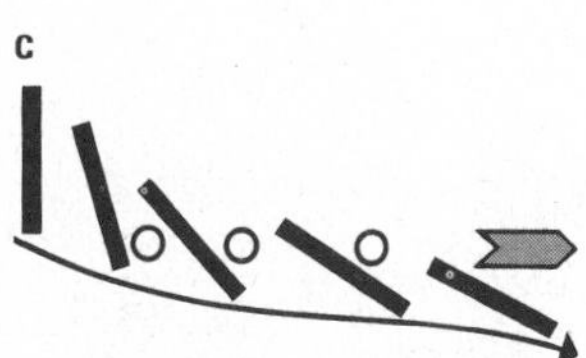

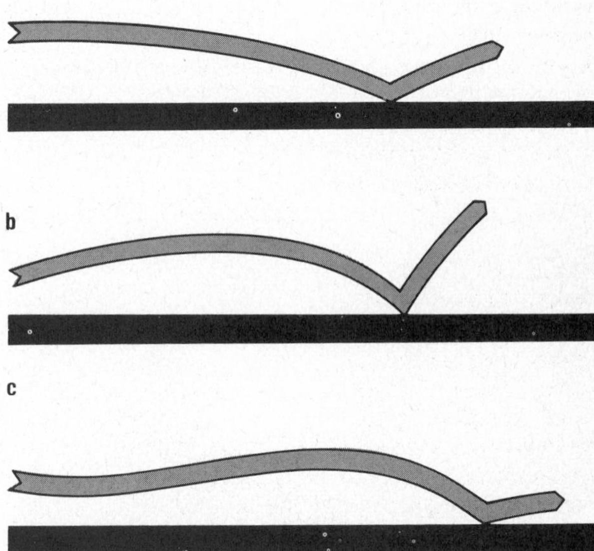


**use of shots**

The various strokes give you all the shots shown on p. 14. But you must also put these shots together, in a successful pattern of play. Here players fall into two types: baseline players, and net rushers. The net rusher likes to move in to volley the ball. As soon as he can, he follows a shot in – often his own service, or any flat, deep drive. He aims to take the next shot from the service line, then go to the net if possible. His shots angle away from his opponent; his first often goes down the line, to be followed by a cross-court point winner.

A baseline player uses deep drives to prevent the net player moving in, and gentle shots to his feet if he starts to do so. Against an opponent who has reached the net, he uses lobs and "passing shots" – i.e., drives that are out of the opponent's reach. His defensive passes are often played down the line, his point winners cross-court.

When one baseline player meets another, the one less good at the net game will use deep drives all the time, varying their pace, spin, and direction, to try to force an error. The other will alternate the same drives with short drives and drop shots, to force his opponent forward.

# Badminton

There is a unique feature to badminton; for instead of a ball, it uses a shuttlecock—a "bird" of feathers stuck in a cork base. Hit hard, this can travel almost faster than the eye can follow; yet the moment it starts to slow, the feathers catch the air, and float it gently to the ground. The result is a game with every kind of appeal. On the one hand, it is a pastime all the family can enjoy. Even a six-year-old can handle the lightweight racquet; anyone has a good chance of keeping rallies going the first time they play; and the game can be played outdoors in summer and indoors in winter. On the other hand, top-level badminton demands both tremendous fitness and tremendous cunning. The shuttlecock can come off the racquet of a champion at over 100 mph, or be abruptly turned in mid-stroke to some totally unexpected speed or direction. Badminton is still a minority sport; but one with great potential.

Badminton grew out of the ancient children's game of battledore and shuttlecock. The first modern developments were in the 1860s, at the Duke of Beaufort's estate at Badminton in England—hence the name. English army officers took the game out to India, while at home it spread to seaside resorts. Gradually, rules were standardized—though it was only in 1901 that the original "hour-glass" court was made into a rectangle. Today, the International Badminton Federation has links with more than seventy countries, and in some of these — such as Denmark, Malaya, Thailand, and Indonesia — badminton is the major national sport.

Many features of badminton are very similar to tennis. The most obvious differences in court and equipment are the high net and use of a shuttlecock instead of a ball.

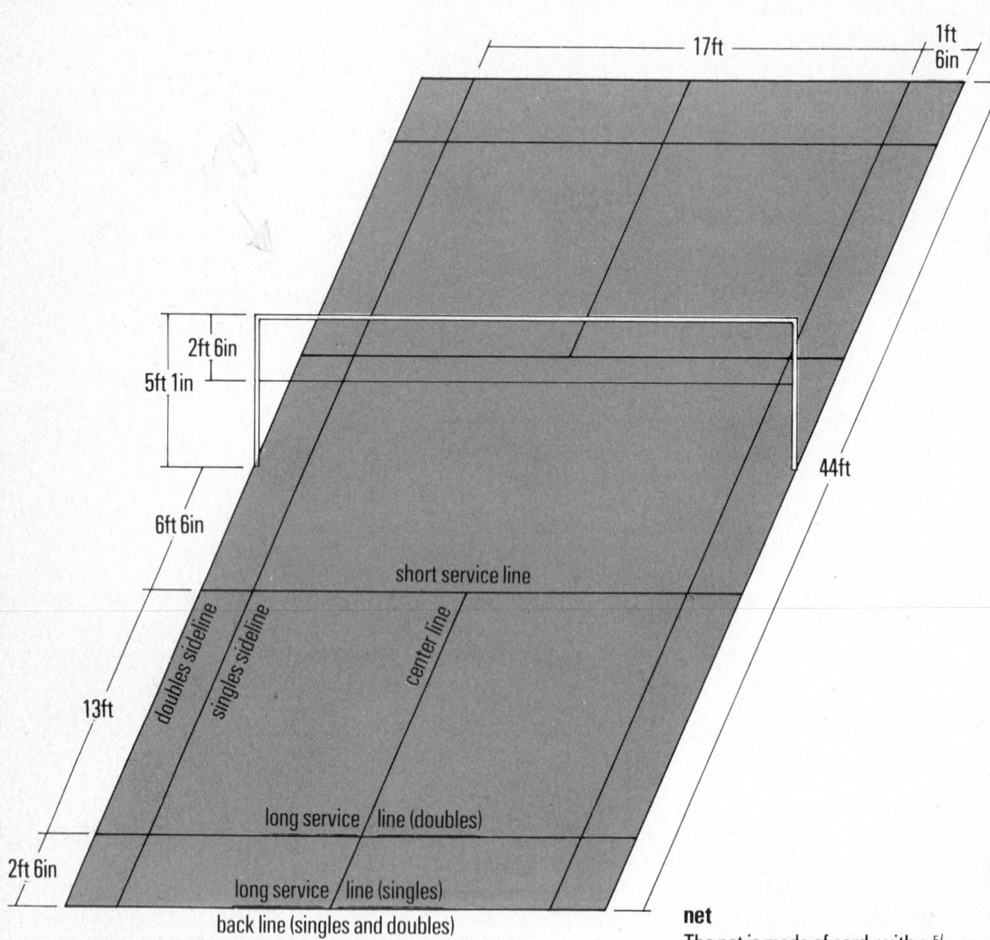


**net**
The net is made of cord, with a 5/8 to 3/4 inch mesh. It is tightly stretched, so that its top edge is virtually level with the top of the support posts. (The posts must be strong enough to allow this.)
If the supports are outside the court area, a post or strip of material is fixed vertically from the boundary line to the top of the net. This marks off the part of the net that is "out of court."

**court**
Badminton can be played out of doors, but it is better indoors as there is less air movement to affect the shuttlecock. (Ventilation drafts should be avoided.)
The court is marked out as shown, with lines 1½ inches wide. As in tennis, the lines count as part of the areas they enclose (the center line counts as being in both service courts). Space around the court should be at least 3 feet to any side wall, 4 feet to an adjacent court, and 5 feet to a back wall.
The court surface should be non-slip, and is usually wood.

**singles and doubles**
As in tennis, the outside alleys are not used in singles. But singles and doubles also use different service areas: the doubles areas include the outside alleys, but do not go right back to the base line.

service areas

rest of playing area

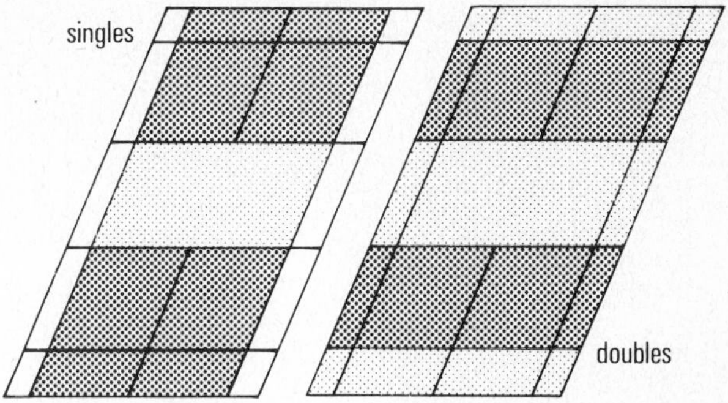

singles

doubles

**racquet**
Racquets are about 26 inches long. Shafts are usually metal, heads metal or wood, strings synthetic or gut. Wooden heads give more control, metal more power; synthetic strings last longer, while gut is more responsive. Racquets also vary in weight (4 to 5½ ounces), string tension, balance, grip, and "whip." A beginner should choose synthetic strings, even balance, comfortable weight, and moderate whip (the bending should be even along the shaft, not confined to the throat). The grip should be leather or toweling (which helps with sweaty hands), and small enough to let the fingers almost touch the palm. A thong on the handle is useful. A wooden-headed racquet needs to be stored in a press.

**dress**
Items needed are as for tennis. Special lightweight shoes are available. A track suit can be very useful for waiting or practicing.

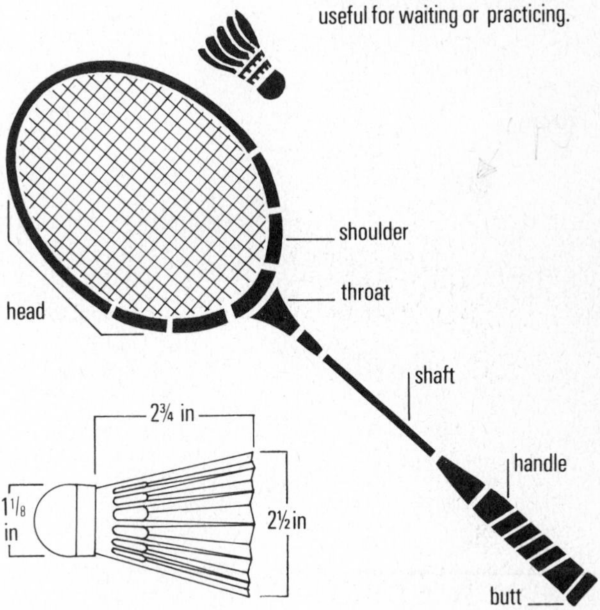

shoulder

throat

head

shaft

handle

butt

2¾ in

1⅛ in

2½ in

**shuttlecock**
The traditional shuttlecock has 14 to 16 feathers fixed in a cork base, but nylon and plastic shuttlecocks are often used, and are allowed for competition by some national associations. Feathers give better control; synthetics are cheaper and last longer. A good synthetic shuttlecock is best for a beginner. To deal with different atmospheric conditions, shuttlecocks are made in about 15 different weights, from 73 to 85 grains (⅙ to ⅕ of an ounce). The weight is set by a small metal pellet in the base. Under equal conditions, heavier shuttlecocks travel further and faster. The shape of the feathers also makes a difference: round feathers travel slower than pointed. The shuttlecock chosen for a game should be one that, when hit up from above one back line with a full underhand stroke, falls between 1 foot and 2 feet 6 inches short of the other back line. Use of too-slow shuttlecocks is a common mistake. It results in over-hard hitting and an over-defensive game.

Shuttlecocks should be kept in a cool, moist atmosphere, handled carefully, and their barbs kept smooth. Never use badly worn shuttlecocks.

Many of the people who take up badminton have a knowledge of tennis. So it is useful to point out the main ways in which badminton is different.

The badminton shuttlecock will not bounce—so to hit it back, it must be volleyed. In fact, it is a "fault" against you if you let the shuttlecock touch the ground on your side of the net. (A fault in badminton is any infringement, whether on service or in play.)

The main aim in badminton, then, is simply to hit the shuttlecock to the floor on the opponent's side of the net.

As in tennis, the service is a diagonal shot, hit into whichever service court is diagonally opposite. It is not taken from the base line, though, but from the server's own service court.

The service is also taken not overarm, but underarm, with both feet on the ground. The shuttlecock must not be above waist level when it is hit for the service, and the head of the racquet must be clearly below the level of the hand holding the racquet.

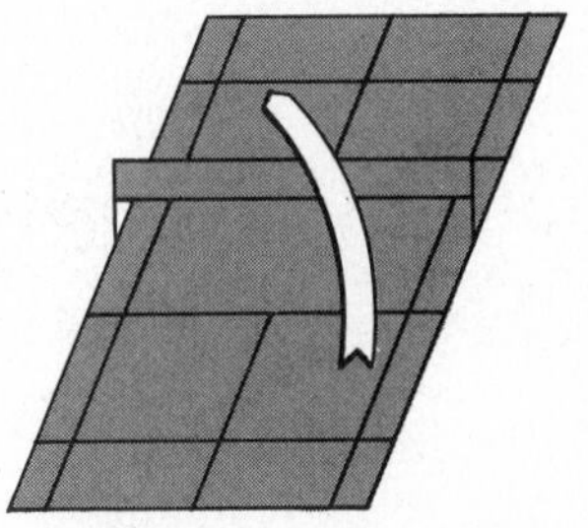

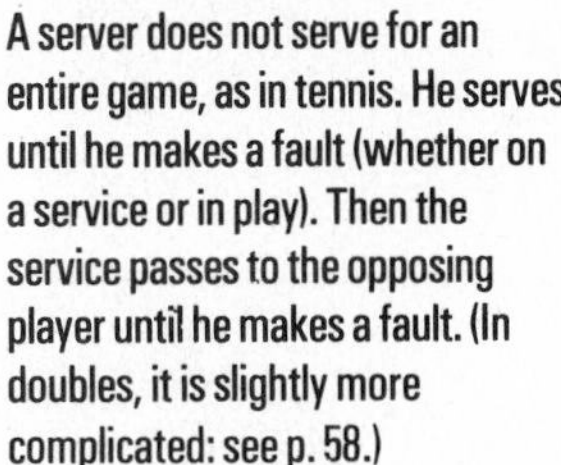

A server does not serve for an entire game, as in tennis. He serves until he makes a fault (whether on a service or in play). Then the service passes to the opposing player until he makes a fault. (In doubles, it is slightly more complicated: see p. 58.)

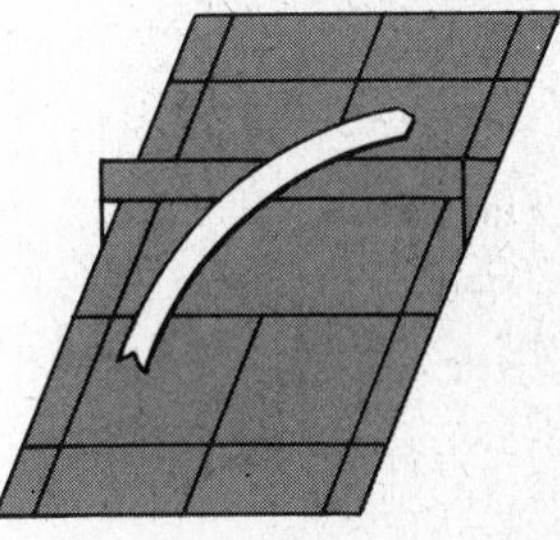

Finally, in badminton only the side that is serving may score. So if the receiving side makes a fault, the serving side wins the point and serves again for the next one. But if the serving side makes a fault, they only lose the service—their opponents do not score that point.

A fault is any infringement that ends a rally. If the serving side makes a fault, the service passes to the other side. If the receiving side makes a fault, the serving side wins the point.

bad services

a

b

**serving faults**

It is a fault if the server:
hits the shuttlecock when it is above waist level **(a)**, or when the head of the racquet is not clearly below the level of the hand holding the racquet **(b)**;
or has one or both feet off the ground, or not inside the correct service court;
or deliberately delays or makes a feinting movement before serving;
or does not hit the shuttlecock over the net and into the correct service court on the other side.

**lets**

If there is a let, the point does not count, and must be served and played for again. It is a let if:
the server serves before the receiver is ready;
or server and receiver fault simultaneously;
or there is any unforeseen or accidental hindrance;
or a player serves or receives from the wrong court or out of turn and his side wins the rally (if his side loses the rally, the point stands).
(Note that a receiver cannot claim he was unready if he attempts to return the shuttlecock.)
If there is an umpire, lets are awarded at his discretion; if there is not, lets must be claimed and agreed to. A let must be claimed or given immediately. (Position lets must be claimed or given before the next service.)

**general faults**

It is a fault by either side at any time during play if:
the shuttlecock is hit so that it drops outside the court (**a**), or fails to go over the net (**b**), or touches the roof or side walls (**c**);
or a player hits the shuttlecock before it crosses to his side of the net (**d**), or hits it twice before returning it (**e**), or if it is "caught" or "slung" on his racquet instead of being hit cleanly;
or a player touches the net with his body, racquet, or clothes while the shuttlecock is in play (**f**);

(Note that the server's feet only have to touch a line round the court he serves from, for it to be a fault. But when a serve lands on a line round the court served into, it is still good.)

**receiving faults**

It is a fault against the receiving side if the receiver:
delays or moves before the service;
or does not have both feet in the correct service court when the serve is made.

or a player and his partner (in doubles) hit the shuttlecock with successive strokes (**g**);
or a player is hit by the shuttlecock (**h**);
or a player hits a shuttlecock that is going out of court (unless he makes a good return);
or a player obstructs an opponent.

**not faults**

It is not a fault if:
the shuttlecock is returned outside the post;
or (on service or in play) the shuttlecock touches the net as it passes over it.

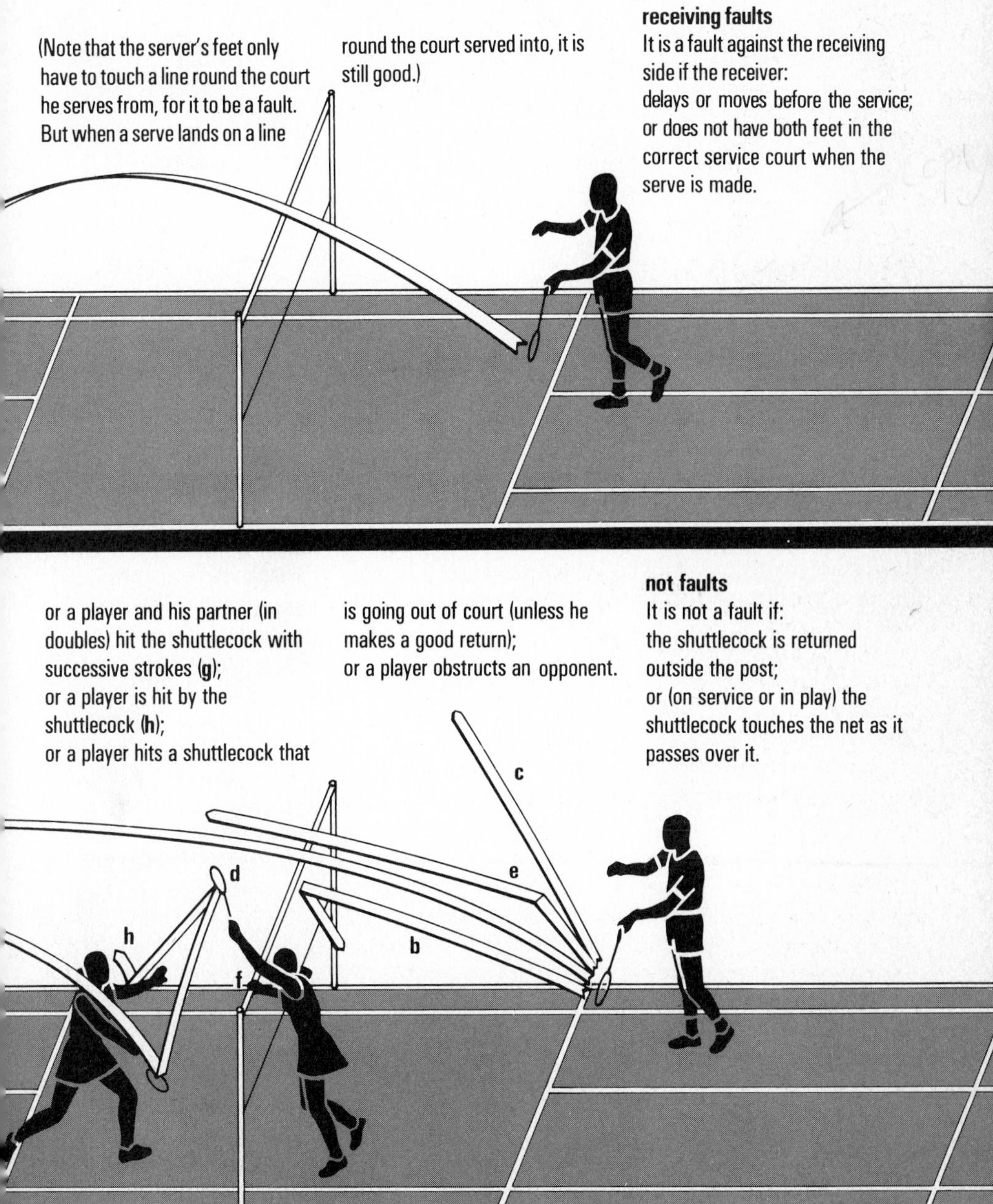

The serving order in singles is quite simple, but in doubles it is a little more complicated.

**first service**

The first service of a match (singles or doubles) is decided by spinning a racquet: see p. 59, start of play. Thereafter, the side winning one game serves first in the next.

**singles serving**

In singles, one player serves until he makes a fault. The serving court is always decided by the server's score. If his score is even (or zero) he serves from his right-hand court; if odd, from his left. (If a game is "set"—see p. 59—it is still the total score in the game that counts.)

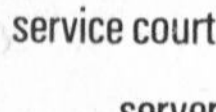


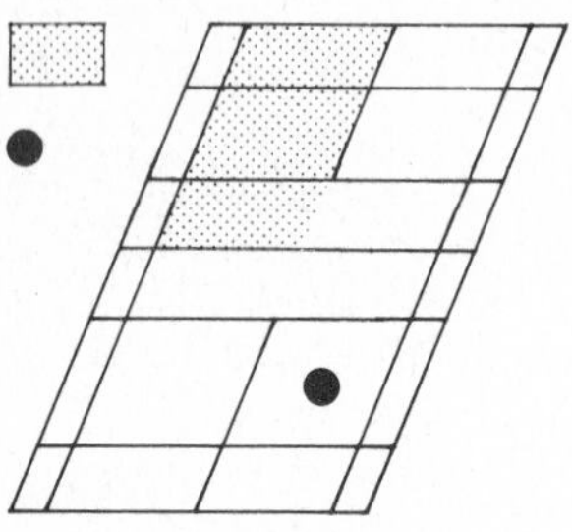

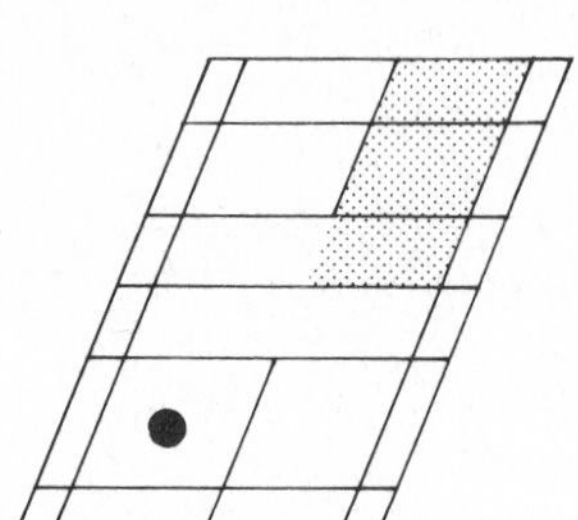

**doubles serving**

In doubles:
one player serves until his side makes a fault;
he changes courts for each point, but the receivers do not;
on the first fault by the serving side in a game, the service passes to the other side;
but thereafter both partners in a side have service opportunities before the service passes to the other side.
For example:
The side with the right to serve first in the game (a and b) decide which of them will take the opening service. They choose a, for example. Similarly the opposing pair (x and y) choose which of them will receive the opening service. They choose x, for example. Player a serves for the opening point of the game (**1**). If his side wins it, he changes to the other service court, and serves to the other opponent, y (**2**). When the serving side makes a fault, the service passes to the opponent who was in the right-hand service court at the start of the rally: x. He serves alternately from that court to whoever was diagonally opposite at the start of the last rally—b, for example (**3**)—and from the other to the other opposing partner, a (**4**), until his side makes a fault. Then his partner, y, takes over, serving first from the court he was in at the beginning of the previous rally. He also serves from alternate courts (**5** and **6**) until his side makes a fault. The service then passes back to the other side, each of whom similarly has a service opportunity before x and y regain the service.

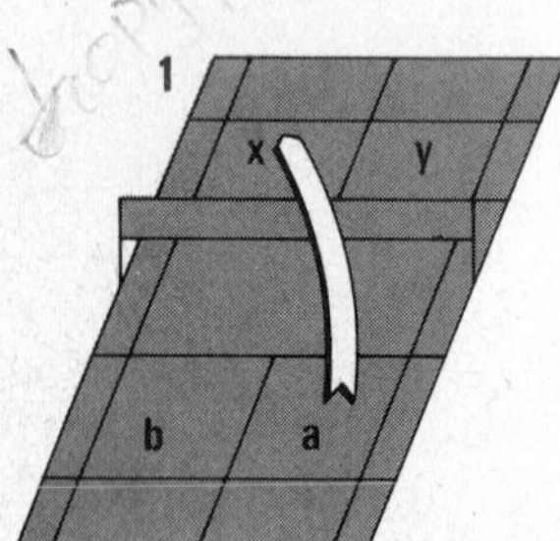


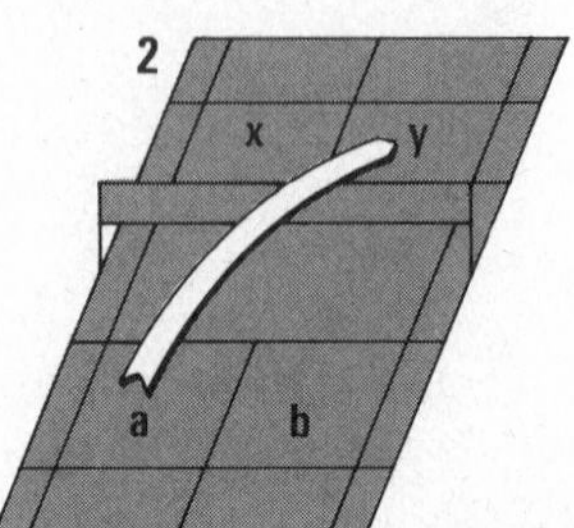


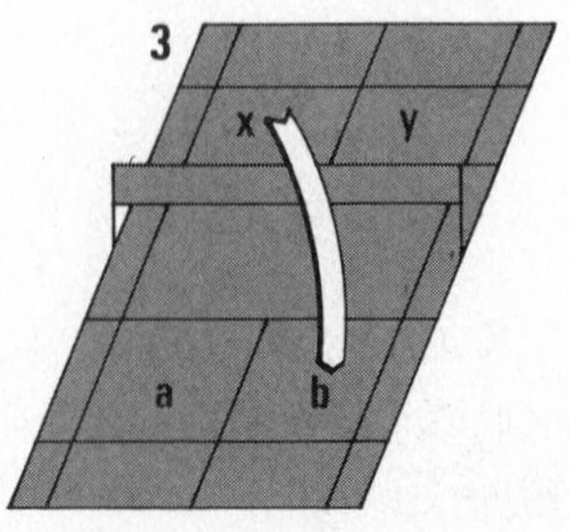

Match procedure is the same for both singles and doubles.

**start of play**
The choice of service and ends is decided by spinning a racquet, as in tennis (see p. 37). The side winning the call can choose to serve first or not to serve first, or can choose ends. The other side then makes whichever choice remains.

**scoring**
The game is won by the first side to reach an agreed points total. In doubles and men's singles, this total is either 15 or 21 points. In women's singles, it is 11 points.
A match is won by the first side to win two games.

**calling the scores**
As in tennis, the score is called after each point, and the word "love" is used for a zero score.

**change of ends**
Sides change ends after every game, and also halfway through the third game (if there is one). The change in the third game occurs when the leading side reaches 8 points in a 15-point game, 6 points in an 11-point game, or 11 points in a 21-point game.

**setting**
If both sides reach the same score in the last stages of a game, play may be extended by setting a new deciding score. For example, if the score reaches 13-all in a 15-point game, the side that reached 13 first may choose to "set the game to 5" —raising the deciding score to 18 points. If this option to "set" is not taken up at 13-all, it may still be taken up at 14-all (by whichever side reached 14 first) and set to 3. In a 21-point game, "setting" may take place in the same way at 19-all (set to 5) or 20-all (set to 3). In an 11-point game, "setting" may take place at 9-all (set to 3) or 10-all (set to 2).
A side wishing to "set" the game must do so before the next service is taken. When the game is "set," the score reverts to love-all, and proceeds to 2, 3, or 5 as decided. (But the final score is recorded as the total number of points scored in the game.)
No setting is allowed in handicap matches.

**tournament play**
In competitions, an umpire supervises play and decides the scoring, helped by service judges and linesmen. There may also be a referee to whom players may appeal on points of law. Play is basically continuous, with no breaks for rest or advice. But most national organizations allow a rest between the second and third games of a singles match, and many allow the same in doubles also.

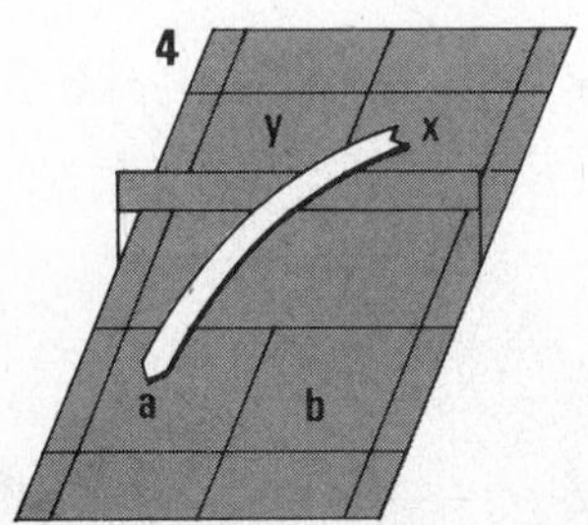


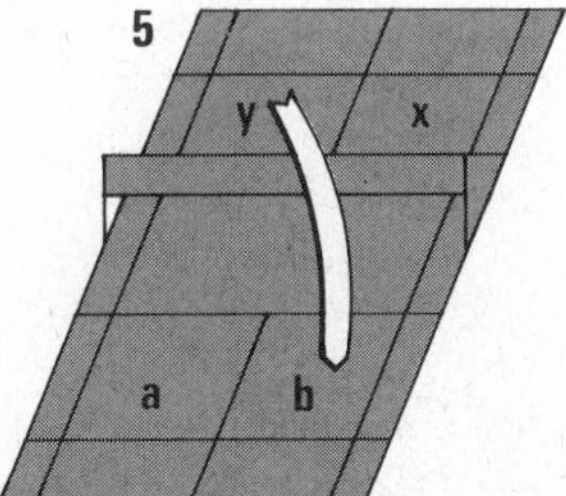


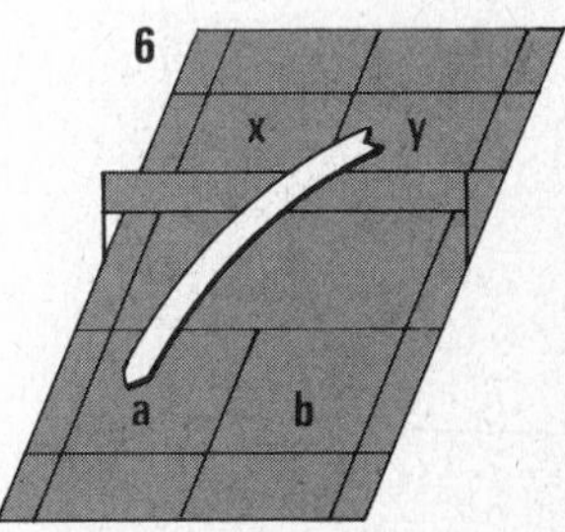

**forehand**
This can be found in the same way as a tennis forehand (**a** – **d**; also see p. 44). The resulting grip has the index finger extended forward, as in tennis. But as badminton uses smaller grip sizes, the racquet is held more in the fingers than in the palm of the hand. Note that the side of the thumb is against the side of the handle.

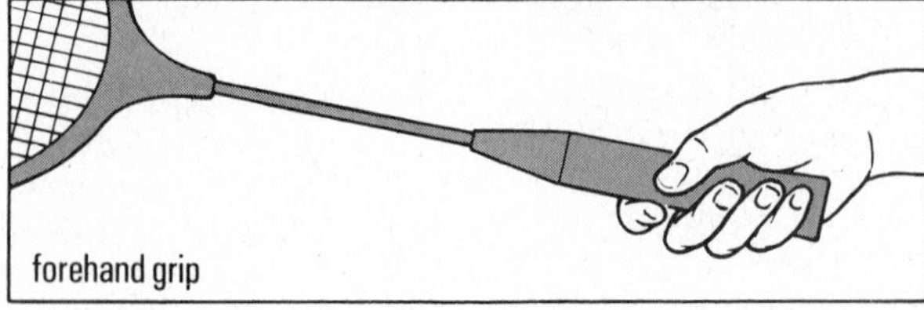


forehand grip

**backhand**
Hold the racquet in front of you in the forehand grip (**a**), and take hold of the throat with your non-playing hand (**b**). Twist the racquet head clockwise by 45°, so the handle twists in your playing hand (**c**). Then turn your wrist so the racquet head is square again (**d**). Also adjust your thumb so it lies flat and straight along the side of the handle.

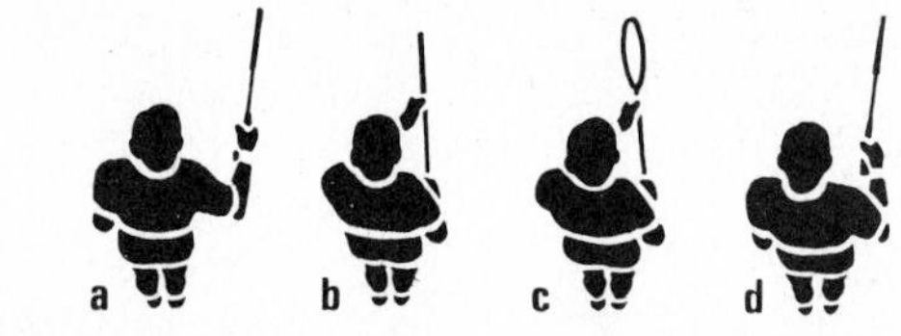


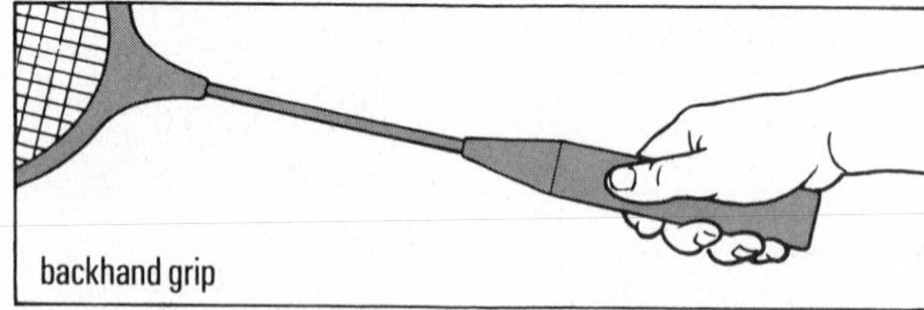

backhand grip

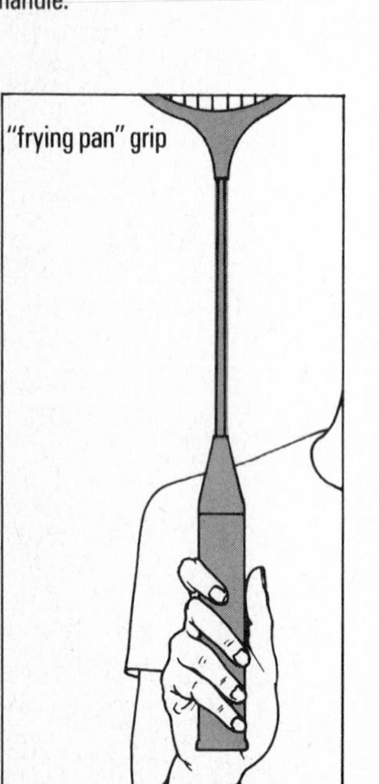

"frying pan" grip

**"frying pan"** (left)
This allows little backswing or follow-through, and is only used for some net shots. The racquet is held like a fly-swat, so the shuttle can easily be hit straight ahead or down, but not up. The grip is as for the forehand, but with the racquet turned 90° clockwise.

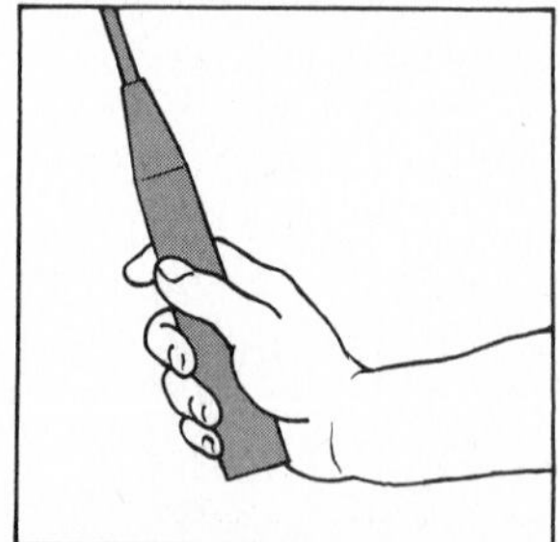

**wrist action** (right)
As racquet and shuttlecock are so light, the wrist can be used to give extra power. It is kept cocked as it leads into the stroke, then uncocked a split second before impact, so the racquet "swishes" through the air. To aid deception, this action is almost always used, whether extra power is needed on a stroke or not.

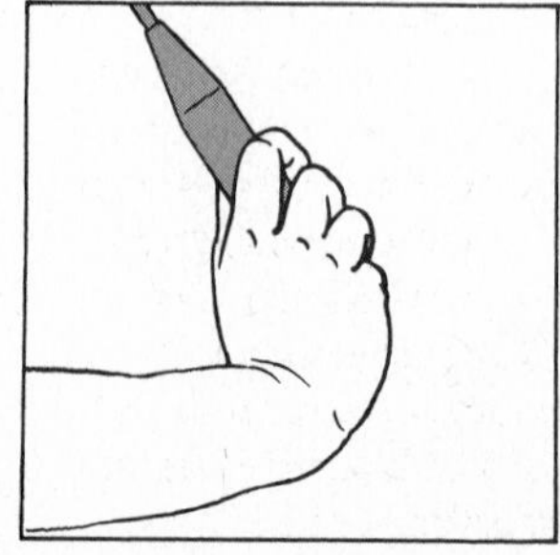

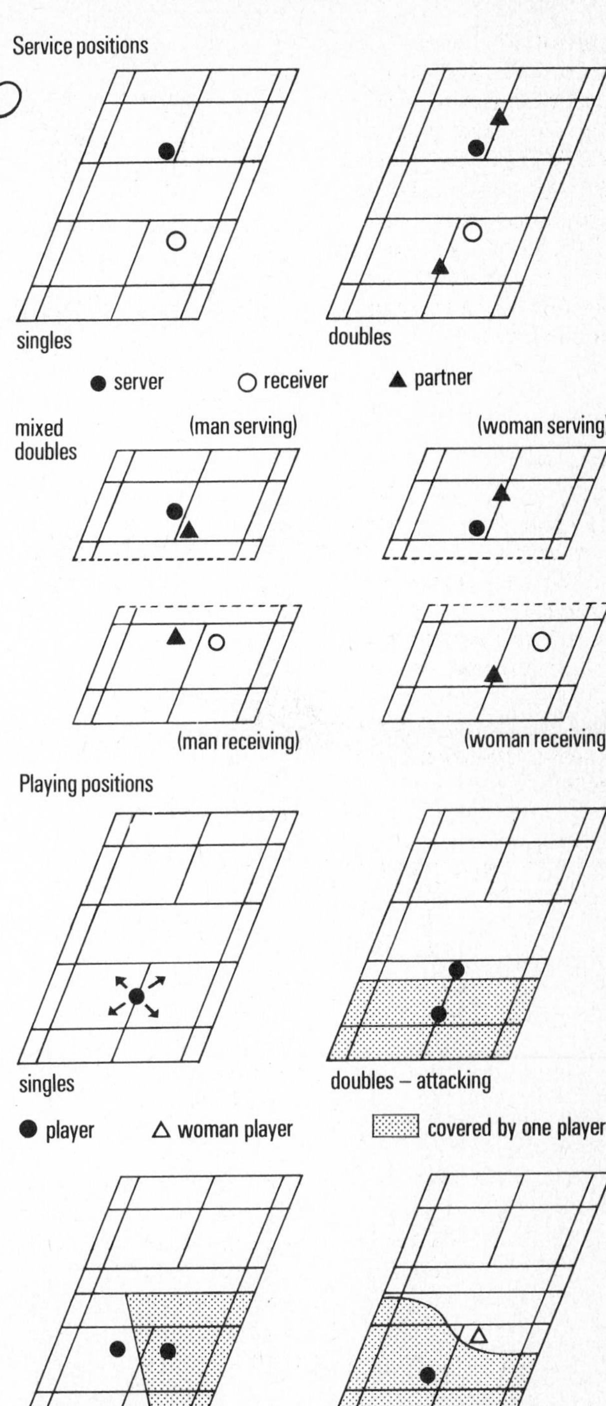


**stance and positioning**
The basic ready stance (**a**) is typical of racquet games in general (see p.18). There are also more aggressive stances for receiving service. The one shown (**b**) is for doubles play.
The service diagrams show positioning for a service to the right-hand court. Those for a service to the left-hand court are generally a mirror image of these.
The playing positions show the bases to which players should try to return after making a stroke – and, for doubles, how partners should divide the court.
Your main aim is to force your opponent to hit the shuttle up, and then be in a position to smash it back down. The singles game demands great fitness and maneuverability. Clears to the back court and drop shots to the front keep your opponent running, while you try to hold to your center-court base. In doubles, clears are more dangerous, as there is more likely to be an opponent in position to smash the shuttlecock back. If there is a situation where the shuttlecock can be hit downward, the other side go into defensive positions at once. In mixed doubles, the woman usually guards the net, and drives and pushes are the main strokes.

**types of service**
Badminton services are defensive, because of the restrictions on the service action (see p. 56). The main techniques used are:
the short service, to the front of the opponent's service court (**a**);
and the high service, to the back of his service court (**b**).
In singles a high service is usual, in doubles a short service.

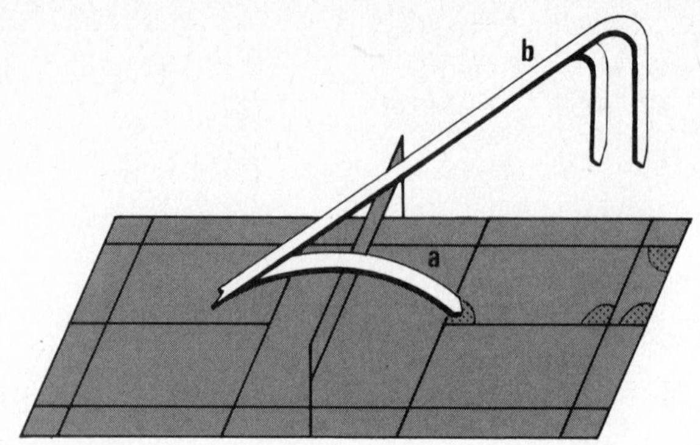


short service

**short service** (above)
**1** Stand with feet as shown, shoulders almost square to the net. Hold the shuttlecock by the tips of the feathers, at shoulder height. Hold the racquet with the normal forehand grip, wrist cocked.
**2** Lean forward, lifting your rear heel and releasing the shuttlecock.
**3** Swing the racquet gently through to meet the shuttlecock. The wrist stays cocked, the heel of the hand leads the stroke, and the elbow almost brushes the hip as it goes past.
**4** The follow-through takes the racquet to shoulder height.
Note: the shuttlecock should reach its highest point before crossing the net.

**high service** (below)
Compared with the short service technique, notice that:
**1** the stance is more sideways, with higher positions of racquet and shuttlecock;
**2** the body leans back on the downswing, and the shuttlecock is thrown a little way forward;
**3** the wrist uncocks on contact;
**4** the follow-through is higher.

high service

**swinging the racquet**
Almost all badminton strokes are derived from the three basic ways in which you can swing a racquet: overhead (**a**), sidearm (**b**), and upward (**c**). On this page, these swings are shown on the forehand side; on the next, on the backhand. Overhead swings are mainly used for attack, upward for defense. Sidearm swings are used for fencing to gain the initiative.

**forehand overhead swing**
From the ready stance, step back with your right foot, and turn sideways as the racquet swings back, up, and over, into the "backscratcher" position (**1**). Sway back, and let your free hand also rise to point at the approaching shuttlecock. Then swing racquet and body weight forward, uncocking the wrist for the impact (**2**). Follow through (**3**).

**forehand sidearm swing**
From the ready stance, step back with your right foot, and lift the racquet back over your shoulder to the backscratcher position (**1**). Then swing the racquet forward level with the floor, uncoiling your body, and strike the shuttlecock between waist and shoulder height (**2**). Uncock the wrist for the impact. Follow through (**3**).

**forehand upward swing**
Begin as for the sidearm swing (**1**), but on the stroke swing the racquet down toward the floor (**2**), so your elbow brushes against your hip. Body weight moves forward with the stroke. Follow through high in front of the body (**3**).

**stances**
The diagram shows how the various swings use different stances in relation to the net. (Of course, they often have to be modified in play.) Note that the descriptions on this page and the last use a backward movement from the ready position, into each stance; but they can also be reached, of course, by moving the opposite foot forward, as the racquet swings back.

**backhand overhead swing**
From the ready stance, step back with your left foot, turning away from the net, and swing the racquet back so your racquet hand comes up by your left ear, with the racquet head pointing downward (**1**). Then swing racquet and body weight at the shuttlecock, uncocking the wrist for the impact (**2**). Follow through (**3**).

**backhand sidearm swing**
From the ready stance, step back with your left foot, and lift the racquet until the racquet head is by your left shoulder (**1**). Then swing the racquet forward level with the floor, uncoiling your body and uncocking your wrist on impact (**2**). Follow through (**3**).

**backhand upward swing**
End the backswing with the racquet pointing upward (**1**). Then swing the racquet down toward the floor, turning into the stroke (**2**). Follow through (**3**).

### playing the shots

Each of the basic swings can be used to give very different results, by varying the impact point, racquet angle, and force. This means that shots can often be disguised until the last moment: deception is very important.

shots from overhead strokes

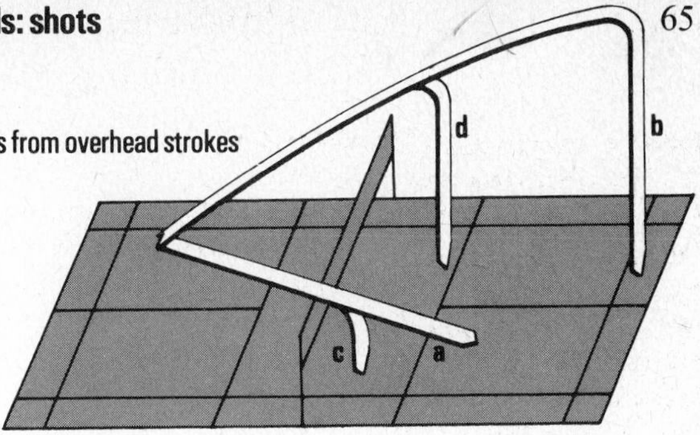

### overhead strokes

The main attacking shot in badminton is the smash (**a**), the main defensive one the clear (**b**). For the smash, the shuttlecock is hit when it is still just in front of you; for the clear, when it is overhead or just behind you, so the wrist is still partly cocked on impact. The fast drop shot (**c**) is played in the same way as the smash, and the floating drop shot (**d**) in the same way as the clear–but in each case the arm and wrist action is eased off.

smash

clear

### sidearm strokes

The drive (**e**) uses the full sidearm swing as already described. The half court push (**f**) is the same but eases up on impact. The drop shot (**g**) is played even more gently, and with the racquet face open instead of vertical.

shots from sidearm and upward strokes

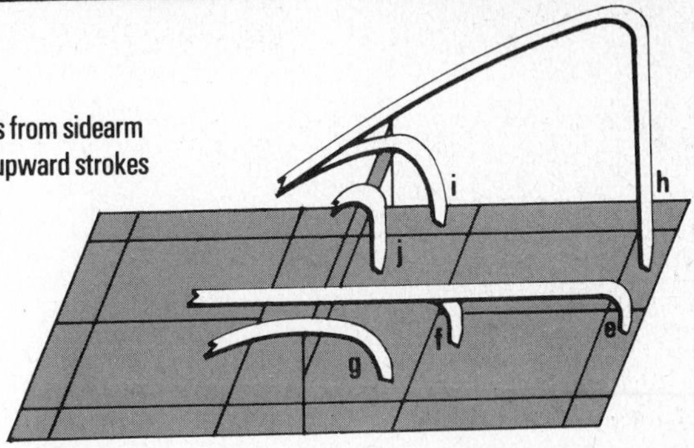

### upward strokes

The underarm clear (or lob) (**h**) is played with a full upward swing that meets the shuttlecock a little in front of the body, as for a high service (p. 62). The low return (**i**) eases off on impact. For the underarm net shot (**j**), the swing meets the shuttlecock well in front of the body, when the racquet face is almost horizontal.

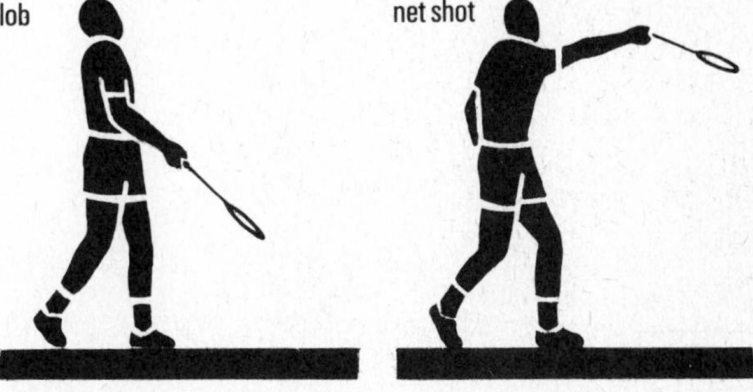

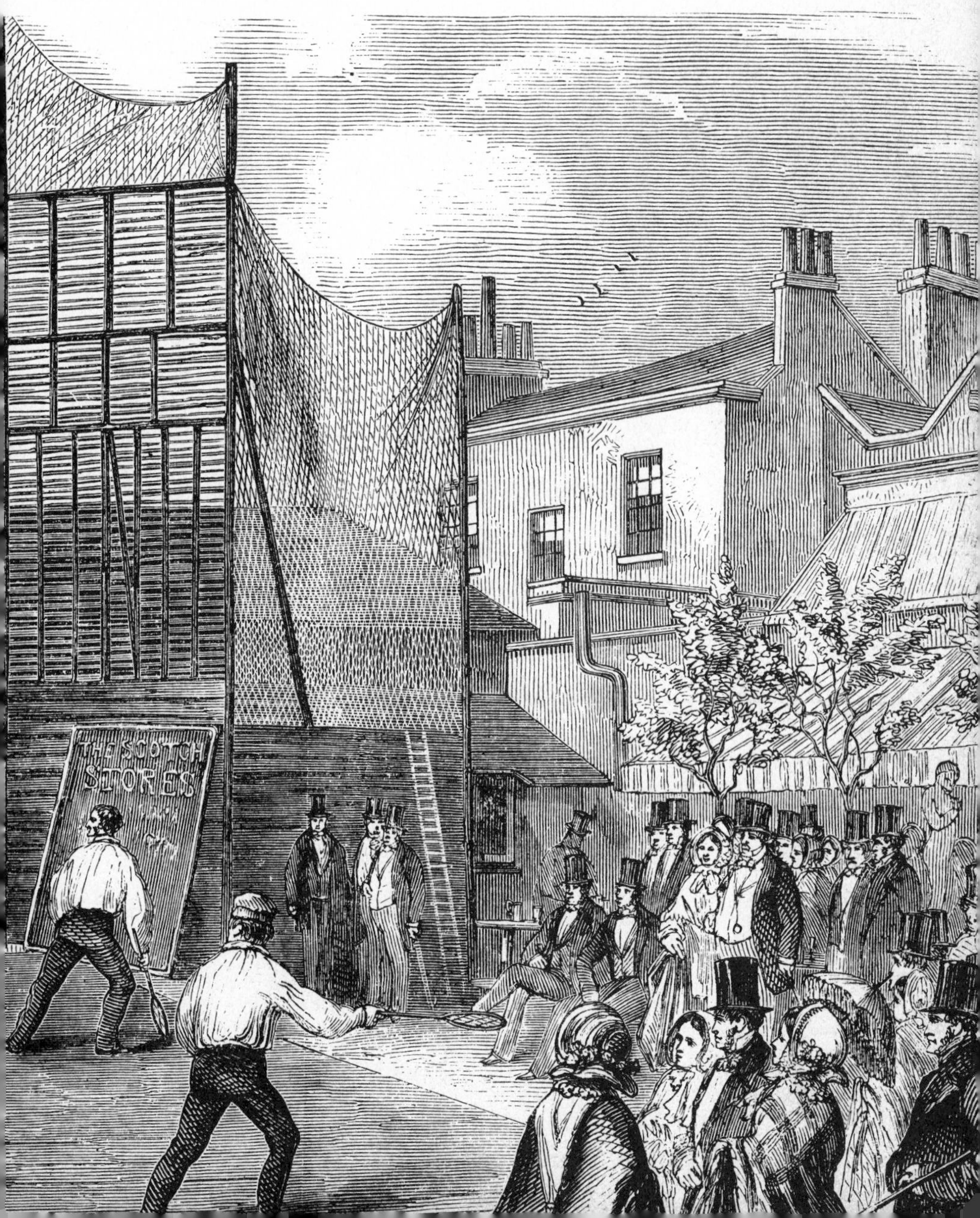
THE SCOTCH
STORES

# Squash

In the last 10 years, squash has grown from a minority activity to an international sport. For the ordinary player, it combines two virtues: it is easy to play enjoyably — and it is tremendous exercise. In a walled court, with no net, the novice is not constantly hitting the ball out of play; he can have an enjoyable game, even against another beginner. But he does have to chase the ball down, and — with the constant starting, stopping, and turning — half an hour's play is as strenuous as 2 hours' tennis or 3 hours' golf. Squash, of course, also has the advantage that it can be played day or night, in any weather, so many busy people find it an easy way to keep fitness up and weight down — whether they are office workers or professional sportsmen.

Like tennis, squash is about 100 years old. It is descended from the similar but older game of rackets, which was played at certain English schools — as well as by prisoners in the confined spaces of London's debtors' prison in Fleet Street. The new game — named after its softer, "squashier" ball — gradually replaced the old one at private schools and among the wealthy, in Britain and the U.S.A. But it was outside most people's experience until World War II and after, when its effectiveness as exercise led to courts being built on many military bases and new college campuses.

In North America, the game has developed along slightly different lines from the International version. The differences are not great; but they are large enough to make it very confusing, if both games are dealt with at once. So in this chapter, even though it has meant there is some repetition, the rules and skills of the two versions are explained quite independently.

Court and equipment specifications are different for the International and North American games.

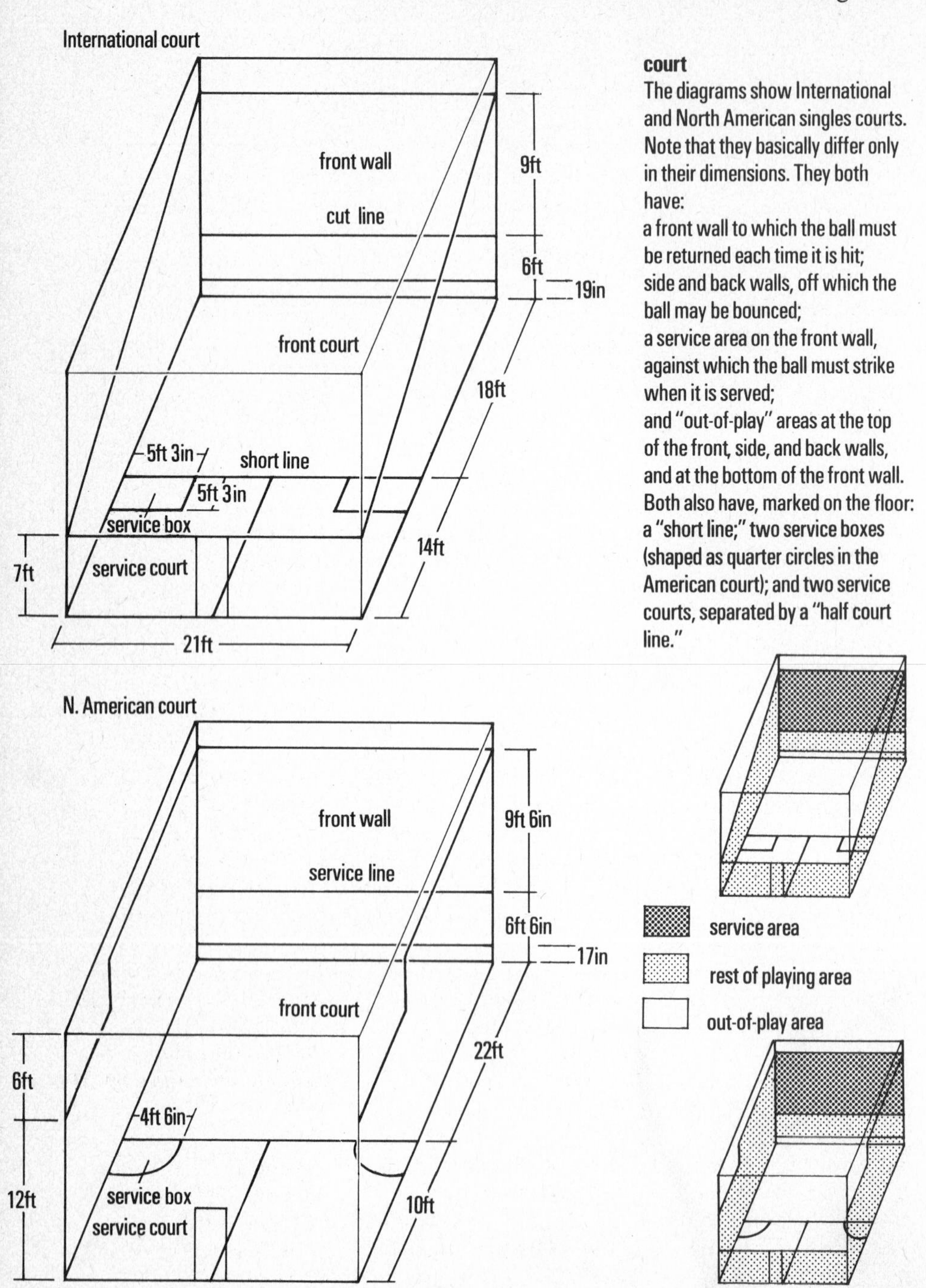


**court**
The diagrams show International and North American singles courts. Note that they basically differ only in their dimensions. They both have:
a front wall to which the ball must be returned each time it is hit;
side and back walls, off which the ball may be bounced;
a service area on the front wall, against which the ball must strike when it is served;
and "out-of-play" areas at the top of the front, side, and back walls, and at the bottom of the front wall.
Both also have, marked on the floor: a "short line;" two service boxes (shaped as quarter circles in the American court); and two service courts, separated by a "half court line."

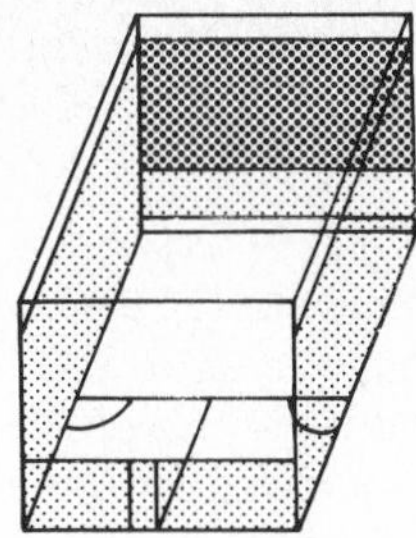

Note that the side-wall playing areas on the American court sometimes extend right back at full height. Where they do not, it is usually because side galleries have been installed, to give extra spectator space.

**tell-tale**

Tell-tale, board, or tin is the name given to a strip of material running along the foot of the front wall. It is not part of the playing area, and makes a distinctive sound when hit by the ball.

**floor and walls**

Floors are normally of wood, walls of either wood (American courts) or concrete/plaster finish (International courts). Walls and ceilings must be white. Floors in International courts are almost always left uncolored, those in American courts usually painted white. All lines are marked in red. The entry door in the back wall has a flush handle so as not to deflect the ball.

**spectator viewing**

Courts are beginning to be built with glass walls, but the usual accommodation for spectators and officials is a gallery above the back wall. As noted, this sometimes extends onto the side walls.

**racquet**

A squash racquet has a long shaft and a circular or near-circular head. The shaft is usually wood or metal, and the head must be wood, (except that American rules now permit molded fiberglass frames, that combine head and handle in one unit). The stringing is gut or synthetic material such as nylon. Under International rules, the maximum overall racquet length is 27 inches. The stringing area must not be more than 8½ inches long and 7¼ inches wide, and the framework of the head must not be more than 9/16 inch across the face and 13/16 inch deep. Under North American rules, the maximum overall length is again 27 inches, and the head is circular with an outside diameter of not more than 9 inches.

The racquet for the North American game has to be much stronger and heavier than that for the International game, because of the heavier ball used. But within each game there is a range of racquet weight, balance, string tension, grip size and shape, and shaft "whip." Primarily, a beginner should simply choose a racquet that feels comfortable – and not spend too much money, for it is easy to damage a racquet on the court walls when learning. However, he should be careful not to get one that is too heavy or has very marked whip, or that is not fairly evenly balanced. The grip material can be important, too: toweling is best for hands that sweat a lot, leather for those that blister easily.

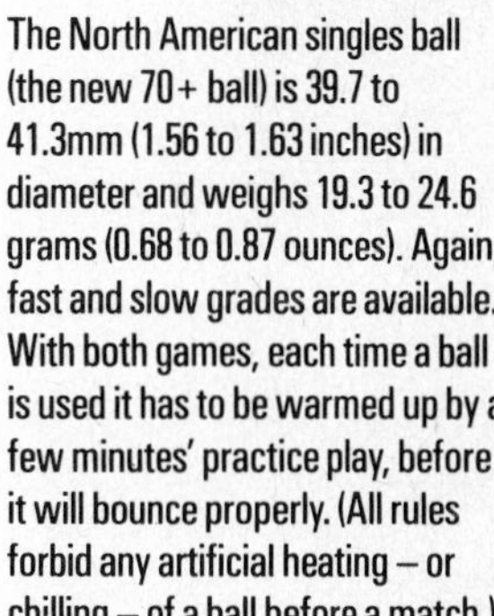

**ball**

The main difference between the International and North American games is in the ball used. Both use a small rubber or composition ball, but the American one is livelier and harder, giving the game a very different character. The International ball weighs 23.3 to 24.6 grams (0.82 to 0.87 ounces), and measures 39.5 to 41.5mm (1.56 to 1.63 inches) in diameter. It is in four grades, marked by colored dots – blue, red, white, or yellow – with blue the fastest and yellow the slowest. Fast balls are used under cold conditions and by beginners; slow ones are used under hot conditions and by skilled players.

The North American singles ball (the new 70+ ball) is 39.7 to 41.3mm (1.56 to 1.63 inches) in diameter and weighs 19.3 to 24.6 grams (0.68 to 0.87 ounces). Again, fast and slow grades are available. With both games, each time a ball is used it has to be warmed up by a few minutes' practice play, before it will bounce properly. (All rules forbid any artificial heating – or chilling – of a ball before a match.)

**dress**

This is as for tennis (see p. 33); white is usually required for competitions. Shoes should not have black soles, as they mark the court.

In squash, a player keeps on serving as long as he is winning points. When he fails to win a point, the service passes to his opponent.

**choice of service box**
Whenever the service passes to a player, he chooses from which service box to make his first service. If he then wins the point on that service, he takes the next service from the other box; then the next from the first one again; and so on, alternately, until he loses the service.
If he serves from the wrong box by mistake, the service still stands – unless his opponent makes no attempt to play it, and demands that it is served again from the correct box.

**serving technique**
To serve, the player simply throws or drops the ball into the air, and hits it before it touches the walls or floor. But at the moment he hits it, he must have at least one foot on the floor inside the serving box (and not touching any of its lines). If he does not, it is a foot fault (see "faults," opposite).

**the service**
In International squash rules, the server is called "hand-in" and the receiver "hand-out."
When a player tries to serve, three things can happen:
he may make a good service – in which case his opponent must return it or lose the point;
he may "serve his hand-out," i.e. make a mistake that immediately loses him the service – in which case his opponent does not try to play the ball, as the service passes to him anyway;
or he may make a "fault" – in which case his opponent has a choice whether to play the ball or not.

**good service**
For a good service the ball must:
reach the front wall (**1**) without bouncing off a side wall (or the back wall), and without touching the floor or the tin;
bounce on the front wall above the cut line but below the out-of-court line (**2**);
and rebound so it first touches the floor inside the opposite back quarter of the court (**3**) – though the opponent may choose to hit it before it reaches the floor.
It is still good if it bounces off a side wall (**a**), or the back wall (**b**), or both, before going into the service court – as long as it bounces off the front wall first, and does not touch any out-of-play area.

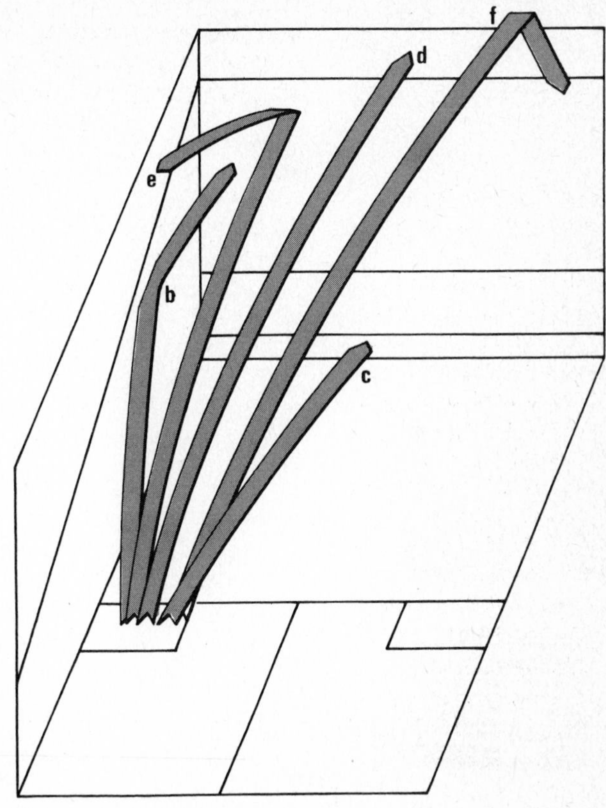


**hand-outs**

The server "serves his hand-out" if:
he does not drop or throw the ball into the air, as he serves it;
or he misses the ball;
or he hits it more than once;
or the ball touches the floor or wall before he hits it (**a**);
or it hits the floor or a side wall before it hits the front wall (**b**);
or it hits the tin (**c**);
or it touches any wall on or above the out-of-court line (**d** and **e**);
or it touches the ceiling, or lighting equipment, or passes over any roof crossbars (**f**);
or it hits the server, or anything he wears or carries, before it has bounced twice on the floor, and before the opponent has hit it.
In any of these cases, the service immediately passes to the server's opponent.

**faults**

It is a fault if:
the server foot faults;
or the ball hits the front wall on the service line (**g**), or between the service line and the tin (**h**);
or the ball first touches the floor outside the correct back quarter of court (**i** and **j**), or on one of the lines marking that quarter.
If the server serves a fault, his opponent must decide whether to try to play the ball or not. If he tries to play the ball, this makes the service "good," and the rally continues in the usual way. If he does not try to play the ball, the server must again try to make a good service, from the same service box. If he again serves a fault the service passes to his opponent.

**receiving service**

The opponent may play the ball before or after it has bounced on the floor – whether or not it was, or might have been, a fault.

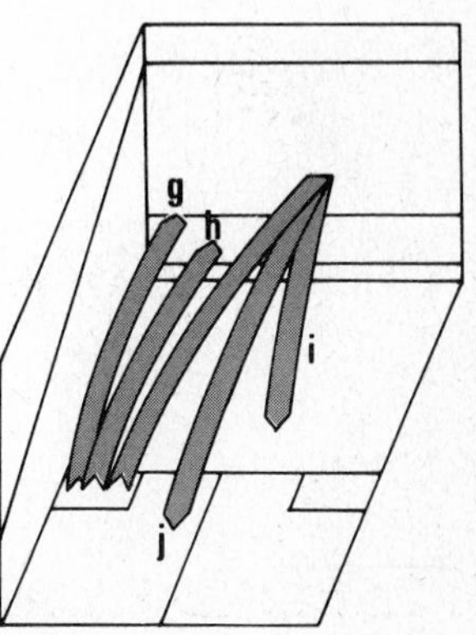

In International squash, only the server can score points. His opponent must win the service from him, before he can score.

**the rally**

Once the ball has been served, the opposing players hit the ball alternately, until one of them fails to make a good return. If it is the server who finally fails to make a good return, the service passes to his opponent. If it is the opponent, the server scores one point and serves again.

**good returns**

It is a good return if a player-
hits the ball before it has bounced twice on the floor (**1**)
so it hits the front wall above the tin and below the out-of-court line (**2**)
and then bounces back without touching any out-of-play area (**3**).
Note that it is still a good return if:
the ball does not bounce on the floor before the player hits it (**a**);
or it bounces off the side or back walls (or both) before he hits it (**b**);
or it bounces off the side or back walls (or both) after he has hit it, on its way to the front wall (**c**).
If a player plays at the ball and misses, he may still try again to make a good return.

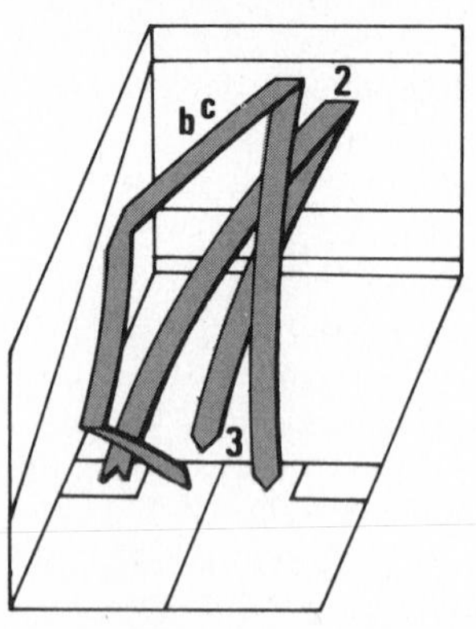

**bad returns**

It is a bad return if:
the ball bounces twice on the floor before the player hits it (**d**);
or it touches the player's body or clothing (**e**);
or it is hit twice by the player (**f**);
or it bounces on the floor after he hits it, on its way to the front wall (**g**);
or it hits the tin (**h**), even if it bounces on another part of the front wall before or after it hits the tin;
or it hits the front wall on or above the out-of-court line (**i**);
or it hits a side or back wall on or above the out-of-court line, either on its way to the front wall (**j**) or on its way back from the front wall before bouncing on the floor;
or, on its way to or from the front wall, it hits the ceiling or lighting equipment or passes over any roof crossbars (**k**).

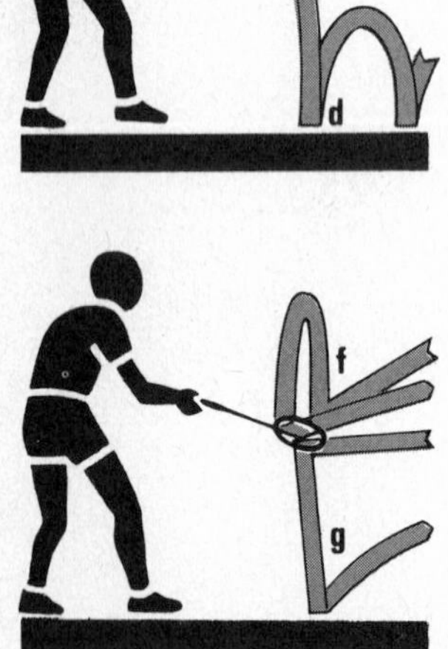


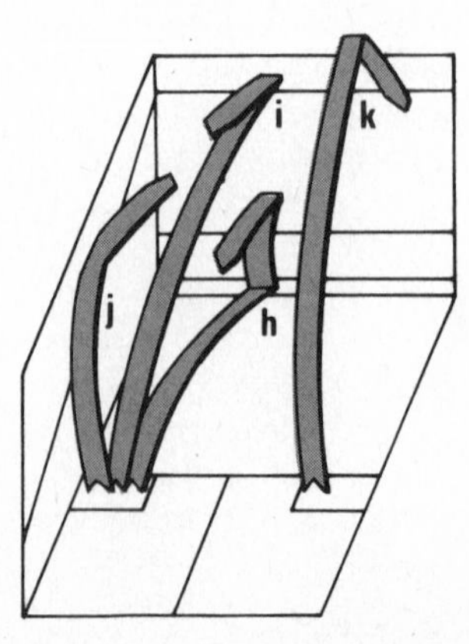

**lets**

If a "let" is given, play stops, and the server takes the service again from the same service box.

A let is always allowed if:
a player is not ready for a service, makes no attempt to play it, and appeals;
or the ball breaks during play;
or, after bouncing once on the floor from a good return, the ball goes out of play by rising to touch the ceiling or lighting equipment or a wall on or above the out-of-court line, or by passing over any roof crossbars.

A let may be given by the referee on appeal if:
a player does not play the ball for fear of injuring his opponent;
or a player is touched by the opponent as the latter plays the ball;
or the referee cannot decide on an appeal;
or a player loses a rally because his opponent distracts him (e.g., by calling out or dropping his racquet);
or the ball hits any article lying in the court.

In the last two cases, a let is not given if the player tries to play the ball.

A let may also be given in some cases where the ball hits the striker's opponent (see "ball hitting opponent").

Note that a let entitles the server to only one service attempt if he has already served a fault on the same point.

**ball hitting opponent**

What happens here depends on whether the ball hits the opponent:
before the player can play it;
or after he has tried to play it but missed;
or after he has played it.

If the ball hits his opponent before a player can play it, then the opponent loses the rally (except that a let is given if the player's position prevented the opponent getting out of the way, or prevented him seeing the ball, or made him think the player would play the ball before it hit him).

If the ball hits the opponent after a player has tried to hit it and missed, then:
if the player might otherwise have still made a good return, a let is given;
but if he could not possibly have made a good return, the player loses the rally.

If the ball hits the opponent after the player has hit it, then:
if it would not have been a good return anyway, the opponent wins the rally;
but if it would otherwise have been a good return, the player wins the rally (except that a let is given if the player had not hit the ball on his first attempt, or he turned to follow the ball around before he played it, or the ball would have touched another wall on its way to the front wall).

In all cases, the same rules apply if the ball hits anything the opponent wears or carries, including his racquet.

**interference**

After playing the ball, a player must make every effort:
to give his opponent a fair view of the ball;
not to interfere with or crowd him, or delay him with an excessive racquet swing;
and not to prevent him playing the ball directly to the front wall or to the side walls near the front wall.

If any such interference does occur, then:
if the player has not made every effort to avoid causing it, the opponent wins the rally;
if he has, it is a let – unless the opponent was prevented from a winning return, in which case he also wins the rally.

**appeals**

A player claims or appeals for a let by calling "let, please." This immediately ends the rally. But a player may not under any circumstances ask the referee to award a rally in his favor.

Scoring in squash is quite simple. The only complication is a procedure called "setting," which is seldom needed.

**knock up**
Players are allowed not more than 5 minutes' knock up before play begins. (This also serves to heat the ball to normal response.) If one player wishes, the players may knock up separately for 2½ minutes each.

**start of play**
At the start of play, the opposing players spin a racquet as in tennis (see p. 37). The winning player chooses whether to serve or receive first in the first game.

**calling the scores**
After each point, the score is called: e.g., "7-6." (The score of the player making the next serve is given first, and he makes the call if there is no referee.)

**winning the game**
The International singles game is won by the first player to reach nine points – unless the game is "set."

**setting**
If the score in any game reaches 8-all, the player to receive on the next service must call:
either "no set," in which case the game ends as usual when one player reaches 9 points;
or "set 2," in which case the game ends when one player reaches 10 points.

**the match**
The player who wins one game serves first in the next.
A match may be over the best of three games (won by the first player to win two games), or the best of five games (won by the first player to win three games).

**tournaments**
In competitions, the game is controlled by a marker and a referee, who sit in the center of the gallery. The marker calls the play and the score. The referee is in overall charge, and decides all appeals, lets, and rallies as necessary.
Play in a competition match is continuous, except for a 1-minute interval between games, and a 2-minute interval if the score reaches 2 games all. (Players may leave court during these breaks.)
Interruption may be allowed for bad light or other circumstances beyond players' control, but not to allow players to recover strength, etc. Time to recover from injury is also not allowed, unless the opponent contributed to the injury. (If the opponent caused it by dangerous play, the injured player immediately wins the match.) If a player continues delaying tactics after due warning, his opponent wins the game in play.
A further knock up is allowed if:
the match is restarted after a long interruption;
or a new ball is substituted;
or (for the period between games) if both players agree.
A new ball is substituted if:
the ball in play breaks;
or the players agree;
or one player appeals and the referee agrees.

**grip**

This is the same for both forehand and backhand. The hand "shakes hands" with the handle (**a**, **b**), so the V between thumb and index finger comes on top of the handle. Note that the fingers are not clamped tight, but spread slightly, with the index finger forward as if on a trigger. The end of the handle projects just beyond the base of the hand. The grip is light, only tightening for a moment as the racquet strikes the ball.

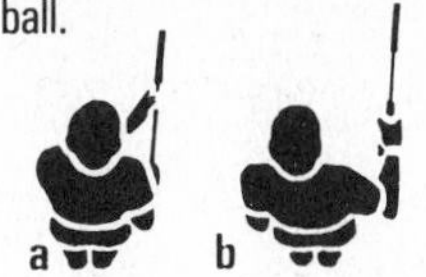


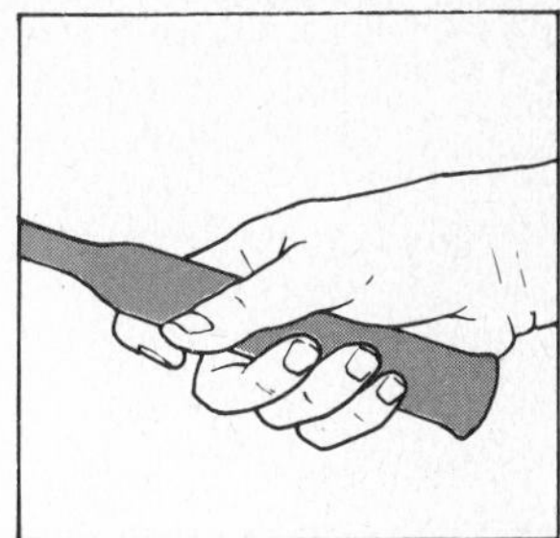

**use of wrist**

The wrist is used in two ways. First, instead of using two different grips, the wrist and lower arm twist a few degrees, to adjust the angle of the racquet face between forehand (**a**) and backhand (**b**). Second, strokes are made with the wrist cocked whenever possible – though it is left cocked on the impact (**c**) and follow-through, not uncocked.

**stance and movement**

The basic ready stance is similar to other racquet games (see p.18), but rather more crouched (**a**). Note that the racquet head is kept well up. Even when watching your opponent play a ball behind you, keep your feet toward the front wall (**b**). For effective court movement, use one or two long strides (**c**) rather than several short ones; and keep the racquet head up.

**positioning and placing**

The command position is the center court "T." Try to take up your ready stance there after each stroke, while sending the ball to front court or back, away from your opponent. Aim your back-court shots "to a length" – i.e., so they bounce into the junction of back wall and floor, making them very hard to retrieve.

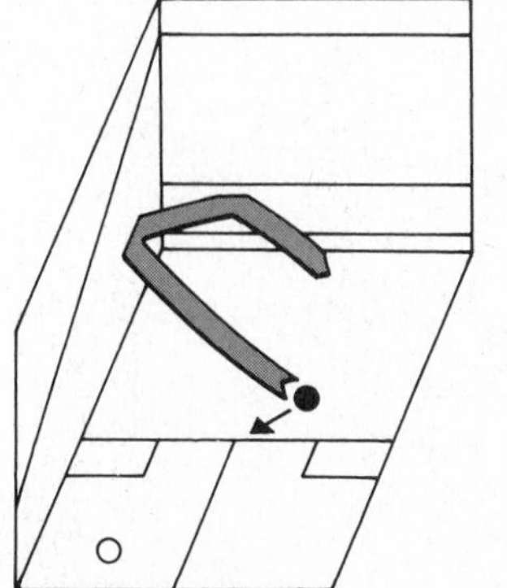

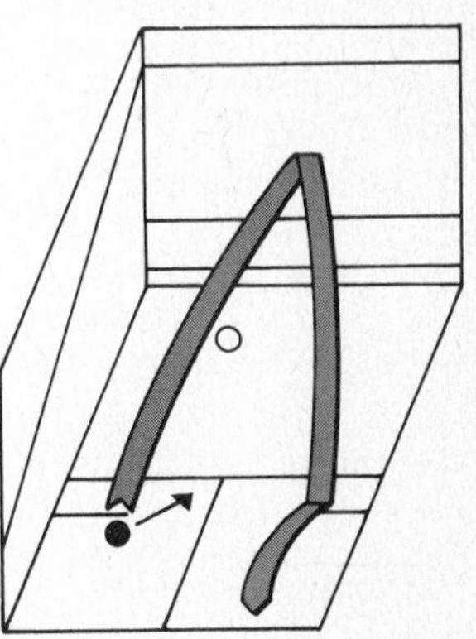

**the drive**

This is the basic stroke.

**1** Turning to the side wall, backswing with bent elbow and cocked wrist, so the racquet is angled behind your head. Get behind the ball.

**2** Lead in with your elbow, only straightening it just before impact. Bend back and knees to get the racquet parallel to the floor. As your weight comes forward, meet the ball at the peak of its bounce, level with your front foot (slightly in front of it on the backhand). Keep your racquet face open, and wrist cocked but relaxed.

**3** Follow through upward, close to your body, wrist cocked, elbow bent.

To angle a ball to the other side of court, meet it a little further forward.

**the volley**

This uses a much shorter stroke, with little backswing or follow-through. On the backhand especially, the action is a forearm chop with locked wrist, rather than a swing of the whole body. Volleying is difficult, but vital – which is one reason why the racquet head should always be kept up between strokes.

**using drives and volleys**

Drives are best used to send the ball to the back wall, when your opponent has claimed the T and you are stuck either behind him (**a**) or in front of him (**b**). Make sure your shot goes wide of his position. Volleys can be used in the same way; or as "stop volley" drop shots in front court; or, defensively, to return difficult back-court balls.

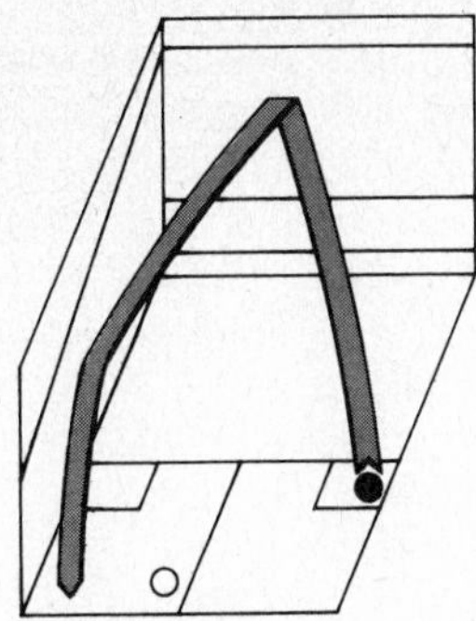

**lob service** (above)
This is the main type of service. It should strike the front wall about center court, and nearer the out-of-court line than the cut line. It then comes back in a slow lob to cross the other service box at about head height and touch high on the side wall, before dropping to the floor and bouncing low into the back corner.

**hard-hit service** (below)
This should strike the front wall on your side of court, just above the cut line. It then comes back to cross the other service box at knee height, bounce early, and hug the side wall before bouncing low into the back corner. As with the lob, the perfect "ace" bounces into the angle of wall and floor.

**service action**
Place your feet so a line joining the toes points at the part of the front wall that is your target. Strike the ball smoothly with the basic drive action, then move at once to the T. Hit the lob from below waist height with an open-angled racquet. Hit the hard-hit service from waist height or above, with a vertical racquet angle.

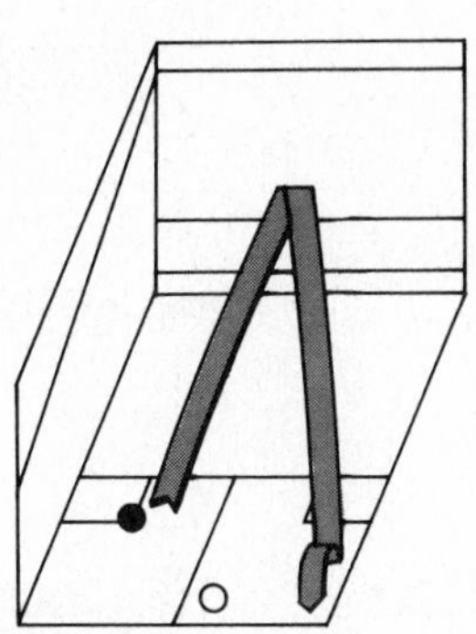

**backhand services**
For a right-handed player, the forehand lob is especially played from the right-hand service box, the forehand hard-hit almost only from the left-hand box. Learning to serve on the backhand allows you to serve from near the side wall from the left-hand box (for a good lob trajectory), and near the T from the right-hand box (for a good hard-hit service trajectory).

**return of service**
It is vital to watch the ball and anticipate. Wait 3 feet from the back wall, and 3 feet inside the court being served to (stance for the backhand court is shown). Then move forward quickly if the service is short or can be volleyed. Volley on easy services, drive down the line on moderate ones, and "boast" difficult ones onto the side wall (see p.80).

**"boast"** (a)
This is used to get the ball out of a back corner. Do not try to drag the ball around, toward the front wall. Instead, hit it up against the side wall, as if you were aiming at the front wall of an adjacent court. Have your feet in line pointing at the back corner, and meet the ball with an open racquet angle, just in front of your leading foot. To prevent an easy kill in reply, the ball needs to reach the front wall near the far side wall.

**angle shot** (b)
This is also played into the side wall, but as a surprise attacking shot from the front court when in front of your opponent, to wrong-foot him or force him forward. (If played to the far side wall first, it is called a reverse angle.) Drive the ball as usual, but with your feet lined up at 45° to the side wall. Better still, volley the ball. The perfect angle shot is a "nick" – i.e., one that ends up in the junction of side wall and floor.

**drop shot** (c)
This is also a front court shot, used only if your opponent is deep behind you, and you are perfectly balanced. Using a good backswing for deception, hit the ball softly at the top of its bounce with an open racquet, so it hits the front wall just above the tin, and drops onto the side wall as near the floor as possible. Play the shot straight or – more riskily – cross-court. (A line joining your toes should parallel the intended path of the ball.) On the stroke, get down low, meet the ball just in front of your leading foot, and use only a short follow-through.

**lob (d)**
Played from the front court when under pressure, this sends your opponent to the back court and gives you time to move to the T. The stroke and path of the ball are as for the lob service (see p. 79). Make sure that the ball is still rising when it hits the front wall. A cross-court shot, which loses speed on touching the far side wall, is safer than one down the line, which may ricochet into court for an easy return. A good lob crosses center court well out of reach, and goes wide to the opponent's backhand.

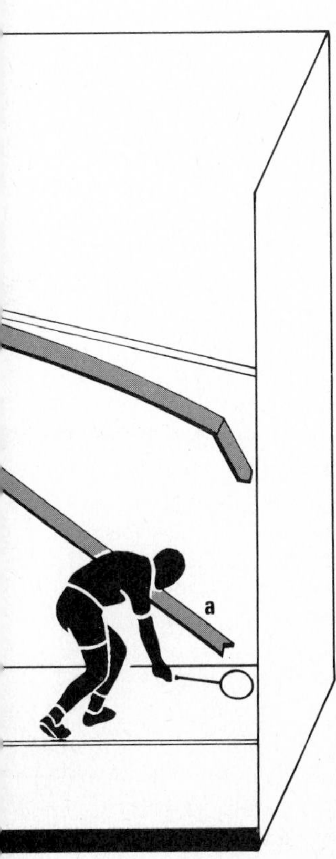


**racquet control**
Any wild swinging at the ball can endanger your opponent, and will be penalized by a referee. In International squash, you should keep your wrist cocked throughout the stroke (see p. 78). This will hold the racquet close to the body on the backswing and follow-through (the two danger points). The illustration shows how *not* to finish your strokes.

**movement**
When your opponent is trying to play the ball, you must not impede his movement or move across the ball's path. So the easiest way to prevent your own movement being restricted is to play the ball away from you into another quarter of the court (not, of course, one that your opponent is in). If you do hit it into the same quarter, you must move to the T in an arc, so as to give your opponent a straight path to the ball (**a**). Also do not hit the ball to the middle of court, or you will have to hold back from the T while your opponent plays his stroke (**b**).

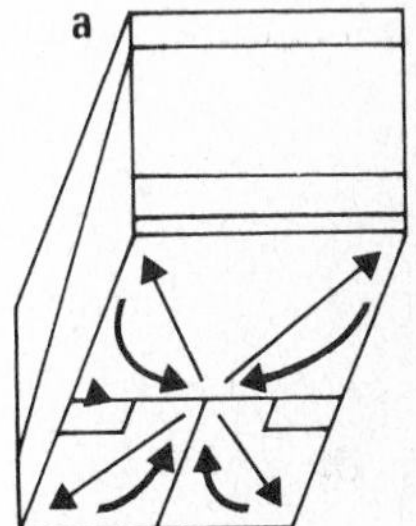


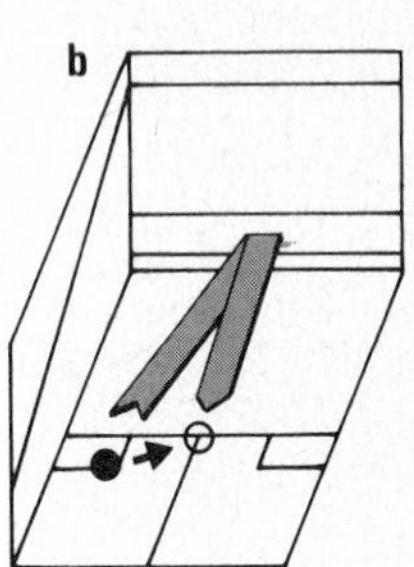


**turning out of corners**
You are allowed to swivel around, in the process of playing a ball that goes into a back corner and then rebounds out again. But the movement can be dangerous to your opponent if your swing is not well controlled; and only a let is awarded if the ball hits your opponent on its way to the front wall.

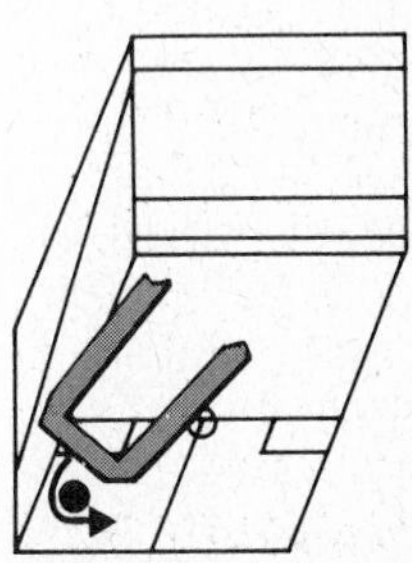

A player keeps on serving as long as he is winning points. When he loses a point, the service passes to his opponent.

**choice of service box**

Whenever the service passes to a player, he chooses from which service box to make his first service. If he then wins the point on that service, he takes the next service from the other box; then the next from the first one again; and so on, alternately, until he loses the service.

**serving technique**

To serve, the player simply throws or drops the ball into the air, or bounces it on the floor, and hits it. But until he has hit it, he must keep one foot on the floor inside the service box (and not touching any of its lines). If he does not, it is a foot fault (see "faults," below).

**good service**

For a good service, the ball must:
reach the front wall without bouncing off a side wall (or the back wall), and without touching the floor (**1**);
bounce on the front wall above the service line but below the out-of-play line (**2**);
and rebound so it first touches the floor inside the opposite service court (**3**)–though the opponent may choose to hit it before it reaches the floor.
It is still good if it bounces off a side wall (**a**), or the back wall (**b**), before going into the service court–as long as it bounces off the front wall first, and does not touch any out-of-play area.
Note that a service that bounces on one of the lines marking the correct service court is not good.

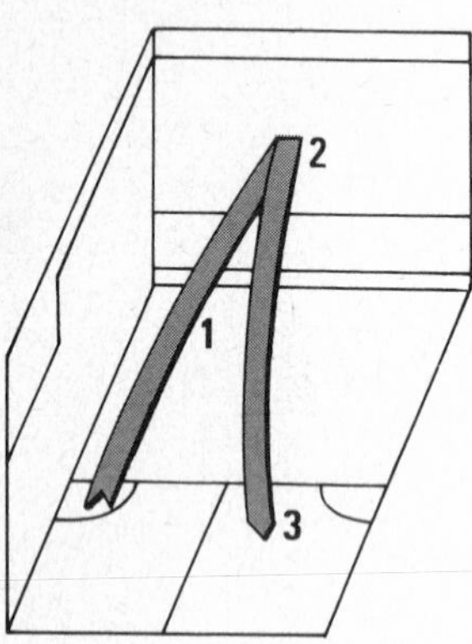


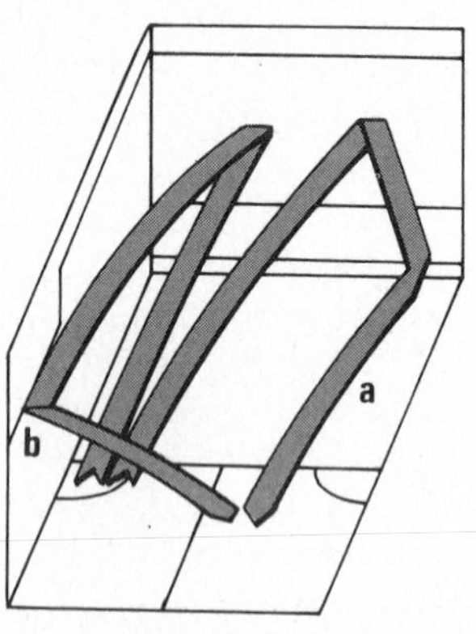


**faults**

Any service that is not good is a "fault." For example, it is a fault if:
the server misses the ball;
or he foot faults;
or the ball hits the floor or a side wall before it hits the front wall;
or it hits the front wall on or below the service line;
or it hits any wall on or above the out-of-play line;
or it hits the ceiling or lights;
or it does not first touch the floor in the correct service court.
If the first service for a point is a fault, the server must try again to make a good service, from the same service box. If he again serves a fault, his opponent scores one point and becomes the server.

**receiving service**

A service that has become a fault must not be played by the receiver. But he may volley a service that has not yet become a fault–even if it is clear that it was going to become one by not bouncing in the correct service court. (Note that, if he tries to volley such a service but misses, the service can still become a fault.)

**service from the wrong box**

If a player serves from the wrong box, the service still stands, unless:
his opponent makes no attempt to play it, and demands that it is served again from the correct box;
or the referee calls a "let" before the opponent can play it (see "claiming a let," p. 84).
If a service from a wrong box is accepted, the service for the next point is taken from the other box, and so on alternately. (If a first service from a wrong box is accepted but is a fault, the second service must be from the same box.)

Under North American rules, both server and receiver have a chance to score (not just the server).

**the rally**

Once the ball has been served, the players hit the ball alternately, until one of them fails to make a good return. Whichever it is, the other player scores one point and is server for the next point.

**good returns**

It is a good return if a player - hits the ball before it has bounced twice on the floor (**1**) so it hits the front wall above the tell-tale and below the out-of-play line (**2**) and then bounces back without touching any out-of-play area (**3**).

Note that it is still a good return if: the ball does not bounce on the floor before the player hits it (**a**); or it bounces off the side or back walls (or both) before he hits it (**b**); or it bounces off the side or back walls (or both) after he has hit it, on its way to the front wall (**c**).

If a player plays at the ball and misses, he may still try again to make a good return.

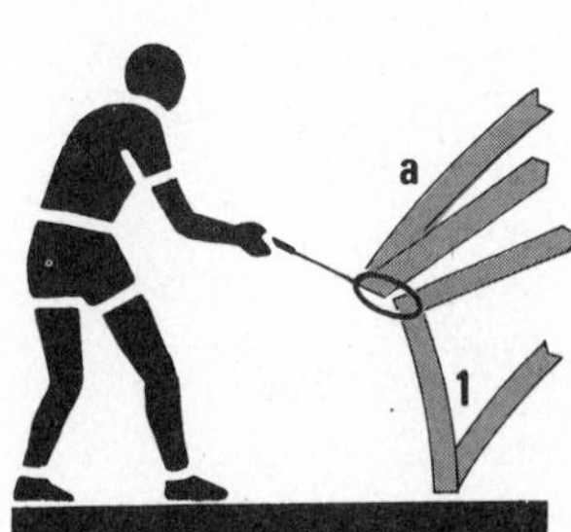


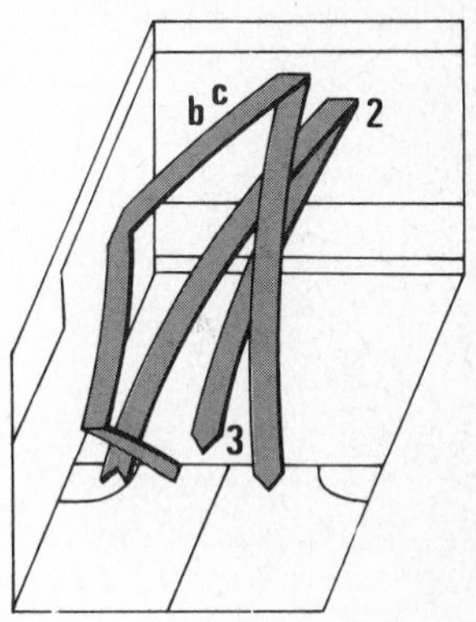

**bad returns**

It is a bad return if: the ball bounces twice on the floor before the player hits it (**d**); or it is hit twice by the player (**e**), or "carried" on his racquet; or it bounces on the floor after he hits it, on its way to the front wall (**f**); or it hits the tell-tale (**g**); or it hits the front wall on or above the out-of-play line (**h**); or it hits a side or back wall on or above the out-of-play line—either on its way to the front wall (**i**), or on its way back from the front wall before bouncing on the floor; or, on its way to or from the front wall, it hits the ceiling or lighting equipment (**j**).

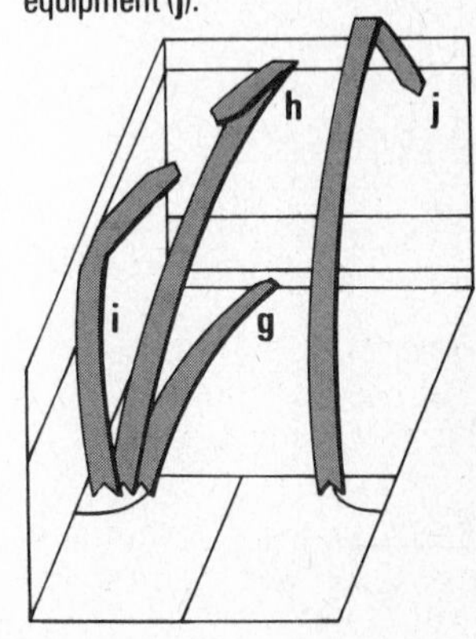

**let situations**

If a "let" is given, play stops, and the server takes the service for the point again. Lets are mainly given for obstruction, but may also be claimed if:
a player does not play the ball for fear of injuring his opponent;
or a player, as or before he plays the ball, is touched by the opponent or his racquet;
or the ball touches the opponent after the player has tried to hit it but missed;
or the ball breaks in play;
or, after bouncing once on the floor, the ball goes out of play by hitting on or above the back wall out-of-play line.
But in all these cases, it is only a let if the player could otherwise have been able to make a good return.

**claiming a let**

If a player thinks the ball has broken, he must play the point to the end, and then immediately ask for a let. If this is turned down after the ball has been examined, the point stands as played.
But in let situations created by players, the player must claim the let (by calling or raising his hand) as he tries to make the stroke. Play then stops, and if the claim is turned down the player loses the point—even if his stroke in fact gave a good return. Claims in competition play are decided by the referee; in other cases, by agreement between the players. A referee may also give a let on his own initiative, to prevent injury, or if there is some distraction beyond players' control.

**taking the let**

If a let is given, the server is entitled to two more service attempts, even if he has already served a fault on the same point. He must serve from the correct box, even if he served from the wrong box originally. But if he was a new server on this point, he may choose a different box from the one he chose originally.

**let point**

If avoidable obstruction occurs and a let is claimed, a let point may be granted to the obstructed player. This is done if the obstruction prevented a winning stroke, or the opponent has been guilty of repeated obstruction.
A "let point" means that the point is not replayed, but given to the obstructed player.
A player who thinks he is entitled to a let point may specifically ask for it.

**obstruction**

After playing the ball, a player must immediately get out of his opponent's way, so as to:
give him a fair view of the ball;
give him a fair chance to get to it and /or strike it from any part of the court;
and allow him to play it to any part of the front wall, or to either side wall near the front wall.
If obstruction occurs, the opponent can ask for a let. It counts as obstruction if the opponent would otherwise have reached and returned the ball—even if the player did not mean to obstruct, and tried to prevent it. But it is not a let:
if it is just that a player, without being in the path of the ball, briefly blocks his opponent's view;
or if it is an unreasonably long backswing or follow-through that is obstructed.

**ball hitting player**

In general, if the ball touches a player, or anything he wears or carries, he loses the point (apart, of course, from when the ball hits his racquet on his turn of play).
But there are three exceptions.
1) If the contact is due to an opponent's obstruction or positioning, it is a let (or let point).
2) If the contact comes after the opponent has tried to play the ball, but missed:
the player touched by the ball scores if the opponent could not still have made a good return;
but if the opponent might yet have made a good return, it is a let.
3) If the opponent has just played the ball, and the player is hit before the ball reaches the front wall:
the player still scores if the return would not have been good anyway;
the opponent scores if the return would have been a good one direct to the front wall—as long as he hit the ball at first attempt, and did not turn to follow it around before hitting it;
a let is played if the return would have been good but indirect, or if the opponent did turn to follow the ball around before hitting it, or if he hit it only after he had tried to hit it but missed.

A squash match usually takes about 40 to 50 minutes to complete.

**knock up**
Players are allowed at least 5 minutes' knock up before play begins. (This also serves to heat the ball to normal response.) If one player wishes, the players may knock up separately for 2½ minutes each.

**start of play**
At the start of play, the opposing players spin a racquet as in tennis (see p. 37). The winning player chooses whether to serve or receive first in the first game.

**calling the scores**
After each point, the score is called: e.g., "7-6." (The score of the player making the next service is given first, and he makes the call if there is no referee.)

**winning the game**
The North American singles game is won by the first player to reach 15 points—unless the game is "set."

**setting**
If the score in any game reaches 13-all, the player to receive on the next service must call:
either "no set," in which case the game ends as usual when one player reaches 15 points;
or "set 3," in which case it ends when one player reaches 16 points;
or "set 5," in which case it ends when one player reaches 18 points.
If the score does not reach 13-all, but does reach 14-all, then the option to set occurs at this score instead. Whoever is then the player to receive the next service must call:
either "no set," in which case the game still ends when one player reaches 15 points;
or "set 3," in which case it ends when one player reaches 17 points.

**the match**
The player who wins one game serves first in the next. The first player to win three games wins the match (except that a player may win the match at any time through the retirement, default, or disqualification of his opponent).

**tournaments**
In competitions, the game is controlled by a referee. Two judges may be appointed to decide any appeals by players.
Play in a competition match is continuous, except for a 2-minute interval between games (if requested by either player), and a 5-minute interval between the third and fourth games (when the players may leave the court if desired). Play may be suspended for circumstances beyond players' control, but not to allow players to recover strength, etc. But up to one hour is allowed for recovery from injury—after which the injured player loses the match. (One suspension of up to 5 minutes only is allowed for cramp or a pulled muscle.) Reasonable time is allowed for a player to use a towel, wipe glasses, etc. But any intentional delaying tactics, if continued after due warning, result in loss of the match.

**replacement ball**
A new ball may be substituted, at any time when the ball is not in play, if:
the ball in play breaks;
or the players agree;
or the referee so rules.
A ball is considered broken if it is cracked through both inner and outer surfaces. When a ball breaks, the preceding point is replayed. (If a damaged but unbroken ball is replaced by agreement, the point is not replayed.)

### grip

The grip is the same for forehand and backhand. To find it, hold the racquet in front of you with your non-playing hand, so the racquet head is vertical to the ground (**a**). Then turn the head slightly clockwise (**b**), before "shaking hands" with the handle (**c**). If you have made the right amount of turn, the V between your index finger and thumb will fall to the left of the top of the handle, in line with the first ridge. Note that the fingers are not clamped tight, but spread slightly, with the index finger forward as if on a trigger. The end of the handle projects just beyond the base of the hand. The grip is light, only tightening for a moment as the racquet strikes the ball.

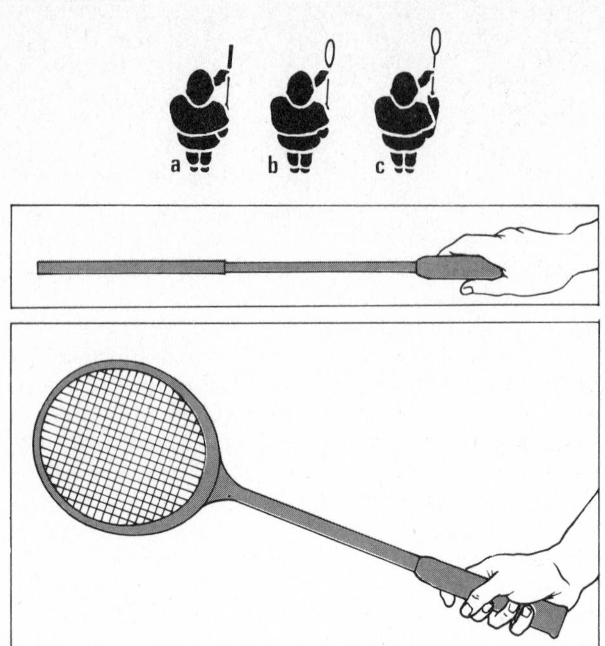

### stance and positioning

During play, the command position is the center court "T". Try to get back there after each stroke, while sending the ball to front court or back court, away from your opponent. Use a ready stance similar to other racquet games (p.18), but rather more crouched. Keep your racquet head well up in front of you, and your body toward the front wall even when you are watching your opponent play a ball behind you (**a**). But to receive service, even as you watch the ball going to the front wall, your body should be facing the side wall of the court being served to, and your racquet already swung back (**b**, **c**). Your best position is about 4 feet from the back wall, and near the center line. (The diagram shows the position for the backhand court.)

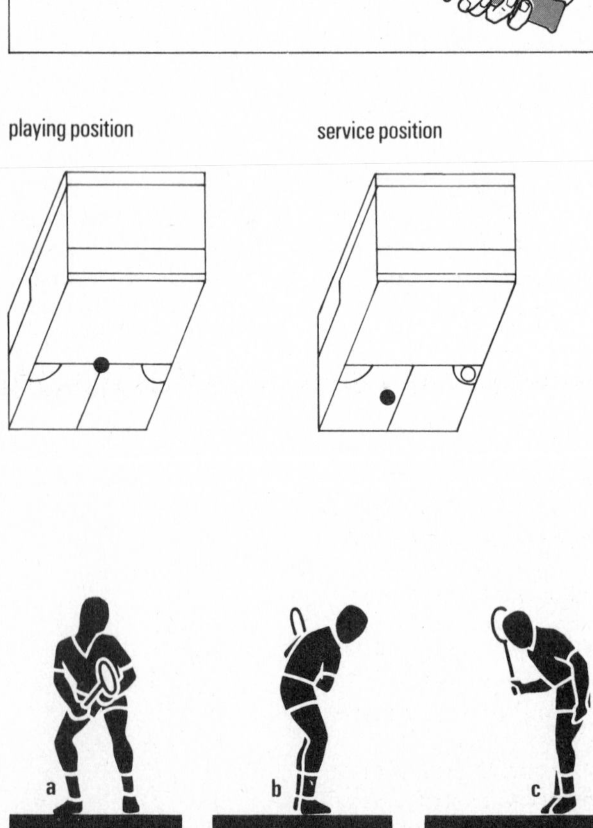

**basic forehand stroke** (above)
**1** Turning to the side wall, backswing with bent elbow and cocked wrist, so the racquet is vertical. Move behind the ball. Keep body crouched, knees bent.
**2** Step into the stroke with your left foot, pointing it at 45° to the side wall for a closed stance.
**3** Dropping your right shoulder, lead into the stroke with your elbow. Only let it straighten just before impact. Bend knees and back to keep your playing hand lower than the racquet head.
**4** As your weight comes forward, meet the ball level with your front foot. Let your wrist snap at the last minute to power the impact. Keep the racquet face open.
**5** Follow through forward and low, as if reaching for the front wall. Keep your knees bent.

**basic backhand stroke** (below)
This is like the forehand, but:
**1** the right shoulder drops on the backswing, as the body coils up;
**2** the right foot steps in;
**3** as the body uncoils, the arm straightens almost immediately;
**4** the racquet meets the ball about 6 inches in front of the leading foot (wrist snap as for forehand);
**5** the follow-through leaves the body half turned to the side wall.

**use of wrist**
The vertical view (**a**) clarifies the wrist snap that usually powers the ball. Of course, the wrist can also be used to alter the angle of the racquet face. But the grip described automatically gives good angles for most shots. On both forehand (**b**) and backhand (**c**), the fairly open angle on strokes below waist level results in useful backspin. On higher strokes, the angle closes.

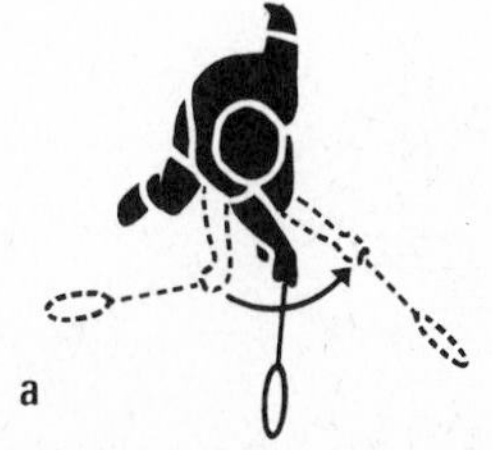

### volleying

Here speed and decisiveness are vital. Do not waste time turning to the side wall or taking the racquet back: move directly forward to meet the ball. Make the final step in with the opposite leg. The stroke itself is as if you were throwing the racquet at the front wall: your arm straightens forward, and at the last minute the wrist snaps to bring the racquet through just as the downward follow-through begins. You meet the ball well in front of you, as you lean into the stroke. Volleying is very important in catching your opponent out of position. But do not try to be too powerful or too accurate. Play the stroke smoothly, and aim for the safe shot.

forehand volley

backhand volley

### half volley

This can also be used to speed up play and catch your opponent out of position. Again, do not turn sideways, or backswing. Bend your knees as you step in, and lean forward to meet the ball just as it comes off the floor. Use a shortened swing and follow-through, and do not snap your wrist. Aim for a safe shot. The diagrams show a forehand stroke.

### front-court strokes

For maximum speed in front-court play you should move in with the racquet still in front of you. Then, if there is no time for a normal stroke, just reach under the ball and flip upward, using wrist snap only (**a**). But if there is time for a normal stroke, use no wrist snap, and "scoop" the ball up for a drop shot by sliding the racquet under it after impact (**b**).

**drives and lobs**

Your aim is to vary your shots unpredictably between front court and back, so as to send the ball away from your opponent and away from the T. Drives and lobs are used to send the ball to the back court. Both use the basic stroke, but the lob is angled so it is moving upward as it hits the front wall, and comes back in a slow arc. Both can be played down the line or cross-court, and are usually played from the back court to bypass an opponent ahead of you. But they can be played from front court if your opponent is also forward. A drive has to hit the front wall 3 to 5 feet above the tell-tale, to travel to the back court. The down-the-line shot should bounce twice before reaching the back wall. The cross-court shot should hit the far side wall near the service line before continuing back. A drive may beat an opponent completely – or may be volleyed for a winning reply. A lob can seldom be volleyed and effectively draws the opponent to back court, but is unlikely to beat him.

drives

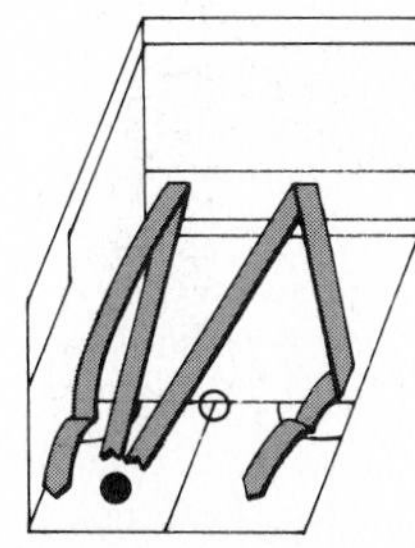

lobs

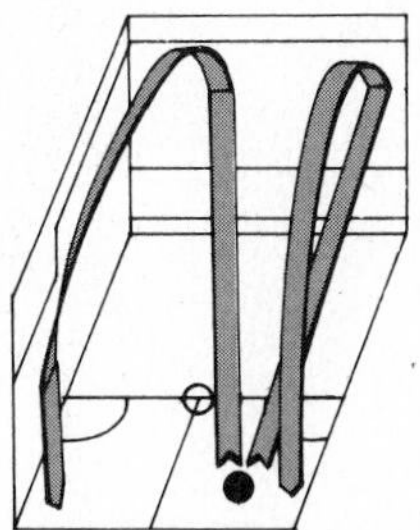

front court to back

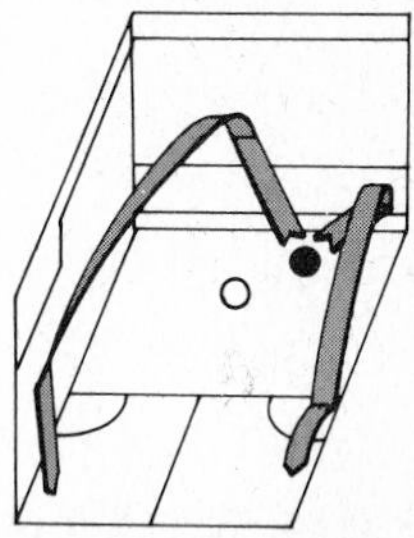

**shots to front court**

a) kills. These are drives that are aimed only just above the tell-tale.
b) drop shots. The stroke for these has been described. Ideally, the ball rebounds into the junction of side wall and floor. A reverse drop is one played cross-court.
c) corner and reverse corner. These strike the side wall first, then die off the front wall.
d) three-wall shot. This is played with a firm wrist and about three-quarter power. Hit into the side wall in the back court, it should reach the front wall just above the tell-tale, before dropping into the junction of side wall and floor.
e) roll corner. This hits the side wall about 5 feet from the front wall, hits the front wall 6 inches above tell-tale, and dies.

drop shots

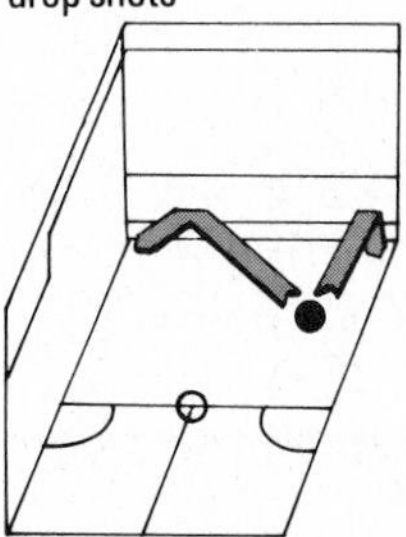

corner and reverse corner

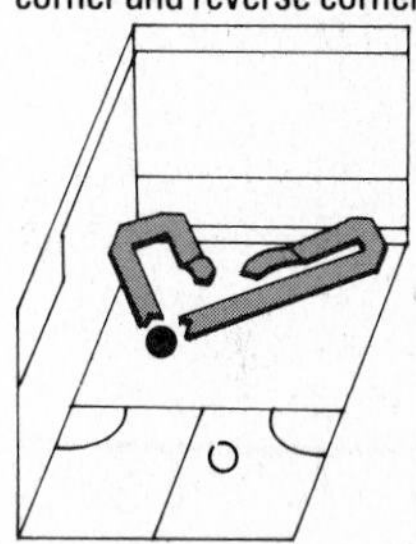

three-wall shot

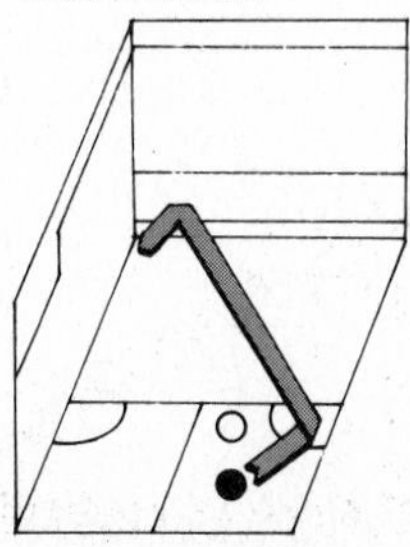

roll corner

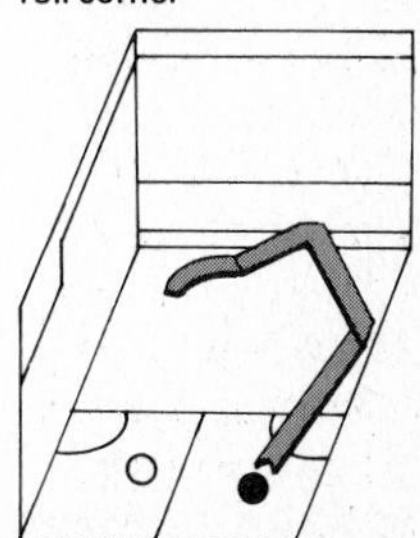

**lob service**

This strikes high up on the front wall, just beyond the center, and then arcs slowly back to touch the side wall near the back wall, before dropping almost vertically to the floor. (It should only reach the back wall after this.) It is the most common and safest service, and gives the server good time to claim the T position. Use an open stance to serve from the right-hand box (**1**), a closed one from the left-hand. Your back foot should be at right angles to your front foot, which points at the front wall. Hold the racquet at waist level, head up and well back, with your elbow close to your body and wrist cocked. Let go the ball as the racquet swings forward and down (**2**), and meet it at knee height (**3**). Do not snap your wrist. Follow through high (**4**).

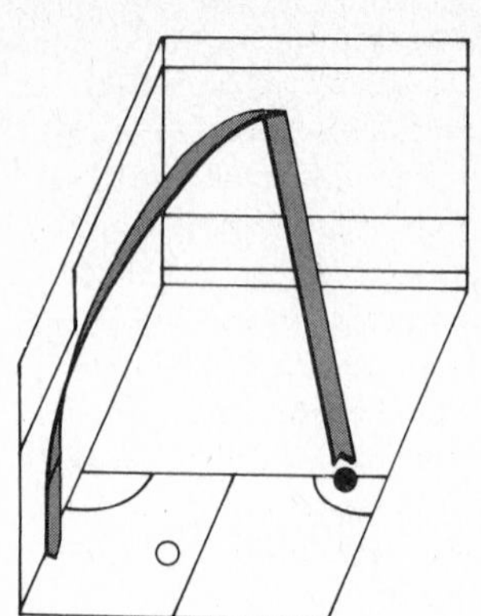

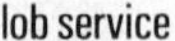

**hard service**

This uses a powerful overhead action. It can score aces, but has to be very accurate, and may leave you off balance. It should be aimed: to your own side of the front wall, to rebound straight at your opponent (**a**); or just beyond the center of the front wall, to go to his back corner (**b**). In each case the shot must come right back to hit the back wall before touching the floor – but you should still aim to hit the front wall as low as possible. Use a closed stance, and throw the ball up in front of your right shoulder as you take the racquet back (**1**). Backswing until your cocked wrist almost touches your right shoulder (**2**), then swing forward as if throwing the racquet at the ball, snapping the wrist when the arm is almost straight (**3**). Follow through (**4**).

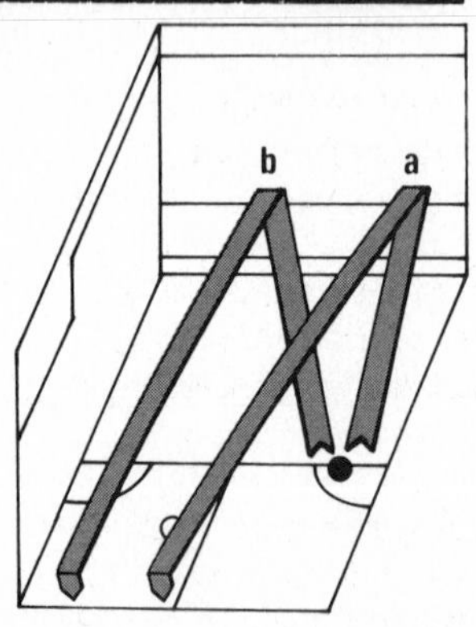


hard service

**slice service**
This is a safer option than the hard service. Use a similar action, but do not throw the ball so high, and swing sideways at it, to meet it at shoulder height, snapping your wrist: this should give it sidespin and backspin. Follow through across the body. The shot should hit the front wall just above the service line, and come back to touch low on the side wall before dying.

**return of service**
Service is an attacking shot, and the server can usually go straight to the T. So unless a service is very bad, your return must be defensive: use maximum control, take no risks, and almost always volley the ball. From the receiving position (p.86), watch and anticipate, then move in quickly. Send your shot down the line, to come back deep to your court.
A lob should be volleyed as it drops from the side wall. Move in, taking the racquet back, and pause in position (**1**). Then swing the racquet upward, straightening your arm (**2**). Snap your wrist for the impact. Follow through toward the front wall, racquet head still up (**3**).
A hard service must be intercepted before it reaches the back wall. Use an open racquet face (**a**), and no wrist snap. Aim about 3 feet above the tell-tale, close to the side wall. Follow through toward the front wall, racquet face still open.
A slice service must be met before it reaches the side wall. Throw the racquet at the ball, to meet it in front of the body, knees bent (**b**). Use wrist snap and an open angle.

YMCA
IN
ACTION

# Racquetball

There were about 50,000 racquetball players in the U.S.A. in 1970; today there are three million or more. The game's rise is perhaps the greatest success story in modern sports history.

In its basic principles, the game is very like squash. The ball must be hit onto a facing wall, but it can also be bounced off side and back walls on the way. The main differences are the court size and the short-handled racquet. It is the racquet — and the fast-moving ball — that have brought racquetball its success. The pace can be even faster than squash. Yet even more than in squash, novices who have never played a sport before find it easy to hit the ball, keep up rallies, and win points. Women find that they can play — and often beat — husbands, sons, or boyfriends. (In fact many married women are making time for a sport for the first time, by playing each other at racquetball during the week: 30 to 40 per cent of players are women.) Finally, the glass-walled courts make spectating easy, and most clubs run leagues and tournaments that add to the interest.

Racquetball grew out of paddleball (see page 148). In about 1949, a player called Joe Sobek decided paddleball would be more interesting if a strung racquet was used. He designed one, and gradually the game spread — mainly through YMCA clubs. For many years there were various rules, and names, for the sport — as well as confusion with paddleball proper. But a U.S. national tournament in 1968 led to uniform rules, a lighter racquet, a livelier ball, and the name "racquetball." The game is now beginning to spread internationally — mainly through the U.S. forces in Japan and West Germany. And in countries (such as the U.K.) with no handball or paddleball tradition, it is beginning to be adapted for squash-court play.

LEACH-SEAMCO

On the racquetball four-wall court, even the ceiling is used as a playing surface.

**governing bodies**
Two different organizations publish racquetball rules: the United States Racquetball Association (USRA) (together with the National Racquetball Club, which promotes professional racquetball); and the International Racquetball Association (IRA).
Despite their names, they are essentially rival U.S. national organizations. But their rules are almost identical, and any significant differences are noted in what follows.

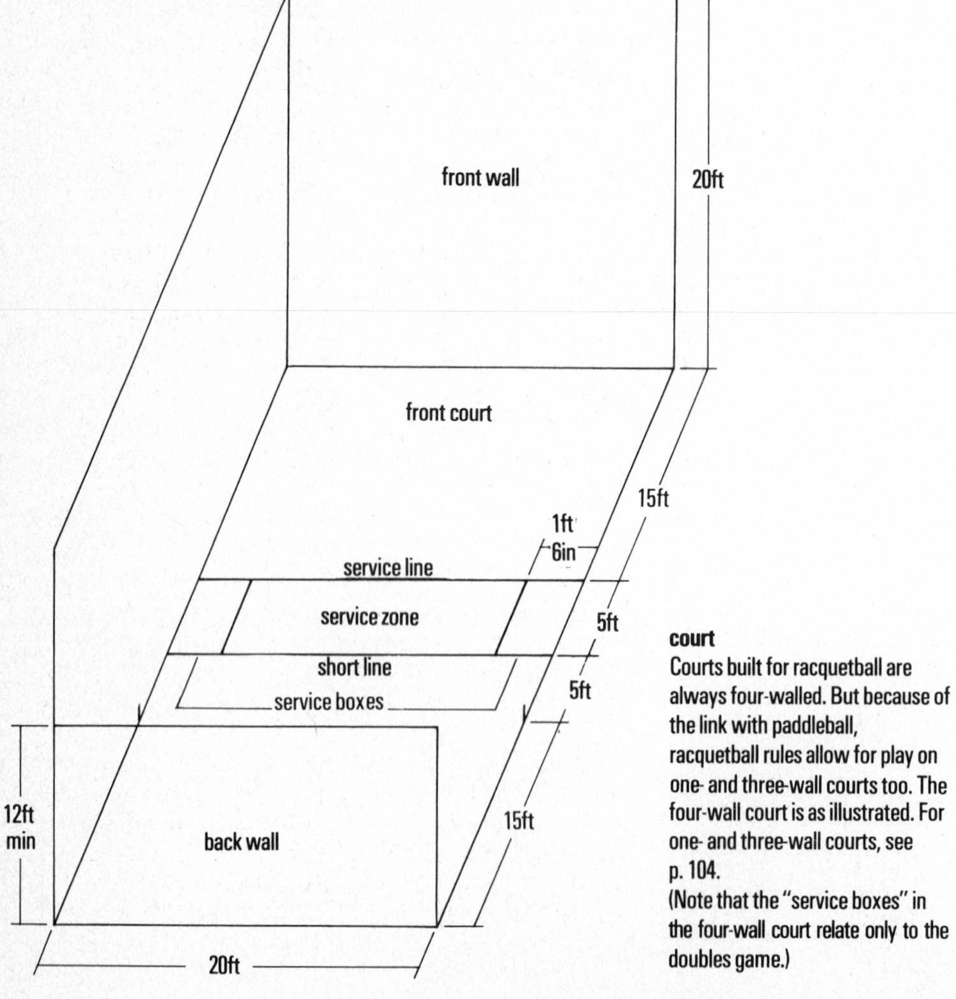


**court**
Courts built for racquetball are always four-walled. But because of the link with paddleball, racquetball rules allow for play on one- and three-wall courts too. The four-wall court is as illustrated. For one- and three-wall courts, see p. 104.
(Note that the "service boxes" in the four-wall court relate only to the doubles game.)

**ball**

The ball is hollow and pressurized. It should weigh about 1.4 ounces and (at 76° Fahrenheit, USRA; 70-74° Fahrenheit, IRA) bounce 68 to 72 inches from a 100-inch drop. Various makes of ball are approved by the USRA and IRA.

**racquet**

Racquetball racquets are distinguished by their short handles. The diagram shows maximum measurements; also the total of length and width together must not be more than 27 inches. (Head measurements are to the outer edges of the rim.) The handle must have a thong, which is kept securely wrapped around the player's wrist during play. Strings must be gut, nylon, or metal. (IRA rules only allow metal strings if they do not mark or deface the ball.)

Racquets vary in shape, hitting area, materials, string tension, and grip size.

1) head shape and hitting area. The main head shapes are: flat-topped (**a**); broad flat-topped (**b**); and "teardrop" (**c**). A few are "tennis-shaped" (**d**). Choice is a matter of personal preference. Some head shapes do give a larger hitting area, but as a result are probably fractionally slower to maneuver. As almost all good shots must come off the center of the strings, a larger head gives no real gain.

2) racquet material. Most racquets are made of either metal alloy, or fiber-filled composition. The latter have a reputation for giving greater ball control because of their flexibility; but they are very liable to break, especially in the hands of a beginner. Metal racquets are stronger and give more power, and some are now being designed for flexibility too.

3) string material. Monofilament nylon is usual; string tensions in current use are too low for gut to make much difference. But the grade of material is important: choose clear nylon, rather than painted, which is often substandard. (However a colored braid intertwined with clear nylon is not a sign of poor quality.)

4) grip material. Leather probably gives a better grip, but wears away with use. Rubber is durable and washable, but less slipproof.

5) string tension. The general view is that string tension for the average player should be as low as 25 to 28 pounds on a composition racquet, and 30 to 32 pounds on a metal one. (In fact, some top players use tensions even lower than this.) Higher tension is thought to give more power but too little control.

**dress**

Usual dress is shorts and shirt for men, and the same, or skirt and blouse, or a dress, for women. Tennis clothes or similar can be used. Tournament dress must be clean, and may be white or a bright color.

Sports shoes and socks are also needed, of course. Important accessories are head and wrist sweatbands, and (especially) eyeguards. To aid grip, some players also wear a leather glove (often with the fingers cut off) on their playing hand.

A player goes on serving as long as he is winning points. When he fails to win a point, the service passes to his opponent.

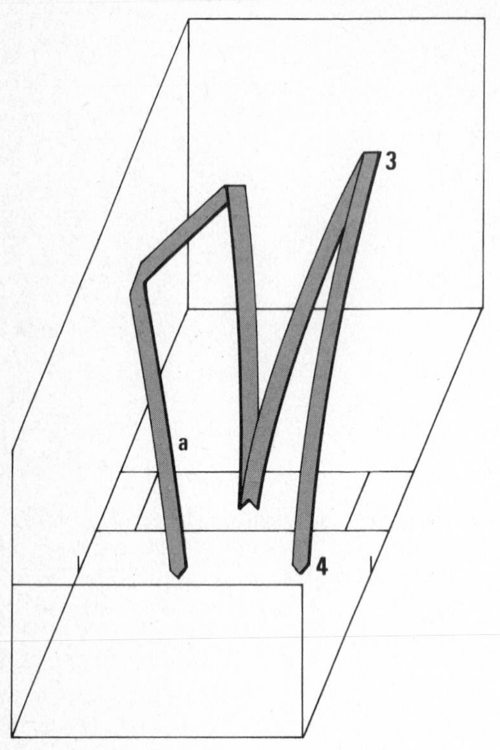


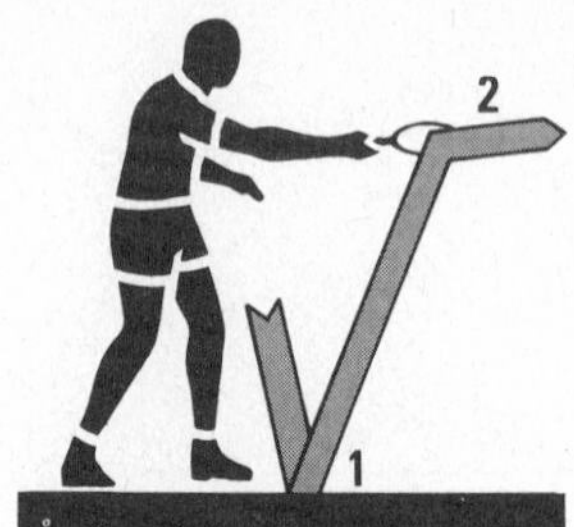


**good service**

It is a good service if-
the server bounces the ball once on the floor, inside the serving zone (**1**)
and hits it on the rebound (**2**)
so it goes to the front wall without touching floor or side walls (**3**)
and then rebounds to touch the floor behind the short line (**4**).
It is still a good service if it touches a side wall on the rebound, before bouncing on the floor (**a**).

**serving position**

The server may stand anywhere in the serving zone, but must have both feet in the zone. (His feet may step on either line bounding the zone, but not beyond.) He must stay in the zone until the ball passes the short line on its way back from the front wall – otherwise it is a foot fault (see "faults," opposite).

**defective services**

There are three types of defective service: faults; outs (also called "hand-outs"); and dead ball services.

a) If a player makes a "fault" service, he must attempt the service again. If he serves two faults in succession, his opponent becomes server.

b) If a player makes an "out" service, his opponent immediately becomes server.

c) If a player makes a "dead ball" service, he must attempt the service again. There is no penalty, but any fault in the preceding service still stands.

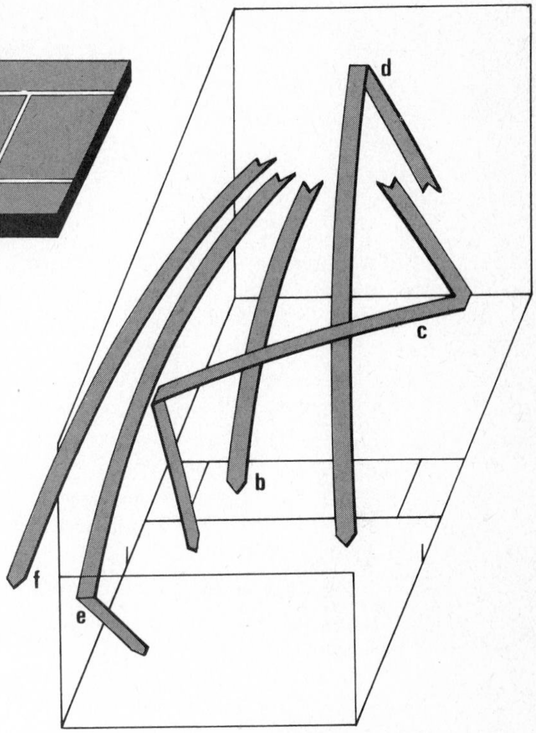

**faults**

It is a fault if:
the server serves before the receiver is ready;
or he foot faults (**a**);
or the ball comes back from the front wall to touch the floor in front of the short line (**b**) (or on the short line, in front of its back edge);
or it hits both side walls before touching the floor (**c**);
or it hits the ceiling before touching the floor (**d**);
or it hits the back wall (or a side wall and the back wall) before touching the floor (**e**);
or it goes out of court before bouncing twice on the floor (**f**).

**out services**

It is an out service if:
the server's body touches the ball as he tries to serve it;
or he misses the ball;
or the ball hits ceiling, floor, or side wall, before bouncing on the front wall;
or it touches one of these simultaneously with the front wall, by bouncing on the angle of the front wall with floor (**g**), side wall (**h**), or ceiling (**i**);
or it touches the server on the rebound from the front wall.
It is also an out if the server bounces the ball outside the serving zone, once he has gone into the zone to serve and the receiver is ready.

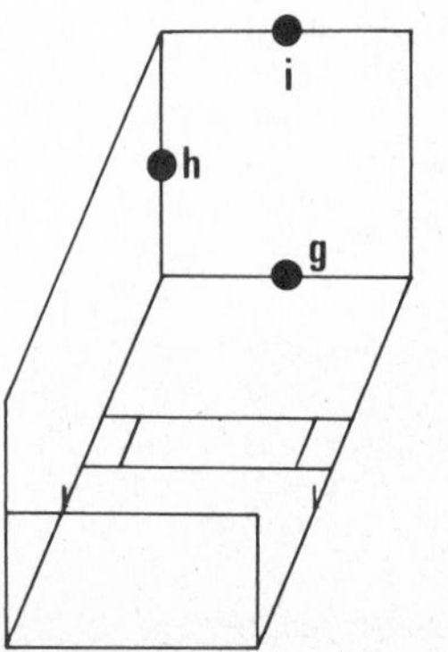


**dead ball services**

It is a dead ball service if:
the ball passes so close to the server as to obstruct the opponent's view;
or it hits any part of the court that is a dead ball under local rules.

**losing service**

A server's turn of service ends (and passes to his opponent) if:
he makes an out service;
or he makes two fault services in succession;
or he fails at any time to keep the ball in play with a good return;
or he makes an avoidable hinder (see p.101);
or he deliberately wets the ball.

In racquetball, as in International squash, only the server can score on any service. His opponent must win the service from him, before he can score.

**the rally**

Once the ball has been served correctly, the opponents hit it alternately, until one of them fails to make a good return. If it is the server who eventually does this, that ends his turn of service. If it is his opponent, the server scores one point and serves again for the next point.

(Note: as in the rest of this book, "rally" here means the sequence of strokes that decides a point. But USRA rules use "rally" to mean simply a good return.)

**receiving service**

Once the rally is under way, players may play from anywhere in the court. But to receive the service, the server's opponent must stand at least 5 feet behind the short line (i.e., behind the receiving lines—see dotted figure). Under USRA rules, he may move forward toward the short line as soon as the ball has been served, but he must not return the ball until it has crossed the short line; and if he plays the ball before it has bounced once on the floor, he must end up with both feet behind the short line.

Under IRA rules, he may not pass the receiving lines until the ball has come back to cross the short line; and even then no part of his racquet or body may pass over the short line.

If any of these rules is broken, the server wins one point.

**good returns**

For a good return a player must-hit the ball before it has bounced twice on the floor (**1**) so it goes back to the front wall without touching the floor (**2**).

It does not matter if:

the ball does not bounce on the floor before he hits it (**a**);

or it bounces on one or both side walls (**b**), the back wall (**c**), the ceiling (**d**), or any or all of these – whether before he hits it, or after

he hits it, on its way to the front wall.
But it is not a good return if it bounces on the angle of the front wall with the floor, striking both simultaneously.
If a player tries to play the ball but misses, he may go on trying, until the ball has touched the floor twice.

**illegal actions**
It is a bad return if a player:
hits the ball more than once;
or carries the ball on his racquet;
or uses anything except the head of his racquet to hit the ball;
or touches the ball with his hand or any part of his body or clothing;
or switches his racquet from one hand to another during play (though he may hold it with both hands, instead of just with his normal playing hand).
(Note that a defectively served ball should not be touched until it has bounced twice on the floor or been called by the referee.)

**ball hitting player**
If the ball touches any player before it touches the floor a second time, the player loses the rally. The only exception is if a ball just played hits an opponent on its way to the front wall – see "dead ball hinders."

**ball out of court**
If the ball goes into the gallery (or through an opening in the side wall), from a player's attempt to return it, the player loses the rally. But if it bounces there before he has hit it, the point is replayed. (This applies whether or not the ball has bounced on the floor – as long as it has not bounced twice on the floor.)

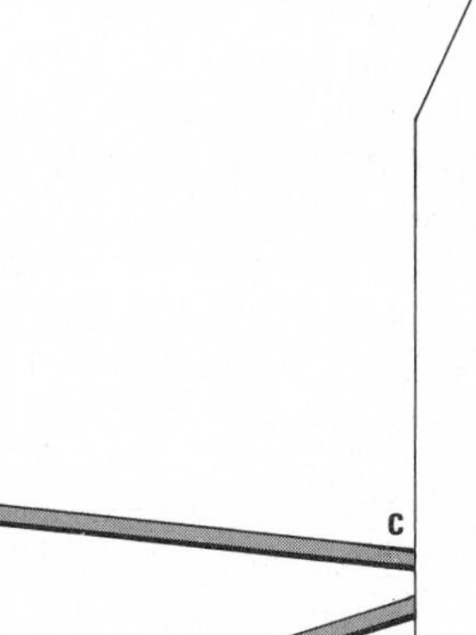


**dead ball hinders**
It is a "dead ball hinder," and the point is replayed, if:
the ball hits any part of the court that under local rules is a dead ball;
or it hits an opponent on its way to the front wall;
or there is unintentional interference that prevents an opponent having a fair chance to see or play the ball, when trying to return it (e.g., due to body contact; or to the ball rebounding from the front wall very close to a player's legs; or to the opponent missing the ball and having to move for a second attempt).
A player may call any body contact on a backswing–or, under IRA rules, if he accidentally steps on an opponent's foot; but all other calls, and all decisions on calls, must be by the referee. His call stops play (anything that happens after his call does not count).

**avoidable hinders**
It is an avoidable hinder, and the offender loses the rally, if he:
deliberately pushes or shoves an opponent;
or does not move enough to allow his opponent's shot;
or moves to a position that blocks his opponent's shot;
or moves and is hit by the ball his opponent has just played.

**other incidents**
If the ball may have broken, the rally should be played out before it is examined. If it has broken, the point is replayed.
If a player loses control of his racquet, the point is still played out, as long as the racquet does not hit an opponent or interfere with play. But if a player loses any other equipment, or there is outside interference, the point is replayed.

In these rules, the "sides" referred to can be either singles players or doubles partnerships.

**winning**
Each game is won by the first side to score 21 points. The match is won by the first side to win two games. (Under USRA rules, if the score reaches one game all, the third "tiebreaker" game is won by the first side to score 11 points.)

**order of service**
A coin is tossed before the start of the match. The side winning the toss serves first in the first game (and in the third, if there is one). The other side serves first in the second game.
(In informal play, instead of tossing a coin, players may bounce the ball against the front wall, and see whose rebound lands closer to the short line.)

**calling the scores**
After each point, the score is called: e.g., "13-9." (The score of the player making the next serve is given first, and he makes the call if there is no referee.)

**officials**
The officials for competition play are referee and scorer – possibly with assistants, linesmen, and record keepers. The referee judges whether shots and serves are good. (USRA rules allow appeals against his judgment if linesmen are present.) He also decides all other issues, and can impose point or loss-of-match penalties for abusive behavior (USRA) or unsportsmanlike behavior (IRA).

**interruptions**
a) rest periods. Under USRA rules, 5 minutes are allowed between the first and second game, and 5 minutes between the second and third. Players may leave the court, but must be back ready when the rest period is over. Under IRA rules, 5 minutes are allowed between the first and second games, and 10 minutes between the second and third; players may only leave the court during the 10-minute break.
b) time outs. During a game, when the ball is not in play, a side may at any time ask for a "time out" – to dry hands, wipe glasses, change or adjust clothing or equipment, etc. Each time out must not last more than 30 seconds, and a side may not have more than three in a single game (or more than two in a USRA 11-point tiebreaker game). IRA rules also allow an additional time out, with the referee's agreement, for faulty equipment or dress. Two minutes are allowed if the defect is in dress, 30 seconds if it is in equipment.
c) injury. Each player is allowed up to 15 minutes' rest per match for injury (no time out is charged). If he cannot play when this time allowance runs out, the opposing side wins the match.
d) deliberate delaying. Any time that a side deliberately delays for more than 10 seconds, the other side wins the service or scores one point.
e) adjournment. If a match has to be adjourned for reasons outside players' control, it is restarted at the same score as when interrupted.

Rules for doubles are exactly the same as for singles, except for the following.

**serving order**
Each side decides its serving order at the beginning of each game, and must keep to that order throughout the game.
Both players of a side normally have a turn of service, in order, before the service passes to the other side. But at the start of a game only the first server, of the side serving first, has a turn of service before his side loses the service.
For example: suppose a and b are playing x and y, and a and b have the right to the first service in the game that is about to start.
So a and b decide which of them will serve first – they choose a, for example; and x and y decide which of them will serve first – they choose x, for example.
Then in the game each player serves till he loses the service, in the order: a, x, y, a, b, x, y, a, b, x, y, etc.

**direction of service**
The server may direct his service to any part of the court. He need not alternate it between opponents.

**server's partner**
For the service, the server's partner must stand in one of the serving boxes – erect, with his back to the side wall and both feet on the floor inside the box. He must stay there until the ball passes the short line on its way back from the front wall.

**defective services**
In addition to the rules for singles, the following are also defective services.
It is a "fault" if the server's partner leaves his service box before the ball passes the short line.
It is an "out" if:
the ball hits the server's partner before hitting the front wall;
or a partner serves out of order.
It is a "dead ball" if:
the ball – after hitting the front wall but before bouncing on the floor – hits the server's partner while he is in the service box;
or it passes between the partner in the box and the side wall.

**losing the service**
A server loses the service if:
he serves an out service;
or he makes two fault services in succession;
or he hits his partner with an attempted return;
or he or his partner fails to make a good return;
or he or his partner makes an avoidable hinder.
As noted, when a player loses the service in doubles, it passes to the next player in the serving order – not necessarily to the other side.

**receiving service**
Both players on the receiving side must be behind the 5-foot mark. Either may return the service.

**good returns**
Rules are as for singles. Note that:
both partners may swing at the ball (though only one may hit it);
and if one partner tries to play the ball, but misses, both partners may go on trying to return it, until it has touched the floor twice.

**dead ball hinders**
Note that both partners are entitled to a fair try at any ball – even if it would naturally be one partner's rather than the other's, and even if one partner has tried to play it or has already missed it. So both can be hindered by the other side. (But one partner cannot "hinder" another.)

**avoidable hinders**
In addition to the singles rules, it is also an avoidable hinder if a player moves in front of an opponent as his own partner is returning the ball.

Racquetball is sometimes played on one-wall and three-wall courts originally built for handball or paddleball. All the relevant rules of the four-wall game apply, with just the few exceptions and clarifications given here. (Note: these modifications are the same for both IRA and USRA; but they do not in fact cover all eventualities, as neither association sponsors one-wall or three-wall tournaments.)

**courts**
The courts are as illustrated. Note that, compared with the four-wall court:
the serving zone is behind the short line;
and there are no serving boxes or receiving lines.

**service**
As in the four-wall game, it is a fault if the ball goes out of court before bouncing twice on the floor. The one exception applies to the three-wall game only: if a service, coming off the front wall, passes over a side wall or side line without having bounced once on the floor, it is an out, not a fault.(If it bounces once before going out, or goes out over the long line, it is a fault as usual.)

**server's partner**
Service rules for the server's partner in doubles are not officially stated, but can be played as in one-wall and three-wall paddleball: i.e., the partner stands outside the side line, between short line and service marker, and it is a fault if he leaves this position before the ball passes the short line (National Paddleball Association rules) or passes where he is standing (American Paddleball Association rules).

**receiving service**
The receiver(s) may stand anywhere in court behind the short line – including in the serving zone.

**playing the point**
The rules for ball out of court become much more important – but these and all "playing the point" rules are just the same as for the four-wall game.

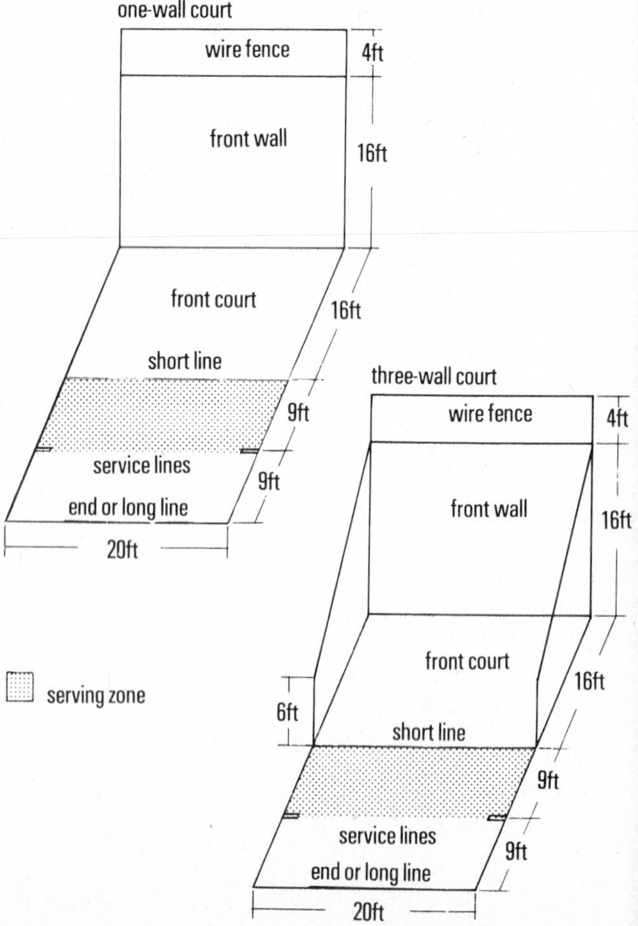

**forehand grip**
You can find this by "shaking hands" with the racquet handle, as in the diagrams. The V between thumb and index finger must fall exactly on top of the handle, in line with the head, or else the racquet face will not be vertical as it hits the ball. Your index finger should be forward, as if on a trigger.

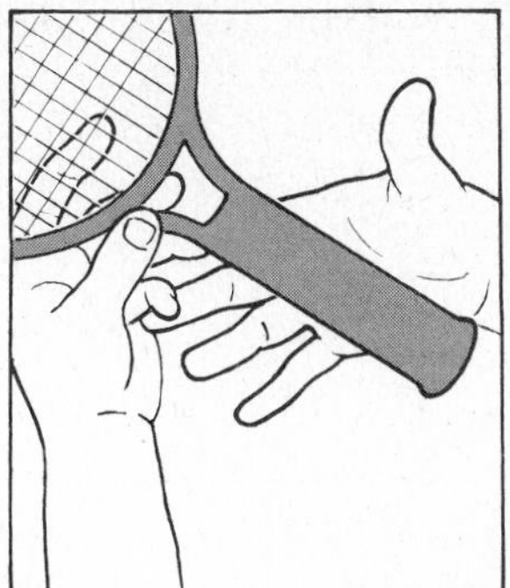

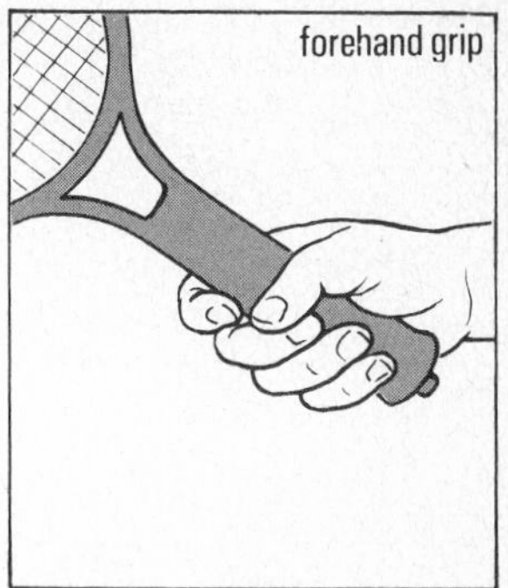
forehand grip

**backhand grip**
Despite the speed of play, your grip must be adjusted for backhand strokes whenever possible. But this only involves turning the racquet slightly in your hand, so the V between thumb and index finger moves about ¼ inch to the left. Otherwise the grip stays the same.

backhand grip

**grip length**
Correct grip length has the butt of the handle just cushioned against the heel of the hand – not projecting beyond it or falling short.

**grip size**
Correct grip size is when your fingers curl around almost far enough to touch the fleshy base of the thumb. A grip that is too small can be thickened with tape.

**positioning – singles**
In singles, players compete for center-court position, which is just a pace behind the short lines (**a**). Each tries to get back to this position after each stroke. On service (**b**), the server usually serves from close to the center position, while the receiver waits near his backhand corner.

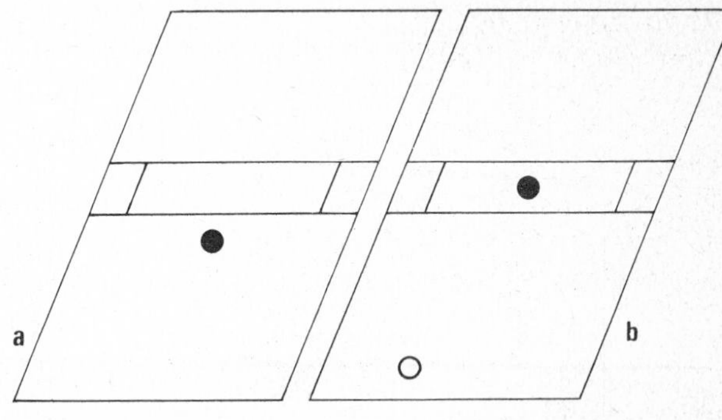


**positioning – doubles**
In doubles, partners use a side-by-side or (less often) a front-and-back formation (**c**). To limit obstruction, it is generally accepted that a side that has just hit the ball has the right to move to center court. Typical serving and receiving positions are as in (**d**).

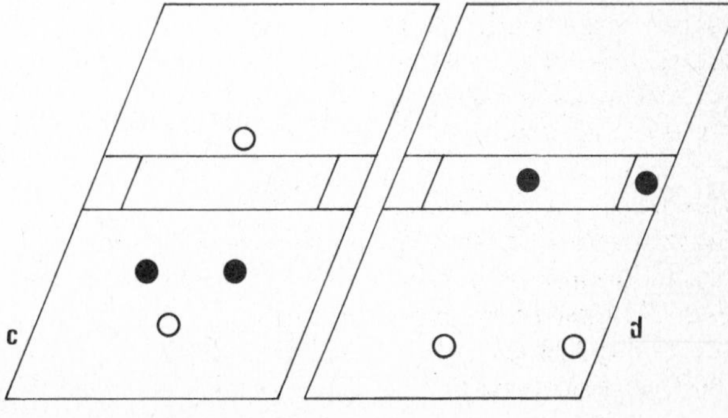

### basic forehand stroke

Get behind the ball, and lift the racquet head-high, wrist cocked back (**1**). Balance evenly on the balls of your feet; then take a long step forward with your leading foot (**2**), and swing evenly into the stroke, bending at knees and waist to get down to the ball. Let your elbow lead into the stroke, powered by the rotation of hips and shoulders – but at the last moment bring your lower arm through, and uncock your wrist with a snap (**3**). Meet the ball at knee height, level with your leading foot, as your weight comes forward. Use about 80% power, or your shot will have poor control. Follow through fairly close to the body (**4**).

### basic backhand stroke

This is basically a mirror image of the forehand, but there are some differences. On the backswing, take your weight back onto your rear foot (**1**), with hips turned away and leading shoulder tucked in. Start the stroke with wrist uncocked. Lean forward, and let hips and shoulders lead the elbow into the stroke (**2**). Take a shorter step than on the forehand (**3**), but bend even more, so at the bottom of your swing the racquet handle is almost parallel with the floor. Meet the ball a little further forward, just in front of your leading foot. Snap your wrist as on the forehand – but this time the snap is from uncocked to cocked position. Finally, for your opponent's safety, be careful with your follow-through (**4**) as it swings away from you.

### adding spin

Spin is regularly used in advanced play. Backspin is added by chopping downward at the ball with an open-angled racquet, sidespin by playing the stroke with sidearm action rather than underarm, so the wrist snap acts sideways on the ball. Topspin is less often used, but can be put on by meeting the ball as usual and then letting the wrist snap roll the racquet over the top of the ball as you start to follow through.

**kill shots**

These are shots that hit the front wall so low they are impossible to return. The perfect kill shot is the "flat roll out," which comes off the front wall onto the floor with no bounce at all. (Of course, if it so much as grazes the floor before hitting the front wall, it is a bad return – not a kill.)

Kill shots use the basic stroke, but contact the ball lower, between calf and ankle height. They are best played: from center court, when in front of your opponent; or (further back) off a ball rebounding forward from the back wall. There are three types: front wall (**a**), front wall-side wall (**b**), and side wall-front wall (**c**). The first is least often successful, the last most often. Use sidespin and backspin on the last two, and backspin alone on the first.

**pass shots**

These aim to get the ball to the front wall and back, past an opponent who is in front of you. If he is in center court, a good pass will draw him back off it, for the return. If he is further forward, it may beat him completely. Pass shots use the basic stroke, but contact the ball higher – from knee up to waist height (though knee height is best).

A "down-the-line" pass shot is usually played on the opponent's backhand. It should hit the front wall about 2 to 4 feet off the floor, and 1 to 3 feet from the side wall, and come back to die against the back wall. Ideally, it should travel back close to the side wall, without touching it: topspin helps keep this line straight.

A cross-court pass (or "V ball") is usually played on the forehand to the opponent's backhand. It can be used to return almost any shot except some ceiling balls. It should reach the front wall about 2 to 4 feet off the floor, and 1 foot beyond center, and come back to die in the far back wall-side wall corner.

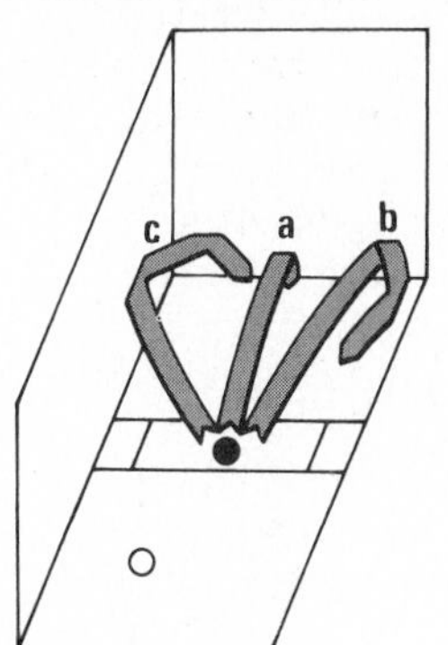


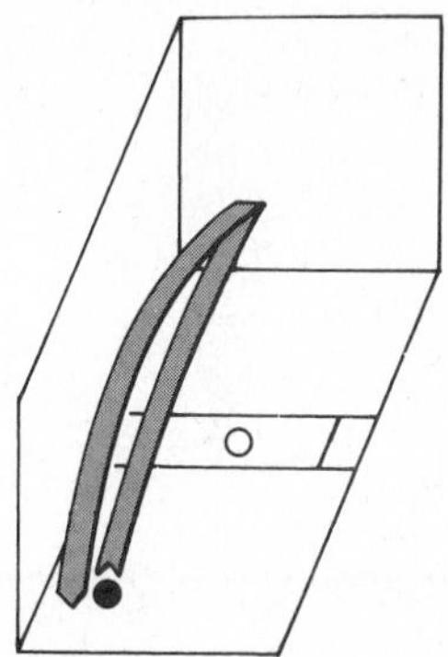

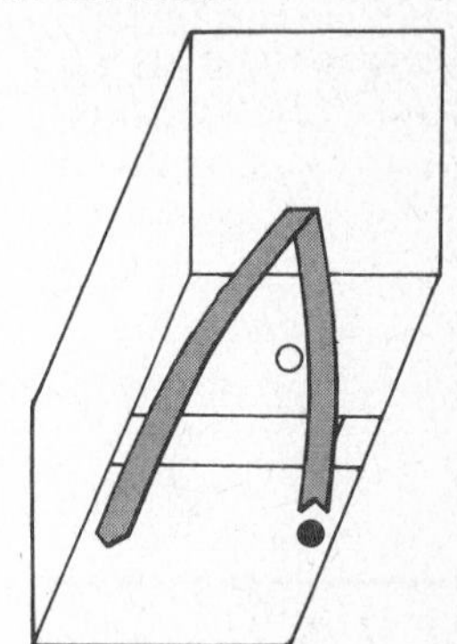

**volleys**

These are used to intercept passes and other shots that may die against the back wall; also to change the rhythm of play and catch your opponent out of position. Charging the ball if necessary, you should meet it between knee and waist height (not overhead), and play it for a kill or pass shot. The stroke is as usual, but often played with the wrist stiff on impact (not snapped).

**ceiling ball**

This is the basic defense shot – played from back court, to strike the ceiling 1 to 5 feet from the front wall. It then comes down off the front wall to bounce high before dying against the back wall. Its steep descent makes it hard to volley, and your opponent usually has to retreat to back court and hit it from at least shoulder height. This draws him from center court, and forces a defensive return – usually another ceiling shot. In fact, play often consists of a long series of ceiling balls, until one side makes a mistake. The shot is almost always sent to the opponent's backhand, and ideally clings to the side wall on its way back. But it must not touch the side wall (or hit the ceiling outside the limits given) or it will ricochet into court for an easy kill.

**forehand ceiling ball** (above)

This requires an overarm stroke, generally above head height. As usual, the wrist cocks on the backswing and snaps for the impact – which should come level with your leading foot as your weight swings forward. The shot can also be played at head height with a more sidearm action (right) but the higher stroke adds useful backspin.

**backhand ceiling ball** (below)

This is far more common: your reply to a preceding ceiling shot to your backhand. It is like the basic backhand stroke, only with a higher point of contact and a higher angle to the shot. Note how the racquet comes back near the left ear. Contact is at anything from waist to head height. On the higher strokes, the wrist is kept stiff, not snapped on impact.

**defensive play**
The ceiling ball, and (on this page) the Z ball and the around-the-wall ball, are generally looked on as defensive shots. That is, they are used to draw your opponent away from center court, and to force him to play a defensive shot in return. They should be used in place of more attacking shots if you are off balance or out of position.

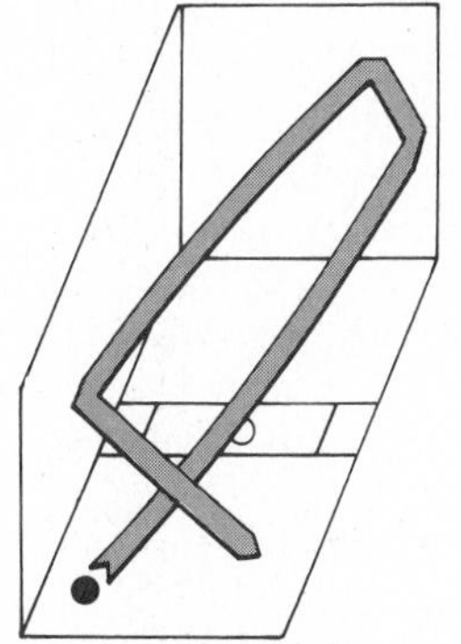

**Z ball** (right)
This is a useful defense shot played from mid-court, preferably near one side wall. The ball is hit hard, to strike the front wall about 3 feet down from the ceiling and 3 feet in from the far side wall. It then ricochets off both side walls, so as to come off the last near the back wall and almost parallel to it. It is usually played to the opponent's backhand.

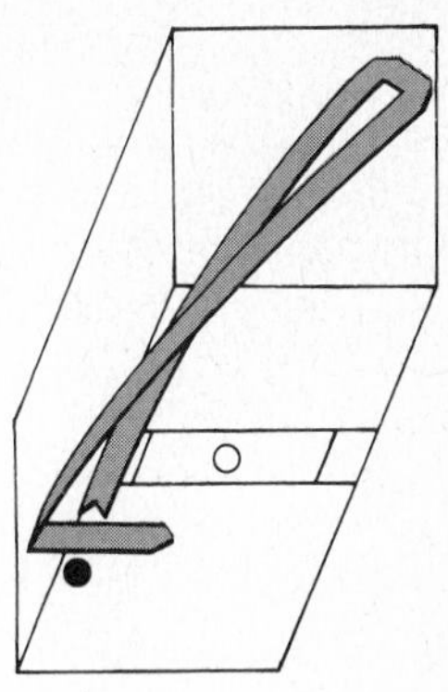

**around-the-wall ball (AWB)** (left)
You can make this shot more easily than the Z ball, and from further back. The ball is hit hard, to strike the far side wall about 3 feet down from the ceiling and 3 feet from the front wall. It then ricochets off the front wall and the other side wall, before dropping sharply into the back court. Before the bounce, your opponent has to take it at shoulder height, as it falls spinning violently. After the bounce, he has to take it as it dies against the back wall. Like the Z ball, it is usually played to the opponent's backhand.

**ball off back wall**
A ball rebounding forward off the back wall often allows a kill or pass attempt – but the right footwork is needed. You should follow the ball back (beginners often stop too far from the back wall). Then wait (**1**), and step forward with the ball (**2**) as it rebounds, to contact it as normal by your leading foot.

**ball into back wall**
If an opponent's shot carries past you – but not strongly enough to rebound from the back wall – you may have to turn and hit the ball into the back wall (aiming about 5 feet off the floor). This should carry the ball back to the front wall on the rebound; but as it also usually gives an easy kill for your opponent, it is used only as a last resort.

**overhead attacking shots**
The standard overhead shots are defensive, but overhead forehand kills and drives are sometimes seen – struck at full stretch or head height, and aimed low to the front wall (with the kill attempts directed to a side wall first to lose momentum). They can work well against a poor opponent, but are seldom used in top-class play.

**other shots**
Most other shots are rarely used.
a) the lob. This is a shot that comes back in a slow arc from the front wall, touches the side wall just enough to lose momentum, and dies off the back wall. It is hard to hit accurately, and is now almost completely replaced by the ceiling shot, though still sometimes used for service returns.
b) half volley. Using the basic stroke, this contacts the ball at ankle height, just as it comes off the ground. In racquetball it is a very difficult shot to make successfully.
c) drop shot. This is also a rare and difficult shot. It demands a stiff-wristed topspin action, either underhand or sidearm.

**the service**

This must be an attacking shot, so it is vital to be accurate, to vary your services unpredictably, and to switch them between forehand and backhand sides. Still, most should go to your opponent's backhand, for a weak return, with occasional ones to his forehand for surprise only. So the services here are all shown to the backhand – although the instructions apply just as well for those aimed at the other side of court.

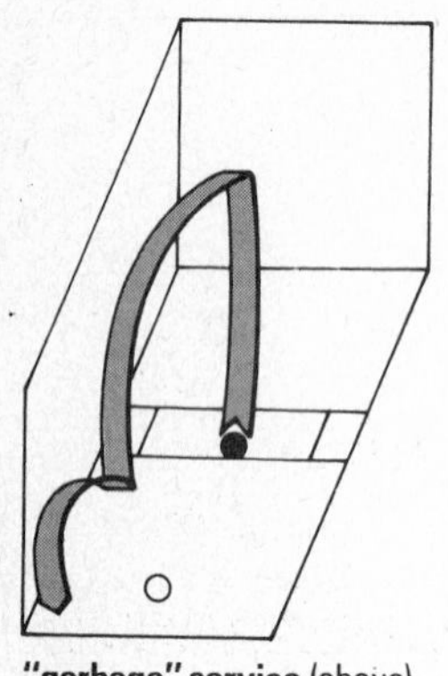

**"garbage" service** (above)

This is the usual service. The ball is hit softly from center court, to strike the front wall about halfway up and about 3 feet off center. It rebounds to touch the floor about 3 feet behind the short line, and bounces shoulder high before dying in the rear corner. It usually forces a ceiling return from shoulder height, so long as it does not touch the side wall before reaching the rear corner, or come forward off the back wall for an easy kill.

For the garbage service, drop the ball to the floor (**1**), so it rebounds to waist or chest height (**2**). Then hit it at the peak of its bounce with a push action rather than a full swing (**3**). If possible add topspin or sidespin.

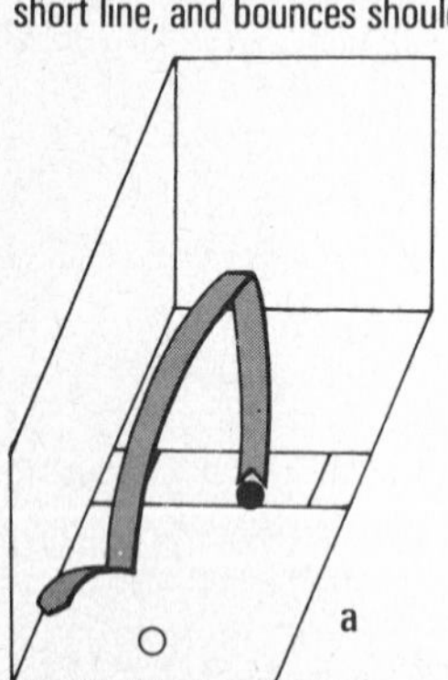


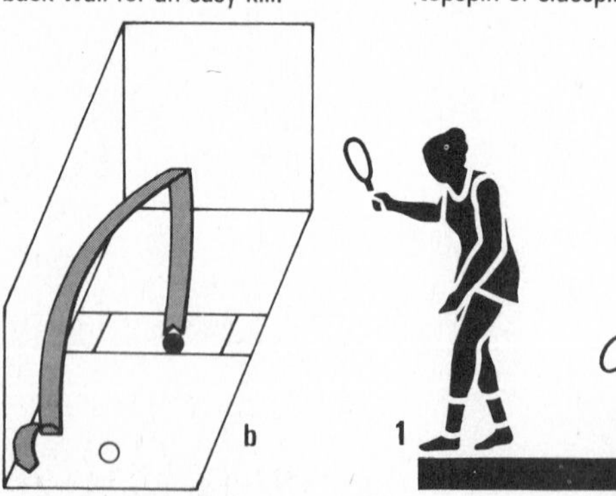


**drive service** (above)

There are two forms: short (**a**), and long (**b**). The short is served from off center, strikes the front wall about 2 feet from the floor and 3 feet from the near side wall, and rebounds to touch the floor just past the short line before bouncing into the angle of side wall and floor. The long is served from the center, strikes the front wall about 3 feet from the floor and 1 foot off center, and rebounds to touch down further back before going low to the rear corner.

For the drive service, drop the ball so that it rebounds to calf or knee height by your lead foot as you step into the stroke (**1**). Hit it at the peak of its bounce with the normal forehand stroke (**2**) at about three-quarter power. (Get well down to the ball.)

**low Z service** (below)

The Z services are easy and effective. The versions to the backhand, as shown here, are known as reverse Z serves. The low Z is served from off center, to strike the front wall about 3 feet from the floor and 1 foot from the opposite side wall. It comes off onto that side wall, ricochets across court, bounces on the floor, and hits the other side wall about 1 to 4 feet from the back wall, to come off spinning violently. Use the same action as for the drive. Do not let the ball hit you as it crosses the court; and do not make this service to your opponent's forehand.

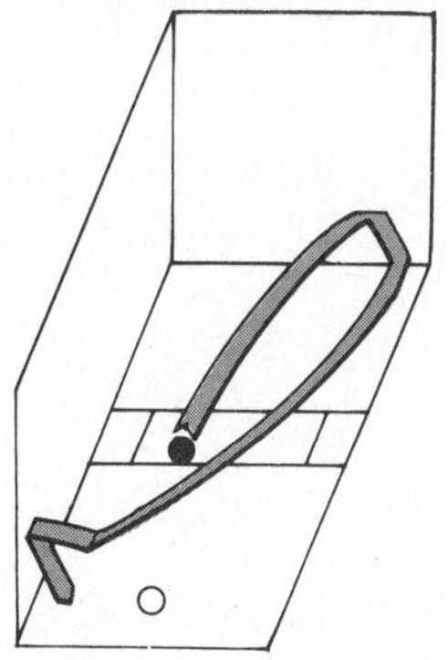

**high Z service** (below)

This is served from the center, to strike the front wall about 8 feet from the floor and 2 feet from the side wall. It follows roughly the same path as the low Z, but reaches the second side wall higher up, about 1 to 5 feet from the back wall. For this service, let the ball bounce between waist and shoulder height. Hit it with half power, sidearm or overarm.

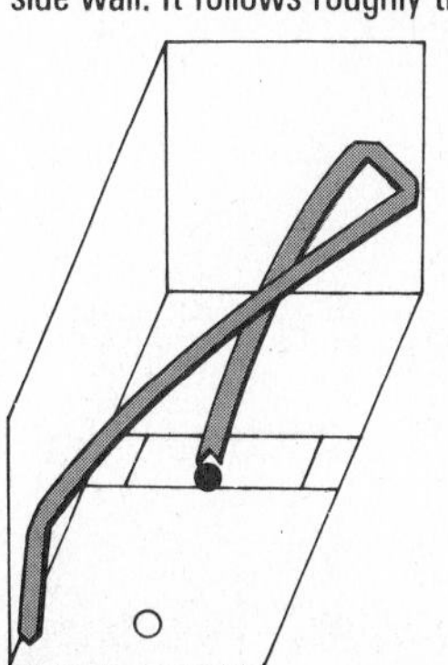

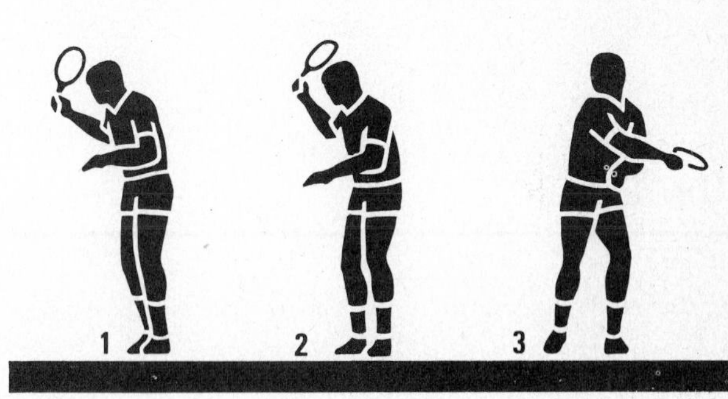


**return of service**

As receiver, you can expect 90% of services to come to your backhand. Wait just left of center, and try to anticipate the shot. Move in to volley it if possible; if not, expect to take it about 4 feet from the back wall. Always have a definite shot in mind. Use the ceiling ball as your basic return: it is safe, can be used against any service, forces the server back, and gives you time to reach center court. Use the drive (usually cross-court) as your main alternative, to change tempo and to attack weak or moderate serves. Occasionally use the around-the-wall ball for surprise against the softer shots. Try to kill only very poor services.

# Paddle games

# Paddle tennis

Paddle tennis is basically a scaled-down version of tennis, with a smaller court, paddles instead of racquets, and a "deadened" low-bouncing ball. It is still scarcely known outside North America; but after years of obscurity, it is now flourishing there, with 200,000 players in the U.S.A. alone.

The game's attraction lies in both its differences from and its similarities to full-size tennis. On the one hand, the short-handled paddle is much easier to get used to than a tennis racquet. So, from their first time on court, novices of all ages can enjoy a fast-moving game with plenty of rallies. Since doubles are usual, this also makes it a sociable sport—families can play together. And the paddles also allow outdoor play all winter, when damp could ruin strung racquets. On the other hand, the game is also excellent training for tennis. Apart from the underarm service, the strokes and skills are identical, and such tennis stars as Bobby Riggs, Althea Gibson, and Pancho Gonzales all started their careers on childhood paddle tennis. Even after turning to the full-size game, many players use paddle tennis as a way of keeping fit and in practice through the winter months: competitive paddle tennis is a highly athletic game.

Paddle tennis was invented by Frank Peer Beal in Michigan, U.S.A., in 1898. He introduced it to New York City in the 1920s, and in the Depression many hundreds of courts were built as part of a government-sponsored program. But the game was hampered by weaknesses in the original court size and playing rules, by being labeled as a children's game, and by confusion in the public mind with platform tennis (which was also referred to as "paddle tennis" for many years.) Its revival from 1959 on, with totally revised court and playing rules, has been almost entirely due to the efforts of one man—Murray Geller, now President of the United States Paddle Tennis Association, and for many years an impassioned advocate for the game.

marcraft
RACQUETBALL

Court and equipment are almost the only features that distinguish paddle tennis from normal tennis.

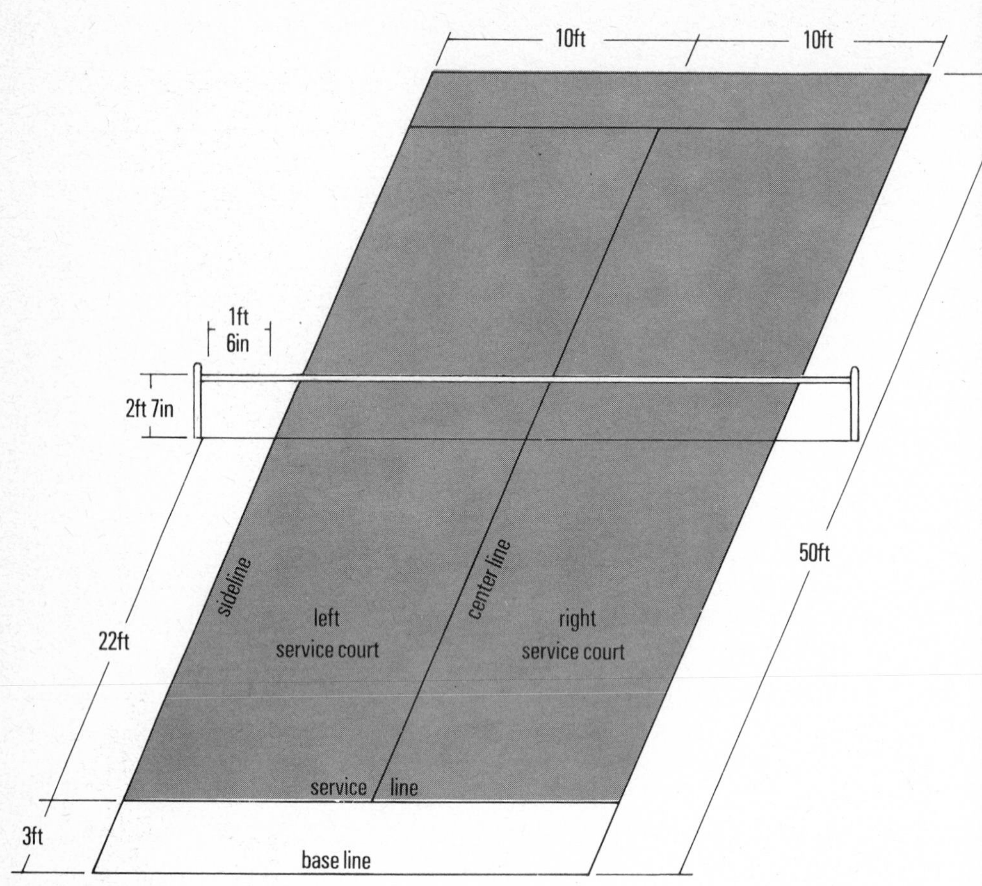


**court**
The court is marked out as shown. It occupies less than half the area of a regular tennis court. The same playing area is used for both singles and doubles: there are no side alleys.
Courts are usually outdoors, but indoor courts are also possible. Any solid surface may be used: asphalt, cement, wood, grass, clay, composition, or synthetic material.

**surround**
There should, where possible, be at least 10 feet of clear space at the sides, and 15 feet of clear back space at each end, between the court and any wall, fencing, or adjacent court.
If there is less than 11 feet of clear back space at the ends, the lob rule applies: see p. 117.

**net**
The net is pulled taut, and should ideally be 2 feet 7 inches high all along its length. However, a 1 inch maximum sag at the center is allowed if there is no steel cable.

**fencing**
Note that, where there is a fencing surround, this serves as a useful backstop only. It is not part of the game (in contrast with platform tennis: see p. 144).

**lob rule**

If there is less than 11 feet of clear back space behind each base line, then the service lines become the base lines, and the base lines the lob lines. The areas between the new base lines and the lob lines become the lob areas. Any ball that lands in a lob area must have reached a height of at least 10 feet above the court surface. Otherwise it is ruled as going out of court.

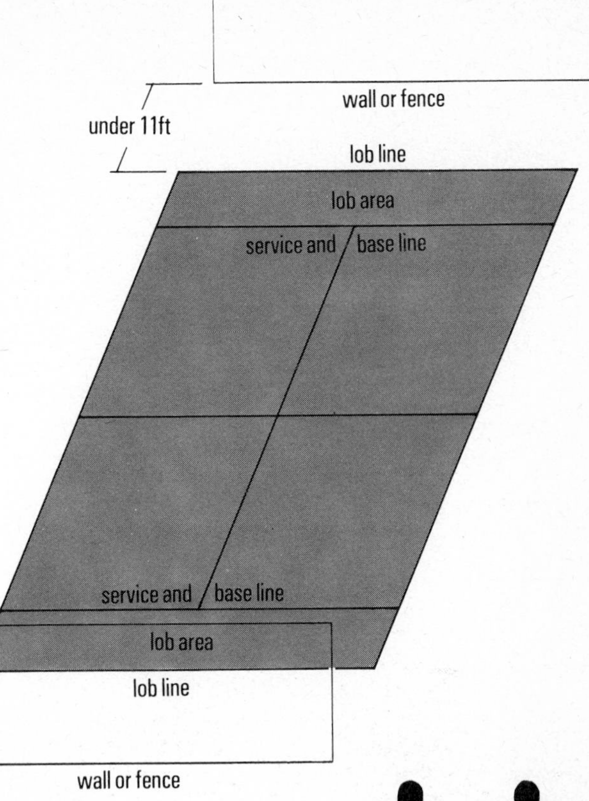

**paddle**

A paddle tennis paddle is oval, and a maximum of 17½ inches long (handle included) by 8½ inches wide. Its face may be solid or perforated, but perforations are usual (without these it is difficult to control the ball).

The paddle face must not be covered with any granular, spongy, or other additional material. No strung racquet of any kind is allowed.

**ball**

Paddle tennis uses a deadened tennis ball. The procedure is to take any pressurized ball that has been officially approved by the national tennis association, and then to puncture it – with a pin or needle, for example. The ball's bounce is then tested on the court it is to be used on: required bounce is between 31 and 33 inches, when the ball is dropped 6 feet to the court surface.

Only one ball may be used during a set – unless opponent or tournament official agrees that the server may change balls. Only one ball may be held when serving.

**dress**

Tennis clothes are generally used in tournaments, but sweater and pants, or a track suit, are useful for playing outdoors in winter. Rubber-soled shoes are a necessity.

The special rules of paddle tennis are given on these two pages. All other rules—and skills—are as for regular tennis (see page 30 on).

**service**

Only one service is allowed for each point. If it is a fault, the server loses the point. (He then serves to the other court for the next point, as in tennis.)

To serve, the server must hit the ball when it is not more than 2 feet 7 inches (net height) above the court surface. The server does this: by releasing the ball into the air, and striking it (**a**); or by bouncing or dropping it onto the court surface, and striking it on the rebound (**b**).

Whichever the server does, he must keep to that method for the rest of the set (changing to the other method at the start of the next set if he wants).

Starting with both feet at rest behind the base line, the server may take one step during the service with either foot (**1**), and also begin a follow-through step (**2**), before hitting the ball. But he must not complete the second step before hitting the ball, nor touch the base line or the ground inside the court with either foot. (Once the player has hit the ball, he may move freely.)

In singles games only, there is a further rule: after a service, not only the receiver, but also the server, must let the ball bounce once on his side of the net (**c**), before he starts any volleying. In other words, the server may not volley the first return of a rally.

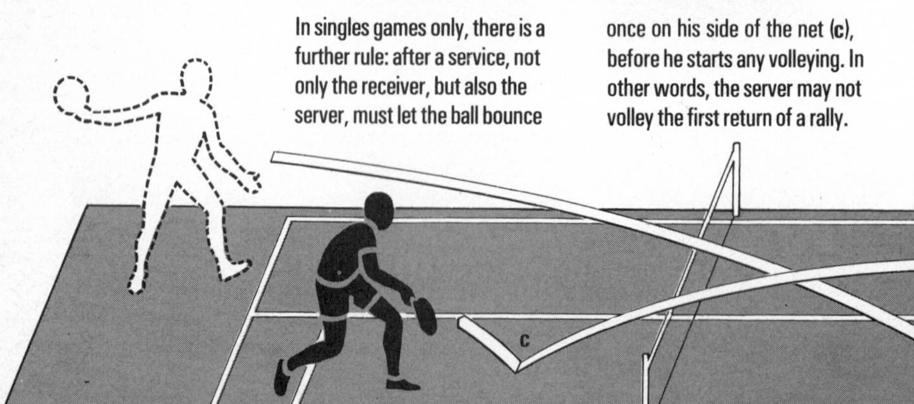

**tie breaker**

Scoring is as in tennis, except for a nine-point tiebreaker, used in national championship tournaments. This is played at six games all (but not in final sets, which must be played out). The first side to win five points wins the set (scored 7-6). First to serve is whoever is next in the usual way. Each player serves for two points. The sequence for doubles is: a, y, b, x (see tennis, p. 38). The ninth serve, if needed, is also by x. Teams change courts after y's second service.

# Table tennis

After soccer, table tennis may well be the most widely played sport in the world. Certainly there are few children who have not rigged up an improvised version at some time or another, at home or in school—perhaps with old books in place of nets and bats. This in fact is the way in which it first developed, in England in the late 19th century, among students and off-duty soldiers. And even when the first commercial versions appeared, there was tremendous variety in rules and equipment. Some paddles were of wood, some of cardboard, others surfaced with cork or sandpaper, and yet others strung like a tennis racquet with gut or wire. Balls were of different materials, nets different heights, and tables different sizes.

In the 1890s the hollow celluloid ball appeared, and there was a brief craze for the game under the name of "ping-pong"—the sound the ball made on the hollow paddles then in use. It soon lapsed back into obscurity, and began to revive only after the First World War. Yet today there are 124 national associations in the International Table Tennis Federation—and one of these alone, that of the Chinese People's Republic, has more than two million members. World titles are fiercely contested, and an application for Olympic status is under way. Table tennis today is still a game enjoyed by all ages, all the year round, anywhere where there is space for a table. But—with ball speeds up to 120 mph—it has also become a major international sport, demanding hair-trigger reactions and considerable athletic agility, and drawing its champions from among the young.

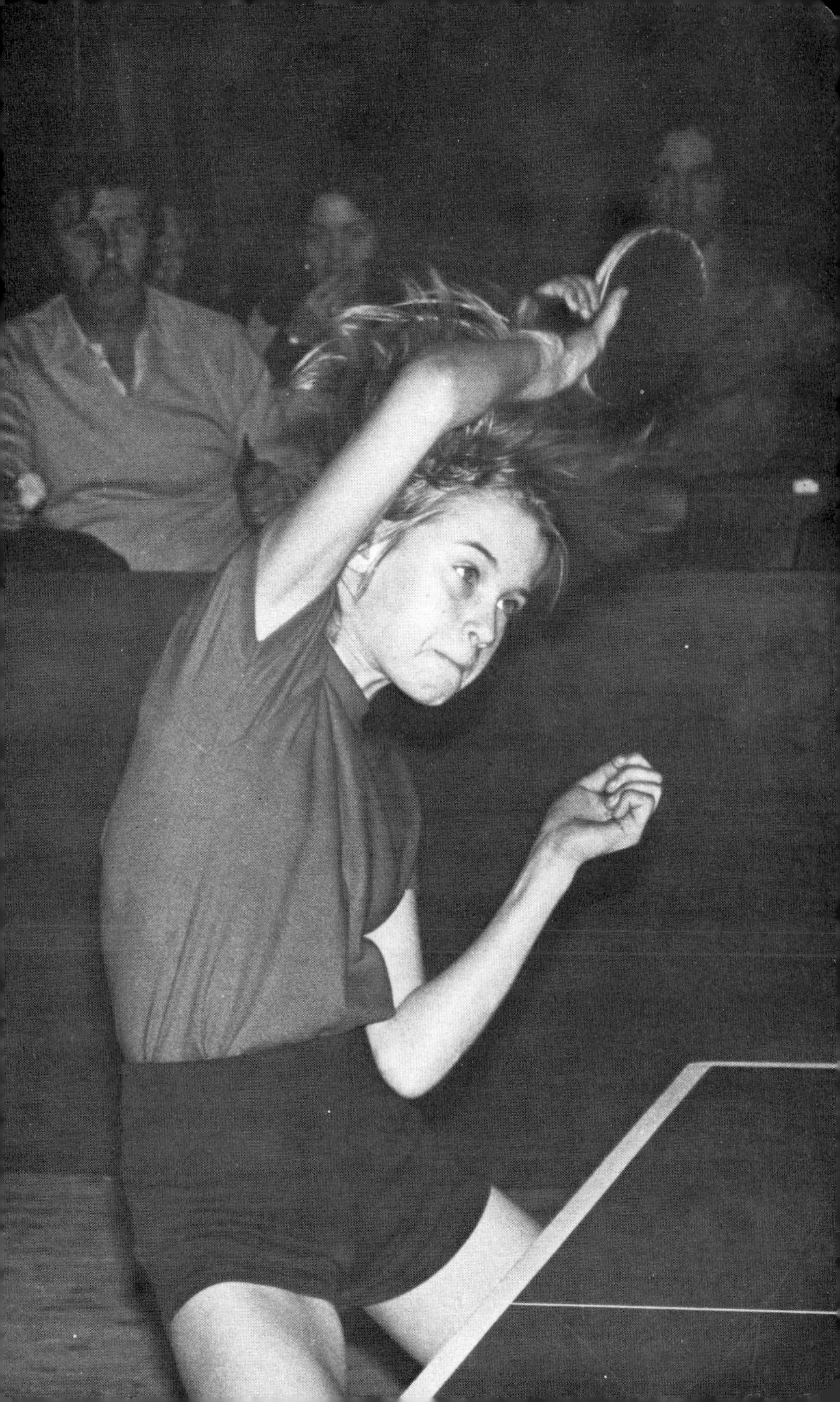

Table tennis is still sometimes thought of as a parlor game, but facilities for serious play require a sizeable investment in space and equipment.

**table**

The top is a dark matt color (preferably dark green), with a white line 20mm (¾ inch) wide around the edges. The thin center line is needed only for doubles play. All the lines count as part of the playing surface.

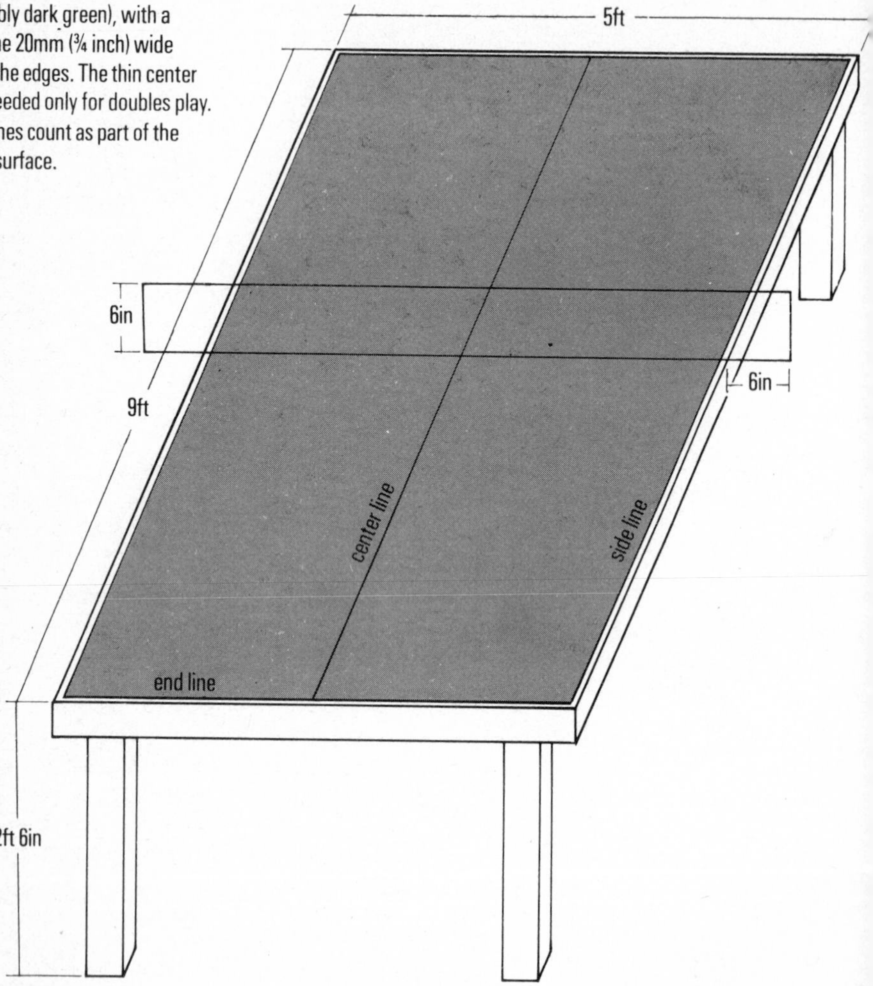

5ft

6in

6in

9ft

center line

side line

end line

2ft 6in

**surface and bounce**

The table surface can be of any material: wood is traditional but metal coated with plastic is now often used, especially for the useful foldaway tables. What is important is that all parts of the surface give the same bounce. (International rules require a bounce of 220 to 255mm–$8\frac{5}{8}$ to 10 inches–when a standard ball is dropped onto it from 305mm–12 inches.) If buying a table, test the bounce at several points, and check that construction is solid (avoid thin wood over battens).

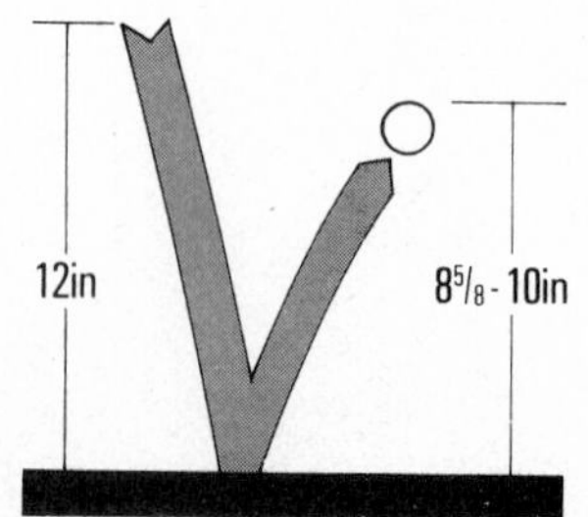

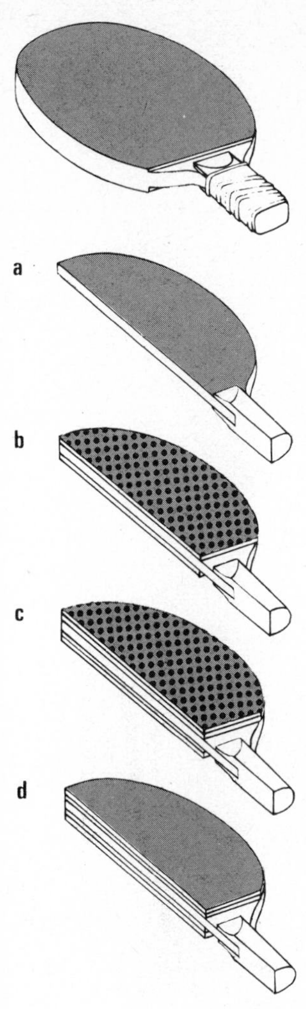


**paddle**

The table tennis paddle is often called a "racquet" or "bat." It may be of any size, weight, or shape; but the blade (the head) must be made of wood, of even thickness, flat, rigid, and unperforated. The sides (faces) of the blade may be:
uncovered (**a**);
covered with plain pimpled rubber, with the pimples pointing outward (**b**);
covered with a layer of cellular ("sponge") rubber and, on top of this, with a layer of plain pimpled rubber, pimples outward (**c**);
or as for (c), but with the pimpled rubber laid pimples inward (**d**).
(The pimpled rubber may not be more than 2mm–0.08 inches–thick, and the combination–"sandwich"–of cellular and pimpled rubber not more than 4mm–0.16 inches–thick.)
Both sides of a blade need not have the same covering; and one side may have any kind of covering, so long as that side is not used for hitting the ball. Also the sides may be differently colored. But the color of any side must be uniform, matt, and dark. (A plain wooden face used for hitting the ball may be stained but not painted.)

**care**

A table tennis paddle should be kept in a cover when not in use, and wiped with a damp cloth once every two weeks (a dirty paddle has no grip on the ball). A regular player will probably have to replace worn rubber at least once a season, and will find an identical spare paddle saves adjustment problems if the regular one gets broken.

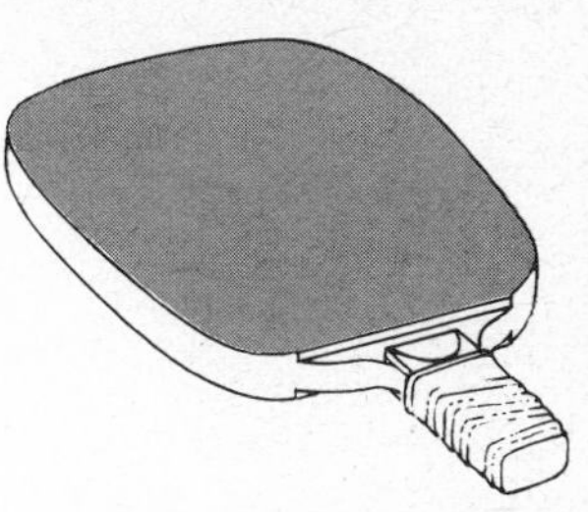

**choosing a paddle**

The different blade surfaces play differently. Even the size of any pimples is significant, with fine encouraging attack, and thick, defense. Single-layer pimpled rubber gives good ball control and encourages all-round stroke play. But it is hardly ever seen in competition today, so a beginner does better to use a "sandwich" bat from the beginning, rather than having to adjust to one later on. All sandwich surfaces allow more spin; that with the pimples inward gives most, but at the expense of speed. Still, the trend among top players is to choose a sandwich with the pimples inward.
Other factors in choosing a paddle are weight, balance, and grip size. But the rule here is simply to choose a paddle that feels as comfortable as possible: neither too heavy nor too light, a natural extension of the hand. (An extra-light paddle is needed, though, if you are going to use penhold grip: see p.132).

**dress**

Competition wear is usually shorts or skirt and a sports shirt, with sports shoes and socks.
International regulations (and most national ones) forbid white or light-colored clothing, and require a uniform dark color (though white clothing is allowed in competitions in the U.S.A.).

**playing space**

To prevent any interference with play, there should be at least 5 feet clear space at each side of the table, and 8 feet at each end. (International rules recommend a playing area at least 12 meters by 6 meters—39⅓ by 19½ feet—with 3½ meters—11½ feet—ceiling height.)

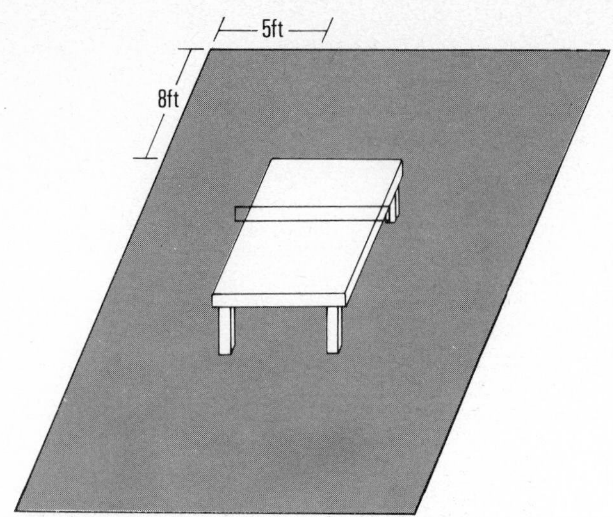


Recommended minimum space

Recommended space for major tournaments

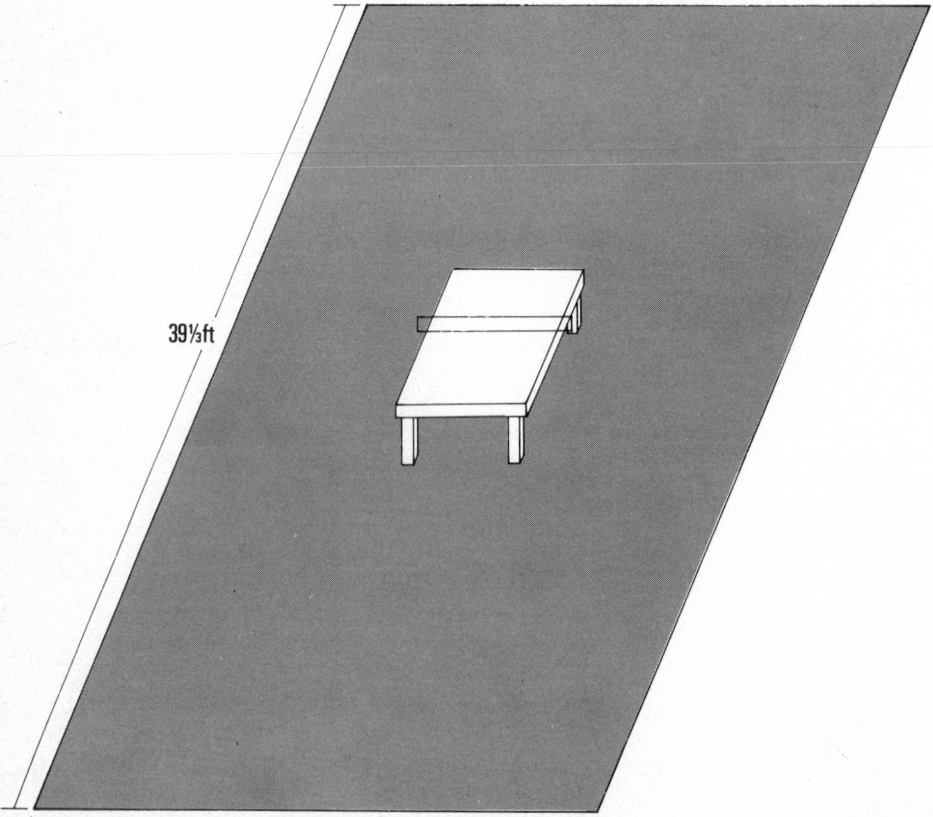

39⅓ft

19½ft

If space is limited it may be best, for serious practice, to offset the table toward one end, so both near and far shots can be developed.

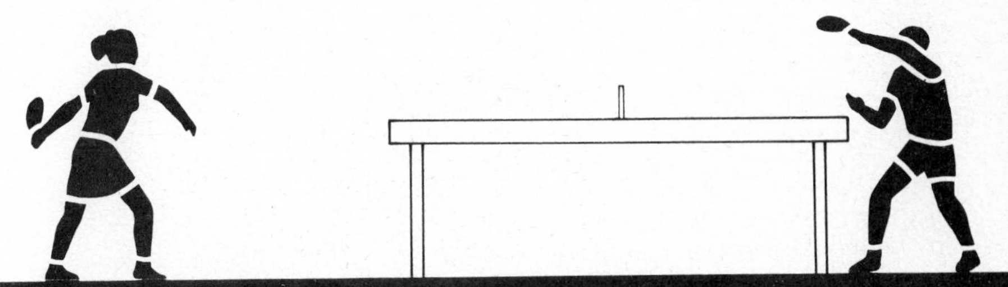

If a miniature table has to be bought, use equipment designed to give comparable stroke play – e.g., a lower net and deadened paddles.

**ball**

The ball must be of celluloid or similar plastic, and white or yellow with a matt surface. Under international rules, its diameter is 37.2 to 38.2mm (about 1½ inches), its weight 2.40 to 2.53 grams (37 to 39 grains), and when dropped 305mm (12 inches) onto a steel block it rebounds between 235 and 255mm (9¼ to 10¹⁄₁₆ inches). (Regulation balls are also classed as low, medium, or high bounce, according to where they fall in this range.)

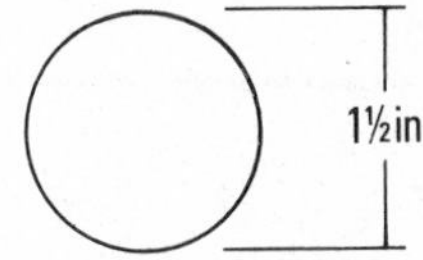


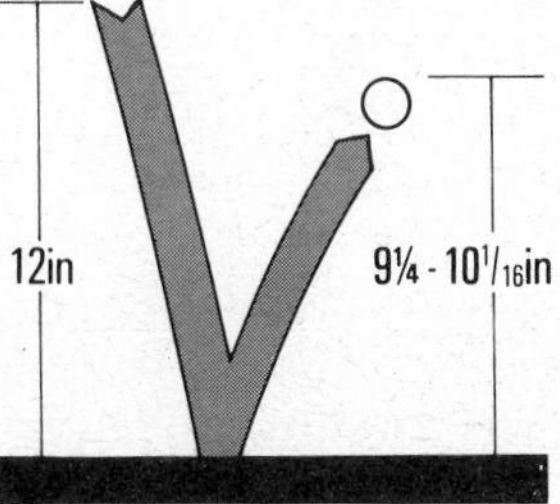

What is unusual about the table tennis service is that it has to bounce on the server's side of the net, before going on to touch table on his opponent's side.

**serving action**

The ball lies in the palm of the server's free hand. The hand has to be still and above table level, and must be flat and open, with the fingers together (thumb position is optional).

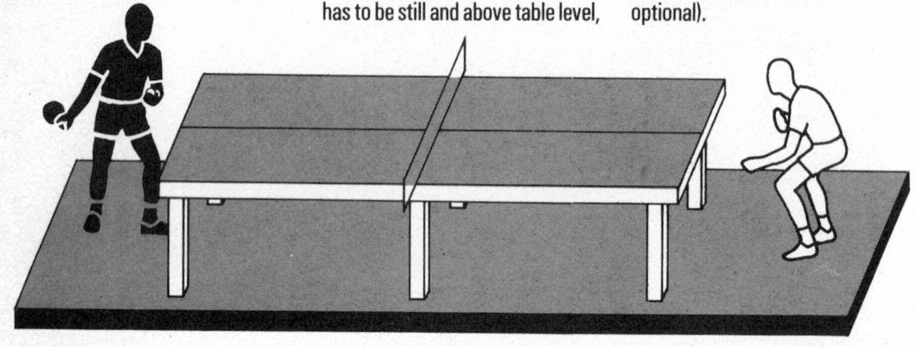

Then the hand throws the ball up without spinning it. The ball must leave the palm and go vertically up—or at least nearer to vertical than to horizontal. (In competition, the ball must be visible to the umpire all the time.)

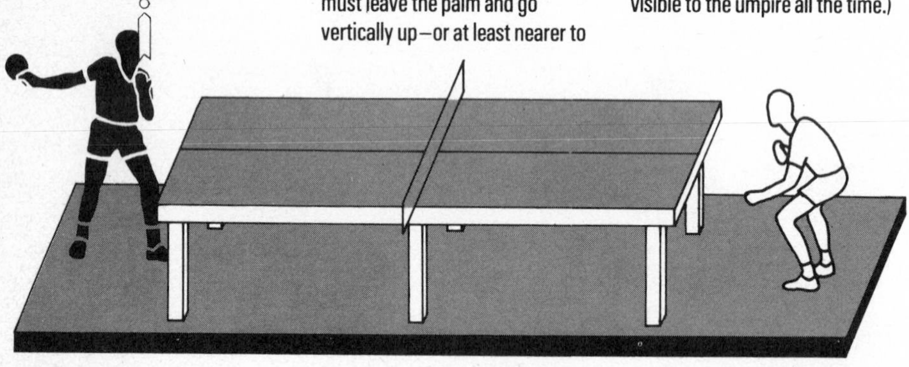

The paddle then has to hit the ball on first attempt, after the ball has started to descend. On impact, the paddle must be behind the line of the end of the table.

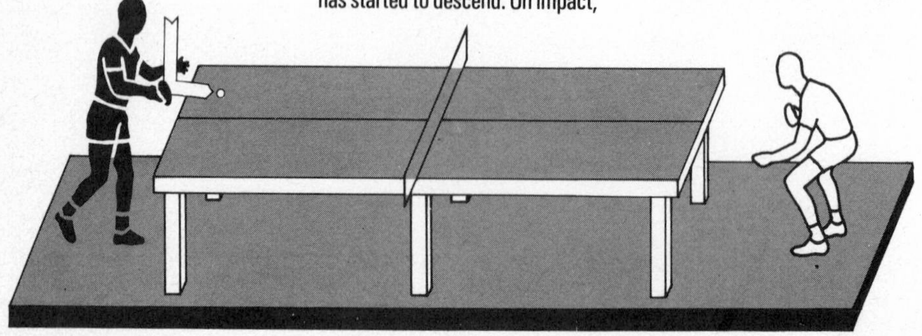

**good services**

In singles, it is a good service if the ball bounces on the server's side of the net, and then passes directly over the net to touch table on the receiver's side (**a**).

It is also good if the ball goes around or under the net outside the sideline (**b**), as long as it still touches the playing surface on each side of the net. (The edge, where table side and top meet, always counts as part of the playing surface, but the side itself does not.)

For the doubles service, see p. 131.

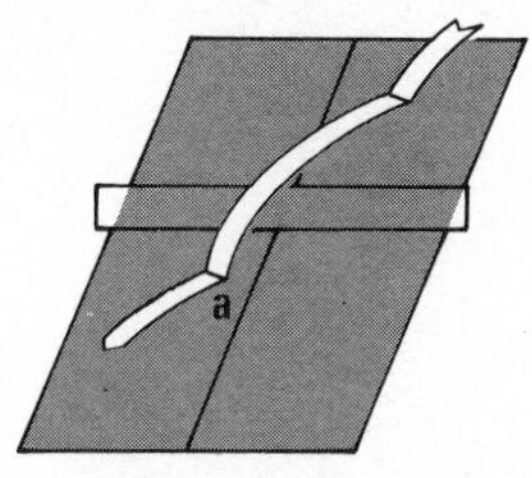


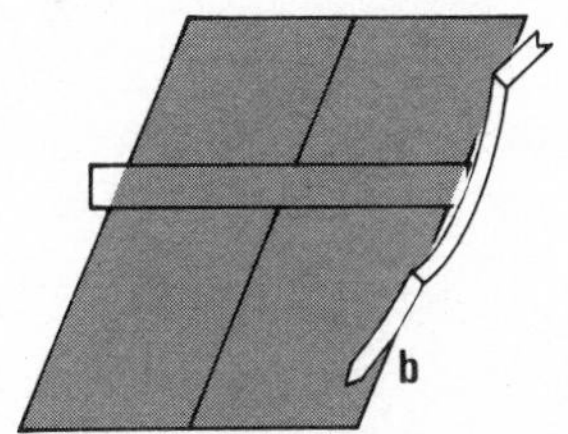


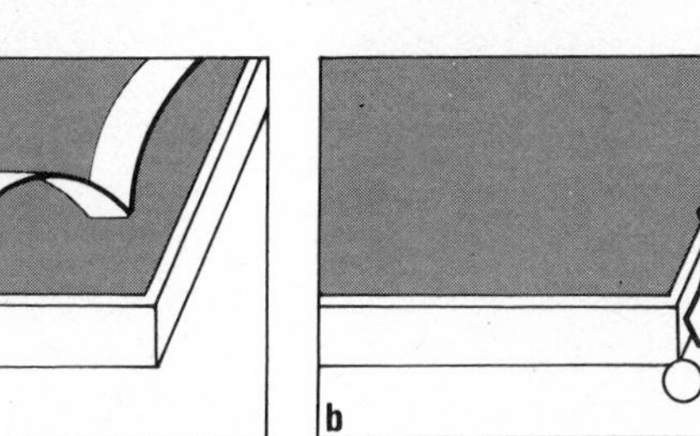


**not good services**

It is a bad service if:
the ball bounces twice before crossing the net (**c**);
or it does not bounce at all before crossing the net (**d**);
or it does not bounce on the opponent's side after crossing the net (**e**);
or the server's serving action is wrong;
or the server makes an illegal action (see p. 129 ).

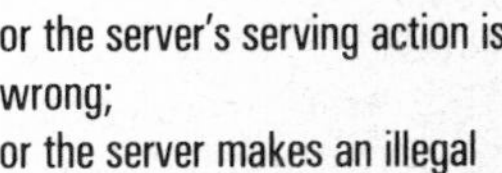

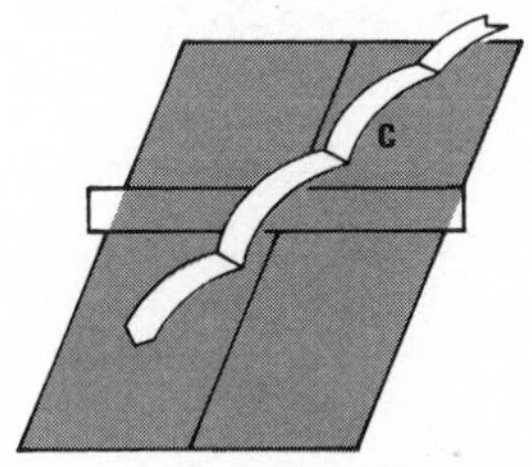


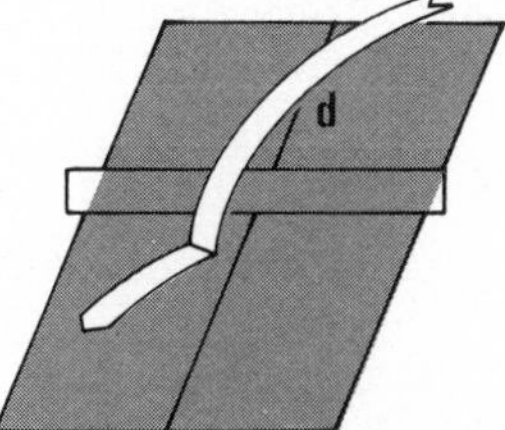


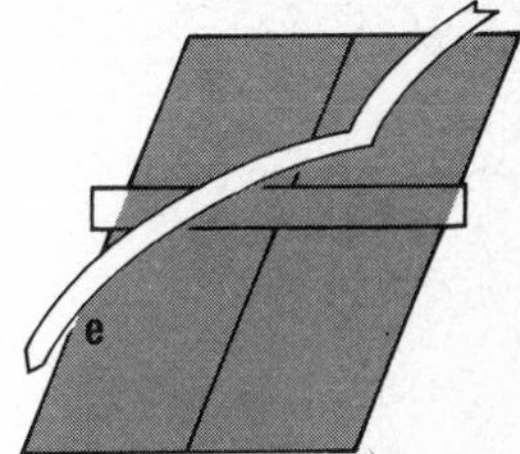


**lets**

If a "let" occurs, the rally is stopped and the service taken again. It is a let if:
a service touches the net or its supports–as long as the service is otherwise good or has been volleyed by the receiver;
or a service is made when the receiver (or his partner) is not ready–as long as they do not try to return the ball;
or a player does not make a good service or return due to an accident beyond his control–such as spectator movement or a sudden noise;
or the rally is interrupted to correct a mistake in playing order or ends;
or the rally is interrupted to apply the expedite system (see p. 130 );
or the ball is broken in play.

If a player does not make a good service, he loses the point straightaway. But if he makes a good service, the opposing players hit the ball back and forth over the net—until eventually one of them fails to make a good return, and so loses the point.

**good returns**
It is a good return if-
the player hits the ball after it has touched the table once on his side of the net (**1**)
so it goes straight back over the net to touch the table on his opponent's side (**2**).

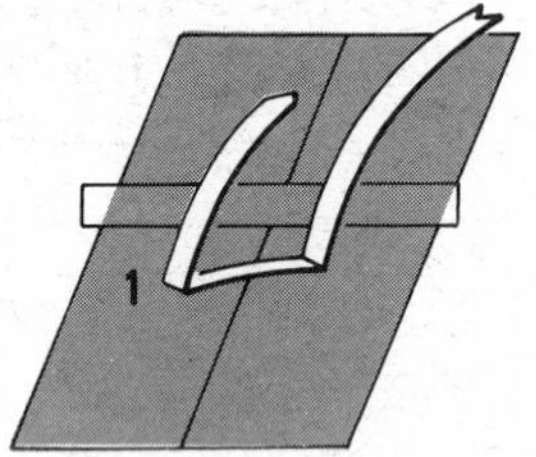


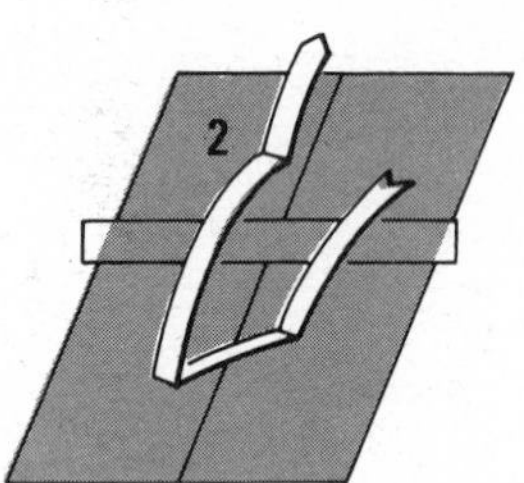


As with the service, returns around or under the net projections are also good (**a**).
The return is still good if:
the ball touches the net or its supports (**b**);
or the ball bounces off the player's paddle hand below the wrist, rather than off the paddle itself (**c**).
Also, if the ball touches the player's side and then rebounds back over the net, he may make a good return by reaching over the net to hit it (**d**)—provided that he or his clothes or paddle do not touch the net.

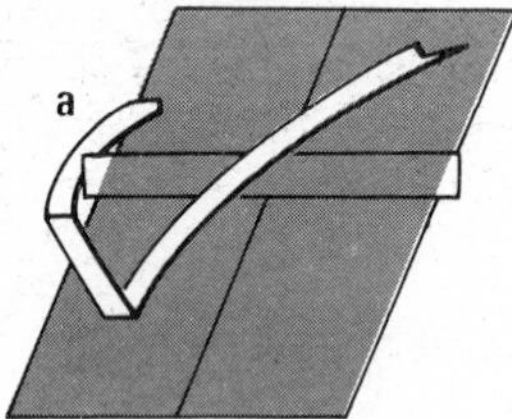


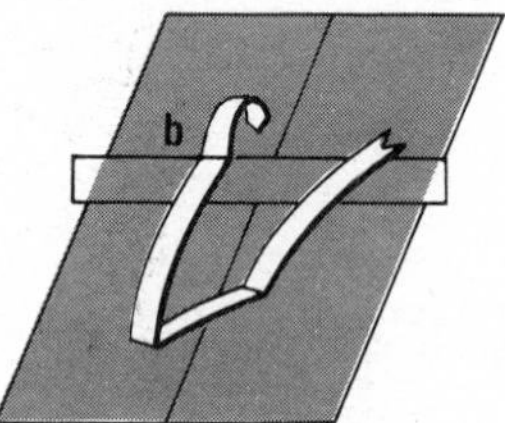


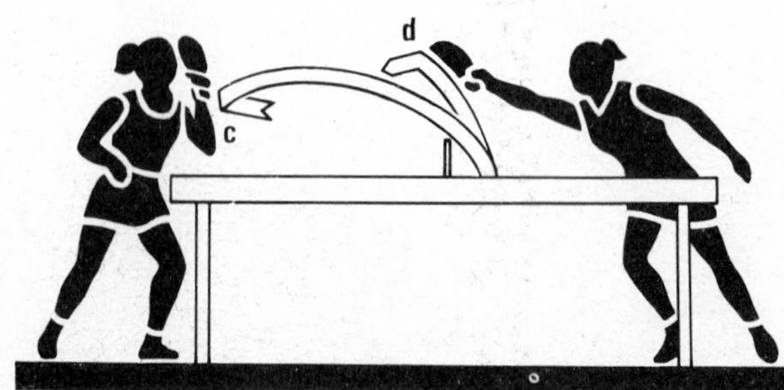

**not good returns**

It is not a good return if:
the ball has not bounced on the player's side when he hits it (**a**);

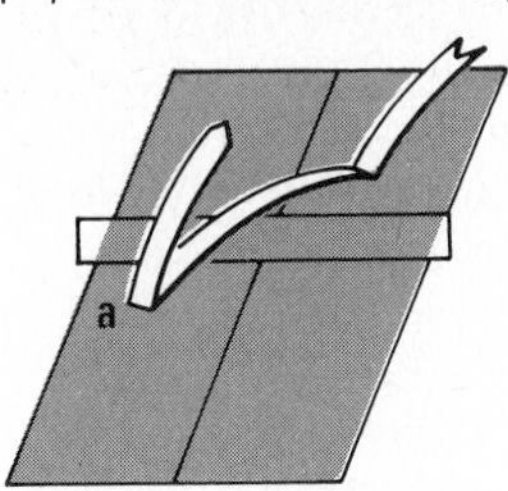


or the ball bounces more than once on the player's side before he hits it (**b**);

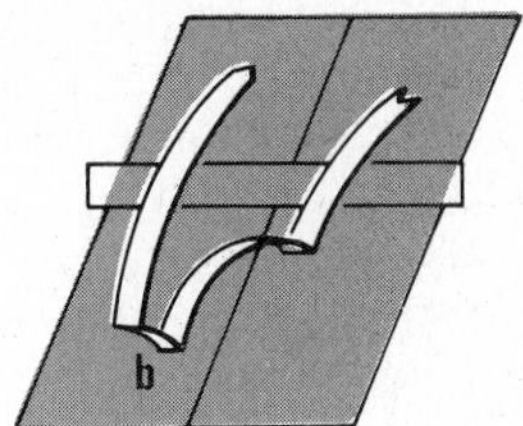


or the ball bounces on the player's side after he hits it (**c**);

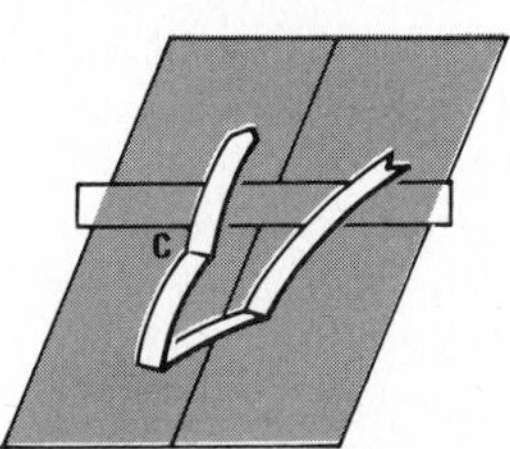


or the ball does not go over the net after being hit (**d**);

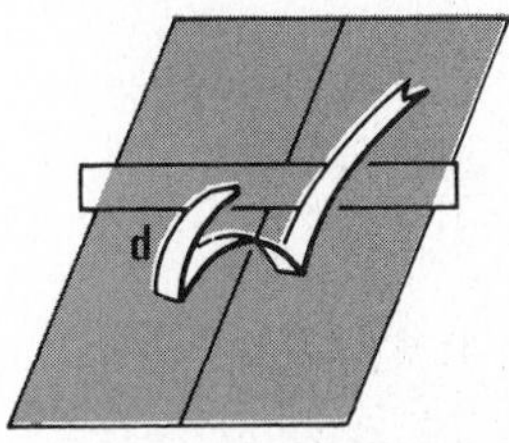


or the ball goes over the net but does not touch the table on his opponent's side (**e**).

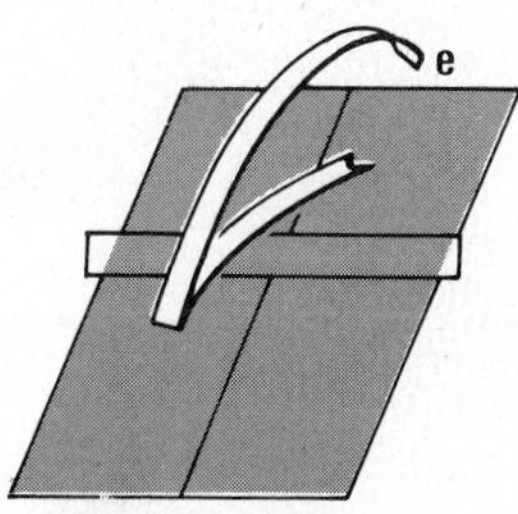


It is also not a good return if the player:
hits the ball so it touches any object off the table before bouncing on his opponent's side (**f**);
or only hits his opponent's good return after it has gone on to touch an object off the table (**g**).
(Note that "objects off the table" include the table sides, legs, and supports, and the floor.)

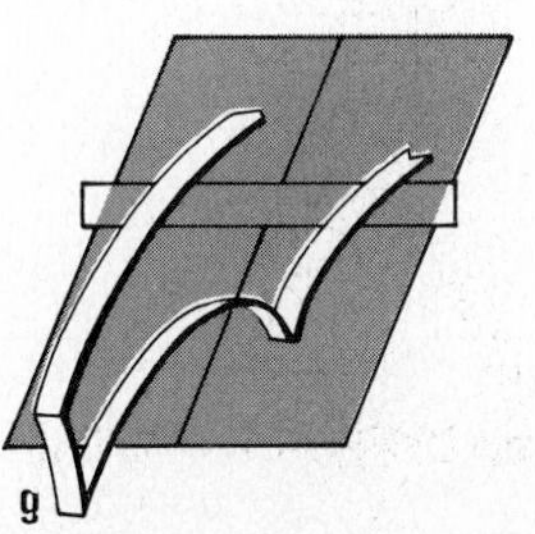


**winning the point**

A player wins the point if his opponent:
does not make a good service;
does not make a good return;
or makes an illegal act.
Under the expedite system (see p. 130), a receiver also scores when he has played 13 good returns in any rally.

**illegal acts**

These include:
hitting the ball more than once to serve or return it;
hitting the ball with the paddle edge;
hitting the ball with the paddle hand after dropping the paddle;
hitting the ball with the paddle after letting go of it;
touching the playing surface with the free hand during play;
moving the playing surface during play;
touching the net or its supports with paddle, body, or clothing during play;
or (however inadvertently) letting the ball touch any part of the body or clothing, apart from the paddle hand below the wrist.
Note that, even if an opponent's return has clearly missed the table and is going to touch the floor, a player who stops the ball with his bat, body, or clothing loses the point in competition play.

All the following rules apply to both singles and doubles games.

**start of play**
Choice of ends and first service is decided by tossing a coin. If the winning side decides to serve first or receive first, the losing side has choice of ends, and vice versa. Alternatively, the winning side may tell the losing side to choose first.

**serving**
The first server serves five times (not counting lets). The opposing side then serves five times, and so on alternately. But if the score reaches 20-all, or if the expedite system is brought in, then each side serves only once before the service passes.

**scoring**
Each point scores one. The current score is called after each point: e.g., "16-13" (the serving side's score is given first). If both sides have the same score, the call is (for example) "16-all."

**winning the game**
The first side to score 21 points wins the game—unless the score reaches 20-all, in which case one side must get a two-point lead to win.

**subsequent games**
The side serving first in the first game receives first in the next, and so on. Sides change ends after each game, and again in the last possible game when one side reaches 10 points.

**the match**
A match can be one game, the best of three games, or the best of five. Play should be without breaks, except that either side can claim up to five minutes' rest between the third and fourth games of a five-game match, and up to one minute between the fourth and fifth.

**expedite system**
This is brought in if a game is not finished 15 minutes after its start. The umpire interrupts play, and the system is then used for the rest of the match. On each rally, the return strokes of the receiving side are counted out loud. After 13 good returns in any rally, the receiving side wins the point.

**errors**
Any mistake in ends, or in serving and receiving, must be corrected as soon as it is discovered, but all points scored still count.

Most of the doubles rules are the same as those for singles, with the following exceptions.

**service**

The server must hit the ball so that it bounces in the righthand half of the table on his side of the net (**a**); passes over the net (**b**); and then first touches the half of the table diagonally opposite (the receiver's righthand half) (**c**). He loses the point if the serve touches his own or the receiver's lefthand halves of the table. (The center line counts as part of the righthand halves.)

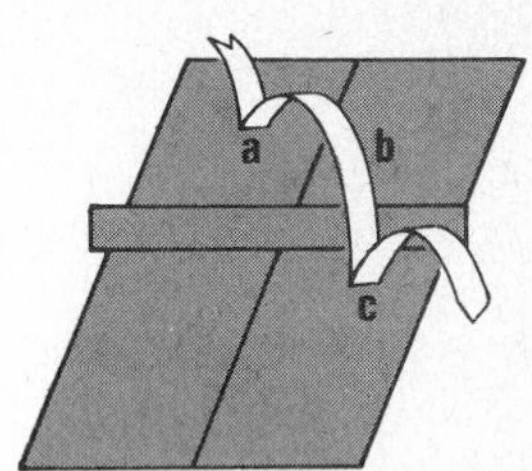


**rally**

In doubles table tennis, players have to hit the ball in a set order, in a rally. Beginning with the service, a rally must follow the playing sequence: server, receiver, server's partner, receiver's partner, back to server, and so on (**a**). It does not matter which side of the center line a ball has bounced: the other partner gets out of the way (**b**).

A side loses the point if one of them hits the ball out of sequence (unless there has been a mistake about the playing order).

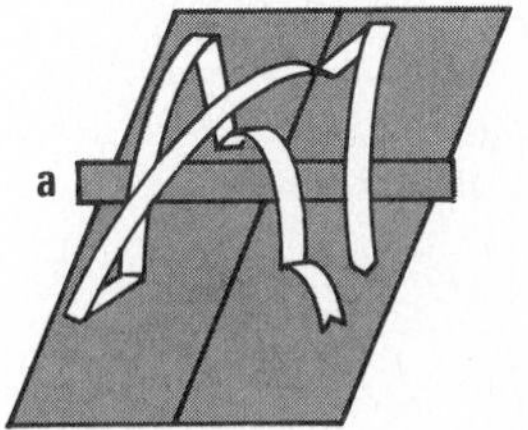


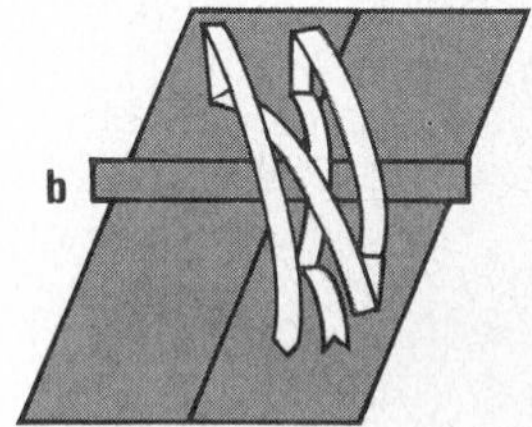


**service sequence**

At the start of the game, ends and first service are decided in the usual way.
The side serving first (a and b) decide which of them is to take the serve: a, for example. The other side (x and y) decide which of them will receive first: x, for example.

The service sequence is then:
a serves five times to x (**1**);
x serves five times to b (**2**);
b serves five times to y (**3**);
y serves five times to a (**4**).
(Any rally follows the rules given below. For example, if b is serving to y, the hitting order in any rally is b, y, a, x.)
In the next game, the other side serves first, and the receiving order changes, i.e.:
x serves five times to a;
a serves five times to y;
y serves five times to b;
b serves five times to x.
In the last possible game of a match, the receiving order changes when one side reaches 10 points.
Any error in the sequence must be corrected as soon as it is noticed, but all points scored still count.

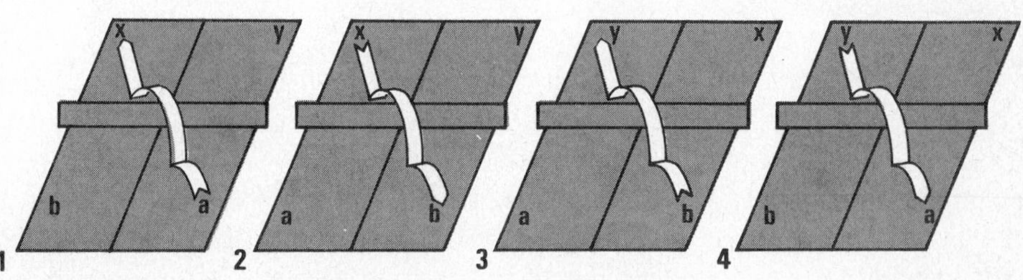

**grips**

There are two ways of holding the table tennis paddle. Almost all Western players use the western or "shake hands" grip, while almost all Asian players use the "penhold" grip. All techniques in this book are shown with the western grip – but use whichever you find more comfortable.

western

penhold

**western grip**

This is a "shake hands" grip, with three fingers around the handle, and index finger and thumb on opposite sides of the blade. Both sides of the paddle can be used to hit the ball. Many players move the index finger up for forehand shots, and the thumb up for backhand shots (the dotted lines show this).

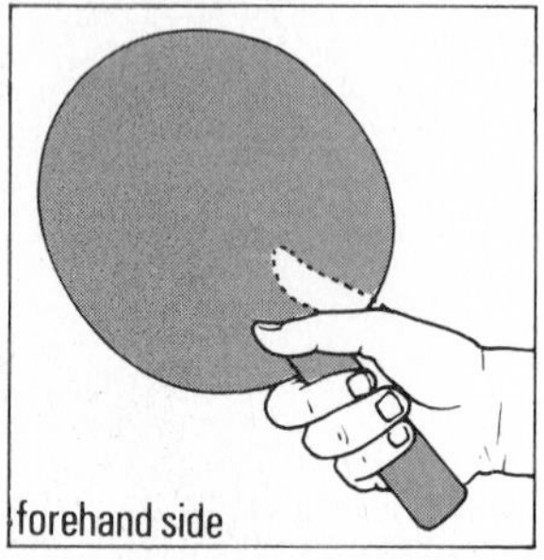

forehand side

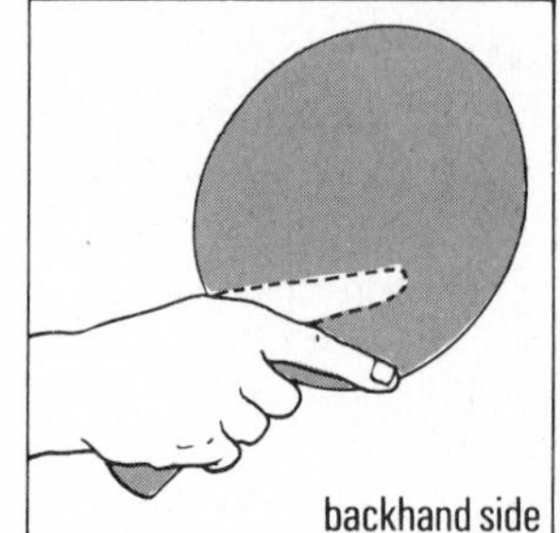

backhand side

**penhold grip**

The handle of the paddle passes between index finger and thumb. These are on one side of the blade, and the other three fingers are on the other side. Usually only the side with index finger and thumb is used for hitting the ball, and a player has to be very agile to overcome the limitations of this. Penholders also generally use a very light paddle.

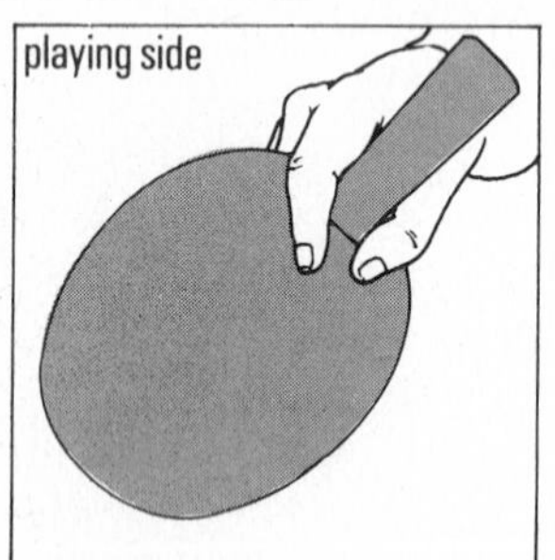

playing side

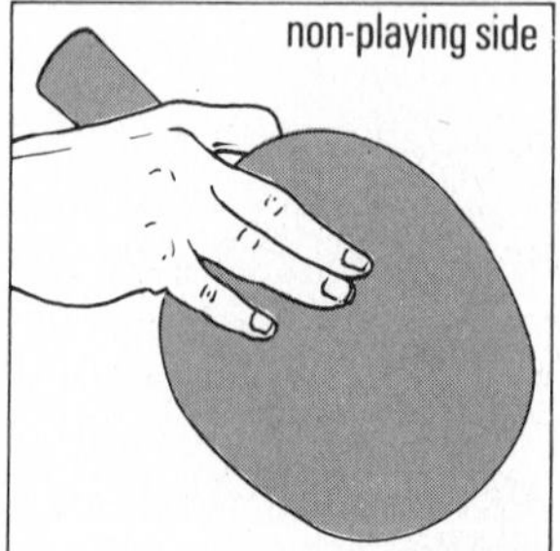

non-playing side

**stance**

The basic stance (**a**) allows easy movement forward (**b** and **c**), sideways (**d** and **e**), and back (**f** and **g**). Note how this movement turns the body into the stroke. To play forehand strokes, the left shoulder is brought nearer the net, with left leg forward. To play backhand, the right shoulder and leg are forward.

**position**
Basic position is behind the center line (**a**), with movement from this as necessary. Ideally the body should turn even for shots arriving down the center. But at match play speed, some shots have to be taken from the basic square stance. Some players, who have a very strong forehand attack, stand to one side and try to cover the whole table with their forehand (**b**).

**positioning the ball**
The most important things here are depth and angle. The white areas in the diagram are where you should try to send the ball: short (just over the net) or deep, but never to the middle of the table (the shaded part). Angling the ball to an unexpected direction is done either by turning the paddle alone (**c**), or by turning your feet and so your whole body (**d**). Angling "with the feet" makes it easier to surprise an opponent.

**movements in doubles**
As they have to hit the ball alternately, partners in doubles need a pattern of movement, so each in turn is in a good playing position. The usual systems are: a backward and forward movement (**e**); or a circling movement (**f**).

**backhand push**

**1** The arm is drawn close in to the body. The right foot is forward; weight is on the left foot. The paddle angle is open.
**2** With body weight shifting forward, contact comes at about the peak of the bounce.
**3** The arm follows through until straight, lifting the ball.

**forehand push**

**1** The stroke starts with the arm clear of the body. The paddle angle is open. Left shoulder and foot are forward; weight is on the right foot.
**2** The paddle moves forward and down. The right shoulder drops as body weight moves forward and the right leg bends. Contact is at the peak of the bounce.
**3** The arm follows through low.

**backhand flat attack**

**1** The paddle starts much lower than for the push, and rises to meet the ball.
**2** Contact is with the paddle vertical or closed, as body weight moves forward.
**3** The arm follows through above the ball.

**forehand flat attack**

This is very similar to the backhand, except that the left hip is toward the table and more body movement is needed.

**blocks**

These are used to return a fast-moving ball. There are two types: straight blocks, which send the ball back along the same line of play; and deflecting blocks, which send it away to a different part of the table. Both can be played forehand or backhand. The diagrams show a backhand straight block and a forehand deflecting block. In both, the ball is taken early, and there is little follow-through. But the straight block uses a slightly closed paddle angle, while for the deflecting block the paddle is vertical and either the whole body or (as here) the paddle alone is angled to one side.

backhand straight block

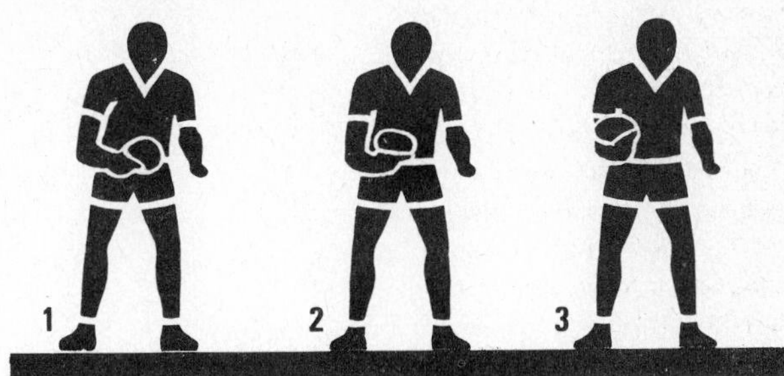


forehand deflecting block

**backspin strokes (chops)**

These are mainly used to return topspin balls. The action is similar to a push stroke, but more vertical: starting high and ending low, so the paddle "chops" downward against the ball. Contact is late in the bounce, with the paddle angle open. Like many other shots, backspin defensive strokes may be taken: close to the table, with the body only half turned away (as in the backhand shown here); or at a distance, with the body sideways to the table (as in the forehand shown). In each case, note how the front knee bends as body weight shifts forward.

backhand backspin defense

forehand backspin defense

**service**

In modern table tennis, the service is an important attacking stroke that can win or lose matches. Spin is almost always used. It is important to study the service rules (pp. 126-127), and to develop a range of different services that allow you to use every part of the table. Then, in play, always take services carefully, deciding beforehand exactly what you are hoping to do, but keeping your opponent uncertain.

The most common service today is a short one, close to the net. It is usually served with backspin, applied by cutting the open paddle down across the back of the ball in the usual way. (Some players also use wrist action, flicking the wrist down sharply on impact.) For a topspin service, in contrast, the paddle moves upward at a closed angle, brushing across the top of the ball when it has fallen to just above table height.

Both backspin and topspin services can also be made on the backhand. For the topspin serve shown, the upward brushing action is achieved by pulling the paddle across the body in an arc from left to right.

More advanced services often add sidespin, to try to beat the opponent. One technique in advanced play is to throw the ball high in the air, and then let it fall to table level before striking it from a crouching posture, well back from the table. This can give heavy top or backspin, and sidespin, with a low trajectory.

forehand backspin

forehand topspin

backhand topspin

forehand topspin with sidespin

**topspin attacks**

In all these topspin strokes, the paddle strikes upward with a closed face, and follows through above the ball. But the precise angle of the stroke has to vary with circumstances: the kind of return your opponent has sent over (you must learn to judge this from his stance and action), and how far from the table you are.

Four versions of the stroke are shown on this page. Three are shown on the forehand, as most players prefer this side for attacking strokes. The first sequence gives the basic stroke–played near the table, against a ball that has no spin. The stroke begins with the hips half turned away from the table (**1**). Contact is at the peak of the bounce (**2**), as body weight shifts forward. The follow-through (**3**) is quite short.

The second sequence shows the stroke against a ball to which your opponent has given backspin (from his point of view–topspin from yours). The stroke is more vertical, contacting the ball late in the bounce, following through high.

The third sequence, by comparison, shows the stroke needed against a ball to which your opponent has given topspin. This is called counterhitting–i.e., countering one topspin drive with another–and is one of the most common strokes in advanced play. The action is again nearly vertical, but quite short, and meets the ball before it has fallen so far from the peak of its bounce. Also the paddle angle is more closed. The final sequence shows: the arm movement for the basic backhand stroke; and the crouching position used to play the ball well back from the table and late in the bounce.

against blocked return

against backspin return

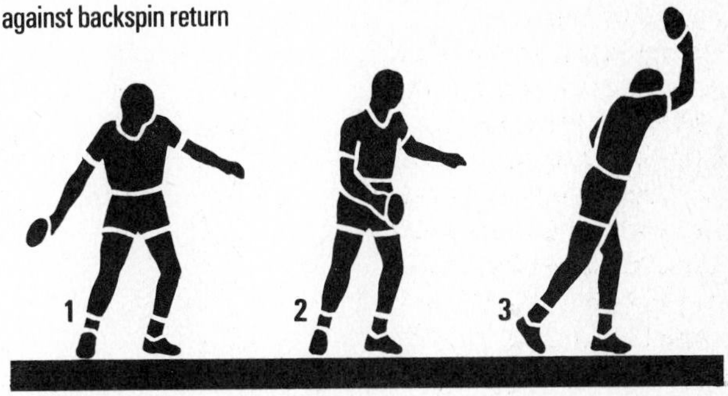

against topspin return

backhand, away from table

**topspin drive with sidespin**
Adding sidespin to a topspin drive doubles your opponent's problems. Start the stroke with paddle low and hips turned away (**1**). Body and arm swing the paddle in an arc, face closed (**2**), dragging the ball around. The follow-through carries across the body (**3**). The stroke does not work well on the backhand, as the body cannot twist sufficiently.

**the loop**
This is an exaggerated topspin drive that makes the ball "kick" violently. The stroke starts low, with hips turned away (**1**). The paddle is almost behind the body, face closed. Body weight shifts forward and up as the paddle rises. At contact the paddle is vertical or open (**2**). The follow-through is high, as the legs straighten (**3**).

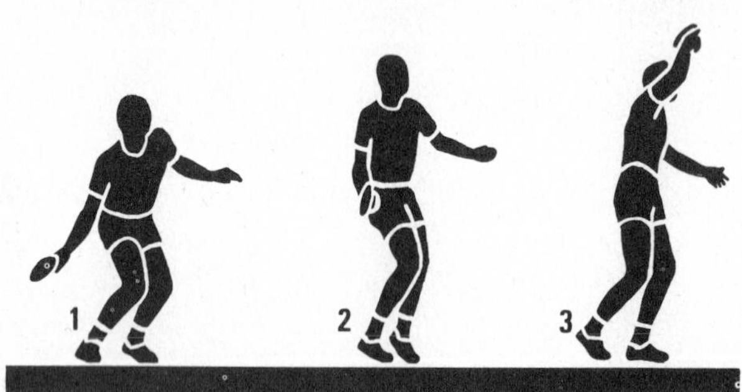


**looping the loop**
The loop is very important in advanced play, and top players have developed various ways to deal with it. One is simply to loop it back again, as shown. Because you must counter your opponent's topspin, the body movement needed is more violent.

**the smash**
A return that is short and bounces high should be "killed" without hesitation. Use a sideways stance, and start high (**1**), so you can hit the ball down from the peak of its bounce (**2**). Meet it flat on, so it takes little or no topspin. Use all your power: aim to hit it out of reach so fast that your opponent has no chance.

**half volley**

This is a simple block, taking the ball straight off the bounce. Very little movement is needed–the surface of a sponge paddle gives a fast return anyway. The face can be tilted to deal with any spin. This stroke is used to upset your opponent's rhythm. It is also one way of dealing with the loop.

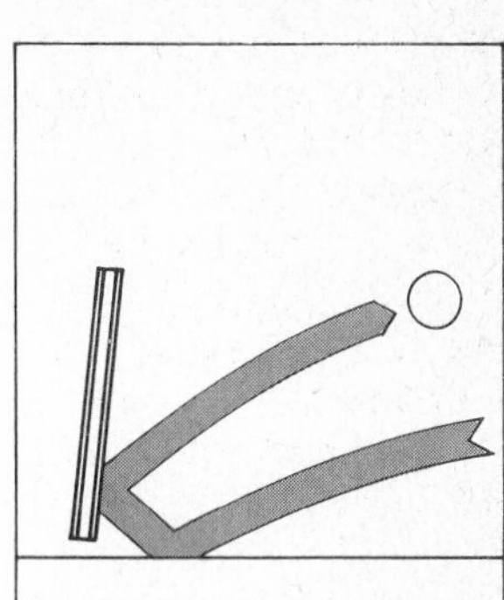

**drop shot**

This deadens the ball, so it just clears the net and "dies." It is used against defensive spin returns that bounce short. Surprise is vital: shape up as for a topspin drive. But the stroke is like a push stroke, deadened by loosening your grip, or jerking back on contact, or (against backspin) sliding the paddle under the ball and lifting (**1**, **2**).

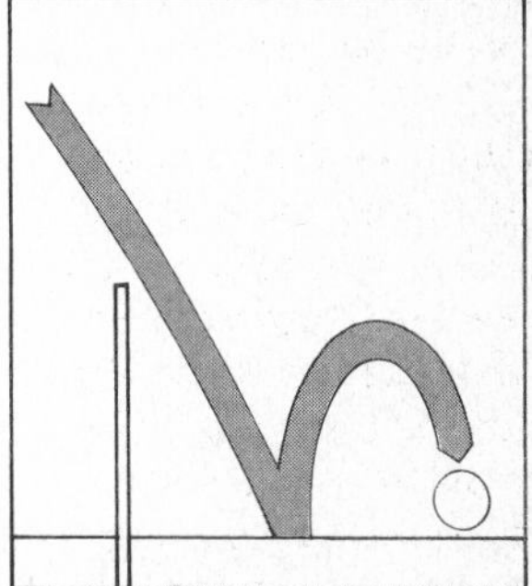

**defensive chop to loop**

You can only use chop against the loop if you take the ball late and well back–at least 10 feet from the table–when most of its spin has been lost. The ball will be low, so the stroke must start at waist height (**1**), and almost reach the floor (**2**). The disadvantage of this return is that the backspin helps your opponent's next loop.

**topspin high defense (lob)**

This is the main defensive stroke in advanced play. The ball is played late, up to 20 feet back from the table, and should go 15 feet or more in the air (ceiling permitting) before bouncing deep to your opponent's base line. Note the low start (**1**), the upward movement to give heavy topspin (**2**), and the high follow-through (**3**).

# Platform tennis

Platform tennis was developed in Scarsdale, New York, in 1928, by two men—Fessenden S. Blanchard and James K. Cogswell—trying to play tennis on a small, wind-swept site. For years it was simply a local New York and New Jersey game. But more recently, under the American Platform Tennis Association, its popularity has spread very rapidly through the U.S.A. (though it is still little known elsewhere).

Like paddle tennis, it is a scaled-down version of tennis, using short-handled paddles instead of racquets. What makes platform tennis different, however, are the taut wire screens around the court. In platform tennis, a ball that bounces in court and then off these screens is still in play—and can be hit back over the net. This gives a player a second chance at his opponent's smashes and passing shots, and the result is a game in which skill counts for more than power. Compared with paddle tennis, it obviously cannot be such good training for full-size tennis; and it is much more expensive to set up. But it perhaps takes even further the important virtues of speed, sociability, rapid success for the novice, and all-year-round outdoor play.

The special feature of platform tennis is the wire court surround, off which the ball may be played.

**court**
The court itself is a scaled-down tennis court, dimensions as shown. Marking lines are 2 inches wide and, as in tennis, count as part of the areas they enclose.

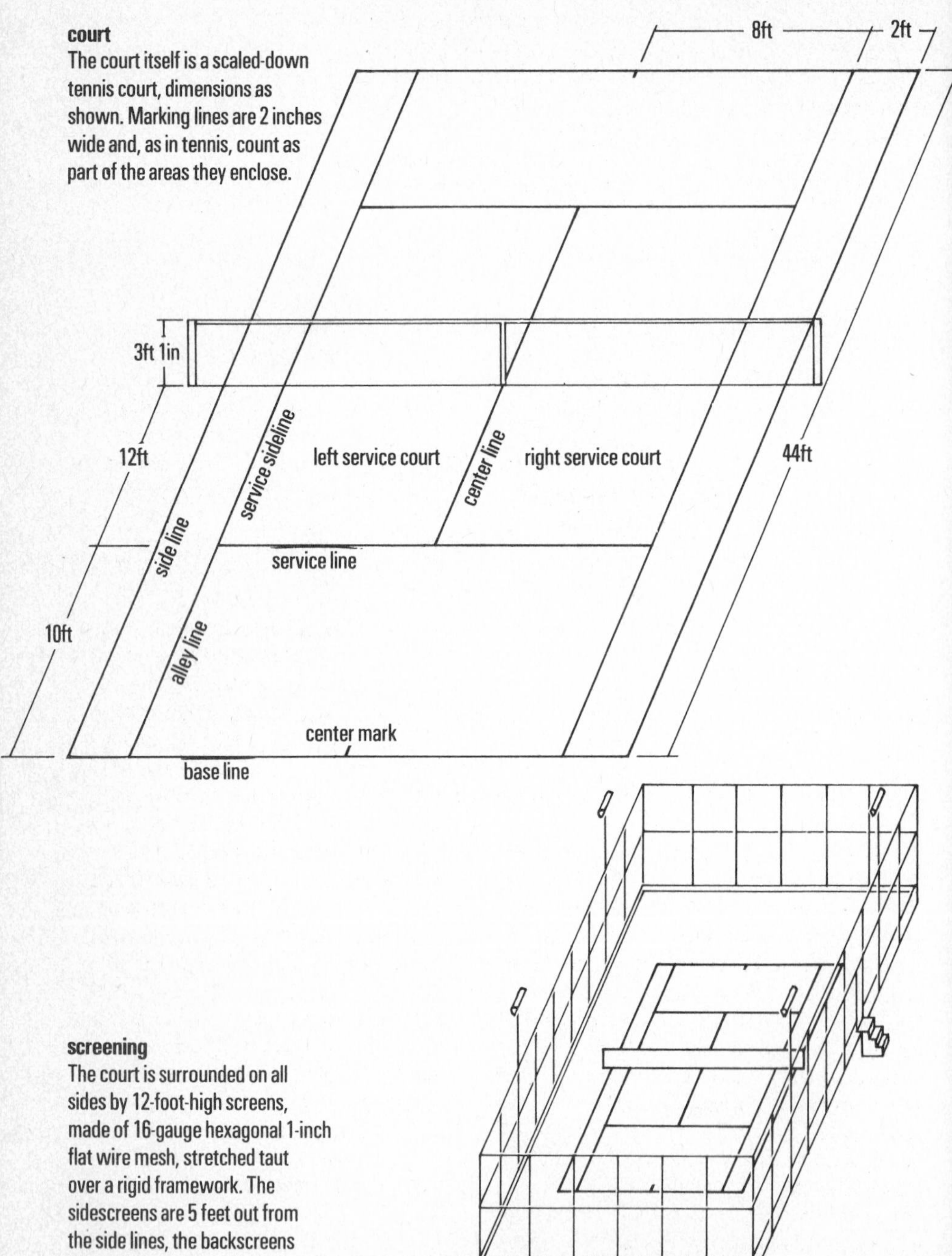


**screening**
The court is surrounded on all sides by 12-foot-high screens, made of 16-gauge hexagonal 1-inch flat wire mesh, stretched taut over a rigid framework. The sidescreens are 5 feet out from the side lines, the backscreens 8 feet back from the base lines.

**platform**
Originally, for outdoor winter use, all courts were built on raised wooden or aluminum platforms, with gates for snow removal. But in warmer climates or indoors, courts may be marked out at ground level on asphalt, concrete, etc.

**singles and doubles**
As in tennis, the side alleys are not used for singles. However, platform tennis is officially always a doubles game. Singles games are only played informally.

**net height**
The net should be 2 feet 10 inches high at the center: the height of two paddles on end.

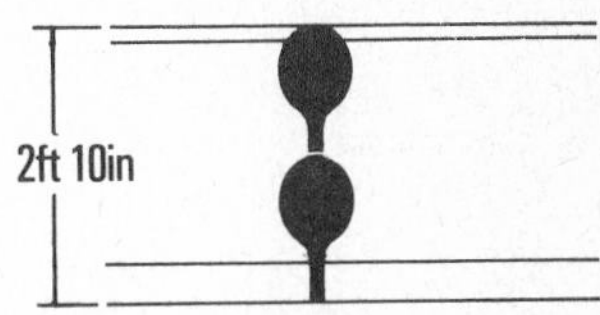


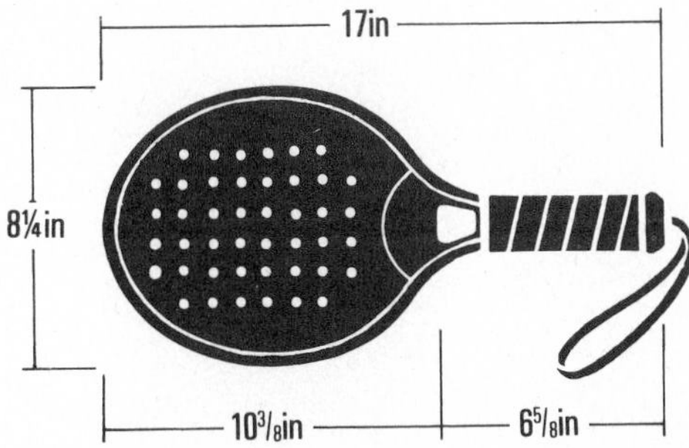


**paddle**
This is oval, with maximum dimensions as shown. The head must be 3/8 inch thick, and flat with a smooth finish. To reduce air resistance the face is perforated with up to 87 holes, each up to 3/8 inch across.
Paddles vary in material and weight. Hardwood (e.g., maple) is traditional; aluminum alloy may absorb more of the ball's impact; plastic is a recent introduction. Wooden paddles for platform tennis usually have a metal or plastic rim or binding to the head, and holes evenly distributed over the face (not in a "U" or "O" shape, as for paddleball). Metal paddles may have only a few holes, but are often open at the throat. Weight differences are more important. Weights vary from 12 to 18 ounces, and it is important to choose a paddle that you find light enough to swing easily. You may also find variations in grip size. Finally, all paddles are made with a wrist strap fixed to the handle, but many players find no use for this so it is better if it is detachable. The rules only allow a player to use one paddle at a time, of course; but he may swap it between his hands at will, or hold it in both at once.

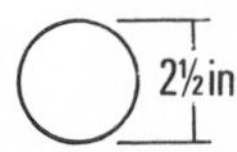


**ball**
The ball is of solid sponge rubber, with a seamless nylon flock coating colored orange or yellow. It is 2½ inches in diameter, weighs 70 to 75 grams, and (at 70° Fahrenheit) rebounds 43 to 48 inches when dropped 90 inches onto a concrete slab. (Balls in this range are divided into "high" and "low" bounce. Skilled players mainly use low bounce, but high bounce balls are easier to keep in play and still give enough rebound in very low temperatures.)
Balls wear out quickly in play, but in competition only one ball may be used per set, unless officials allow otherwise, and the server may only hold one ball when serving.

**dress**
Shorts and shirt are sometimes worn in warm weather or for tournaments. But as platform tennis is mainly a winter game, the usual wear is pants with one or more sweaters. Thin leather gloves are often used to improve grip and keep the hands warm. Shoes wear out quickly: the most suitable have polyurethane soles, well-cushioned insoles, and "breathing" uppers (e.g., canvas, duck, poplin, or denim).

Platform tennis rules are the same as those for standard tennis, with just the following exceptions or clarifications.

**service**

There is only one service for each point. If it is a fault, the server loses the point. (If it is a let, it is retaken.) As in tennis, the rules allow overhand (**a**), underhand (**b**), or sidearm services, at will.

**use of screens**

If the ball bounces once in court and then hits the back or side screens, top bar, or snowboards–or more than one of these–it is still in play (**c**), and can be returned (**d**). It is only dead when it has bounced on the deck twice on the same side of the net (**e**). But a ball cannot be hit back by bouncing it off the screens, etc (**f**). It must be returned directly over the net (**g**).

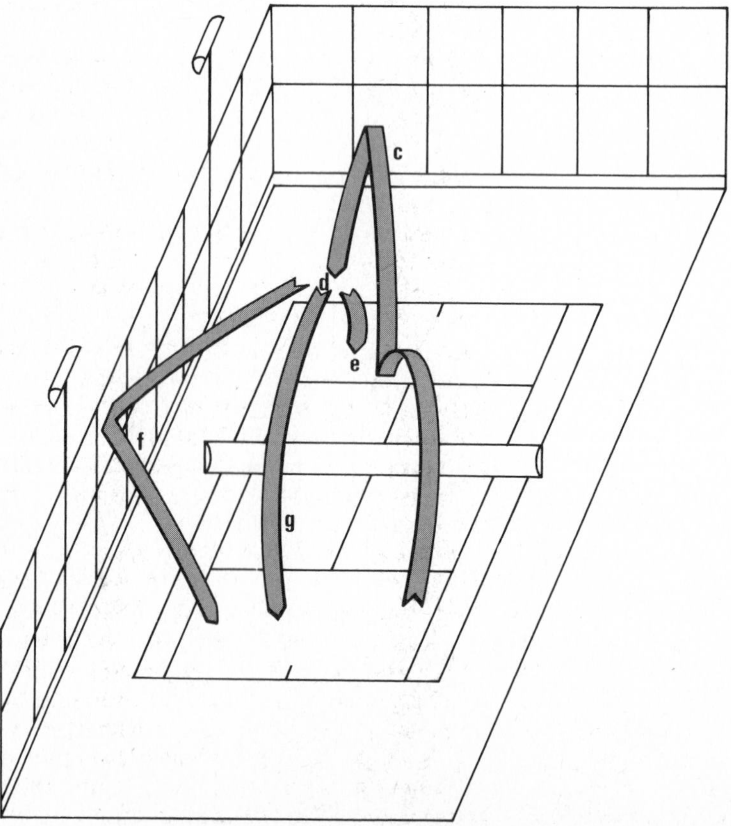

**bad returns**
If the ball hits a light fixture (**h**) or goes over the screen (**i**), the side which last hit it loses the point—even if the ball bounces back in court.
The point is also lost if the ball is hit through the open space between net and post (**j**); or if the ball so much as grazes against a player, his hand, or his clothes.

**lets**
It is a let, and the point is played for again, if:
the ball hits a crossbar (**k**);
or the ball becomes broken during play;
or play is interrupted by an accidental occurrence outside players' control (such as a ball from another court).
But a let must be claimed as soon as it occurs.

**double hits**
If the ball nicks the edge of a paddle, this counts as a hit, and that side cannot hit it again to return it.
But if they merely clash paddles in playing the ball, the return is good so long as only one of them actually hit the ball.
(A side should always admit when a nick has occurred.)

**touching the net**
Note that if a player is standing at the net, and an opponent hits the ball into the net so the net is pushed against the net player or his paddle , the net player loses the point, because he touched the net while the ball was still in play.

**foot faults and line calls**
Where there are no officials, the receivers have the right to make all service fault calls and line calls, so long as they do so promptly. In a case of doubt, they should accept the ball. Foot faults, in fact, are often ignored. If they are called, the first call against a side is treated as a let, not a fault.

**duration**
A match is normally the best of three sets, but the best of five is used in the finals of men's tournaments. A rest period between sets may be allowed; also a 10-minute suspension for injury or difficulty with clothing or equipment.

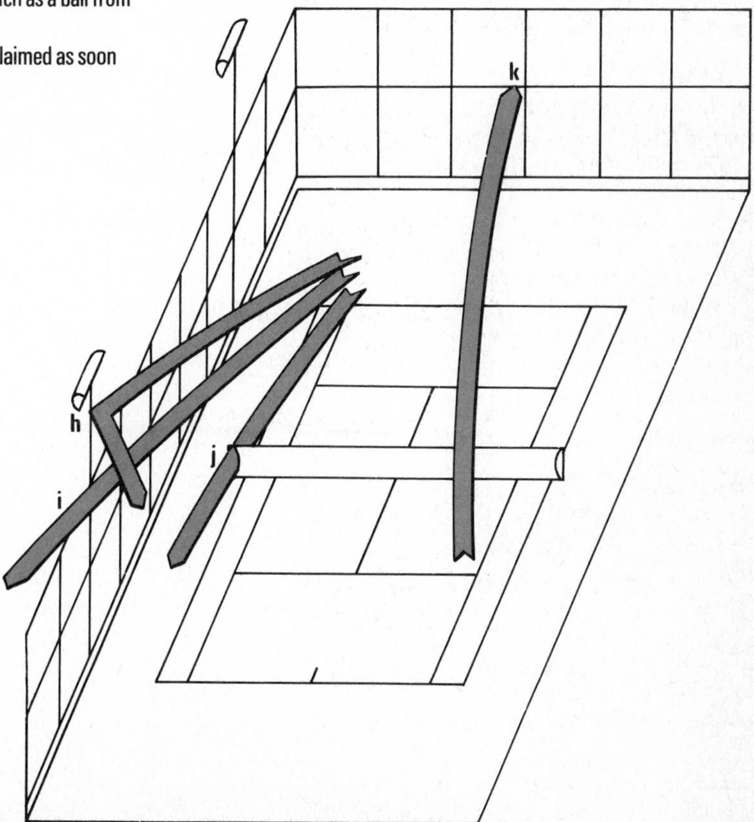

**grip and stance**

For the forehand grip, "shake hands" with the paddle handle. The V between thumb and index finger should come on top of the handle; the fingers should be close together, and the grip firm. For the backhand grip, turn the hand slightly to the left. Ready stance is as for tennis (p.41).

forehand grip

backhand grip

**forehand drive**

From the ready stance:
turn sideways, taking the paddle back (**1**);
step forward as you complete the backswing (**2**) (note the fairly open stance);
and swing paddle and body forward into the stroke, keeping your knees bent, and making contact just in front of you at waist height (**3**).
Follow through.

**backhand drive**

From the ready stance:
turn sideways, taking the paddle back, keeping the knees bent (**1**);
step into the stroke, swinging the paddle forward (**2**) (note the closed stance);
and make contact in front of your front foot, as your weight swings forward (**3**).
Follow through.

**service**

The grip is between forehand and backhand. Compared with a tennis service (pp.44-45), note how the paddle comes up in front of the body. The ball is tossed some way in front of you, so that you lean forward into the stroke. But be careful not to touch down on the platform in front of the base line until after you have hit the ball, or it is a foot fault.

**other strokes**
For the lob, you must get the paddle beneath the ball, and lift as you follow through. For the overhead (or smash), you must get the paddle above the ball: cock the paddle back into the backscratcher position, then reach up to hit the ball downward as your weight comes forward. The volley is a simple block or punch, with the knees bent to keep the body low.

**picking up rebounds**
A simple lob usually works here. The problem is getting into position for it–judging correctly where the rebound will go. Generally you must keep out from the screen, and let the ball come out past you (**a**). But sometimes you must run in to scoop it back (**b**), or reach to take it off a side screen (**c**). Often you need a backhand stroke.

**stroke play**
The screens make the game very different from regular tennis. Power and deep placing count for little: your opponent can simply let the ball bounce off the screens before taking it. Also the small court and doubles play make stamina (and a good backhand) less important. Instead, emphasis is on fast reactions, and on skill, restraint, and patience in placing the ball (especially on the service, because only one is allowed, and the back screens prevent aces). Use of spin is general–usually topspin on forehand shots and backspin on backhand ones. Topspin is applied by rolling the paddle over the ball, backspin by keeping the paddle face open and flicking the wrist on impact. The drop volley with heavy backspin is a very frequent point winner.

**teamwork**
In doubles, teamwork is very important. Partners usually keep alongside each other, moving forward together for attack and back for defense. As one has to move, the other should follow. The stronger player usually covers the lefthand court–unless there is a lefthander to do so. But partners have to keep surprising their opponents by switching courts and–especially–by "poaching" (i.e., volleying balls that are going into the partner's half of the court). Constant verbal instruction between partners is important. (A ball straight down the middle is usually taken by whichever player can take it on his forehand.)

**tactics**
The basic tactic is for both partners to try to get together at the net and volley. A server will usually try to follow his service in. But the platform tennis service travels at only half the speed of a tennis service, and bounces higher. This allows the return of service to be an attacking stroke–usually a forehand topspin drive, between the opponents, or down the alley, or sharply angled to the sideline. Alternatively, the service can be taken off the screen with a lob stroke.

# Paddleball

Paddleball is the game from which racquetball grew: it is racquetball played with solid paddles. But this gives it a completely different character. It is a tough, aggressive game, emphasizing power shots and body-blocking, and often used by sportsmen to keep fit during their off season. Doubles is the main form; singles games are usually less competitive, with few long rallies. And, while most racquetball is played in four-wall courts, a much higher proportion of paddleball games are either the one-wall or the three-wall variety.

Just as racquetball eventually developed from paddleball, so paddleball developed from handball. This happened at the University of Michigan, in the 1920s. Tennis and paddle tennis players there used to practice their strokes in vacant handball courts; and as most of them were also handball players, they gradually realized that paddles and handball could be combined in a new game. The result was still being played at the university during the Second World War, when thousands of armed forces members passed through on training programs; were taught paddleball as part of their physical conditioning; and so spread the game to their bases and, after the war, to their homes. Later, in 1961, the first national tournament brought local groups together, and for a time it was a very fast-growing sport—though hampered by a variety of rules and governing bodies. Today it seems to have been overtaken by the spectacular rise of racquetball. But even if it now seems unlikely to spread internationally, paddleball remains a significant North American sport, with its own appeal and with several thousand enthusiastic players.

ROSENBERG
BRUSCHI
HAMMER

Paddleball inherited from court handball its courts and many of its rules.

**courts**
Paddleball is played on four-wall, three-wall, and one-wall courts. All are exactly the same as those now used for racquetball: for the four-wall court, see p.96; for the three-wall and one-wall courts, p.104. Court materials vary, and can affect the bounce of the ball and so the style of play.

**governing bodies**
The main areas in which paddleball is now played in the U.S.A. are the northern Mid-West and the New York area. Four different organizations govern this following and publish rules. The National Paddle Ball Association (NPA) organizes the Mid-West area. It is mainly concerned with the four-wall game, but also publishes three-wall and one-wall rules. The American Paddleball Association (APA) and the United States Paddleball Association (USPbA), together with the Professional Paddleball Association, organize the New York and East Coast following. They publish a joint set of rules, and are concerned only with the one-wall game.

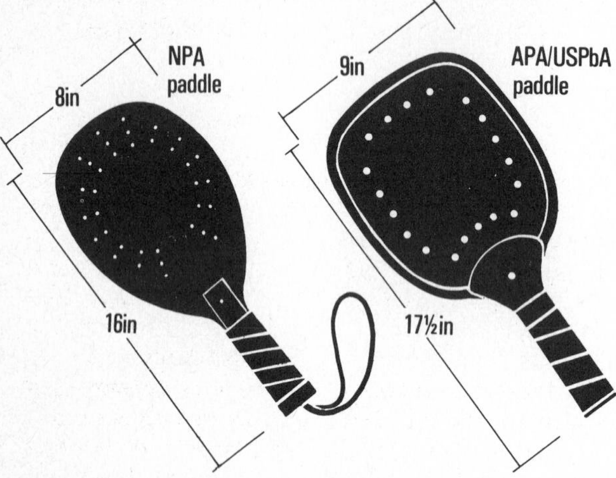


**paddle**
Under NPA rules, the paddle must be of wood, with approximate dimensions as shown, and weighing about 16 ounces. A leather thong must be fixed to the handle and worn around the wrist during play. APA/USPbA rules specify the maximum length and width shown, and require that any exposed metal or wooden edge be covered with tape. (The surface of the paddle may also be covered with adhesive tape, but not so as to create a rough-textured surface.) All rules prohibit strung racquets.
Paddles vary in shape, material, weight, and grip size. Some have perforations in the face, and these possibly reduce air resistance. Get advice on choosing a paddle to suit both yourself and the form of the game you will be playing.
The paddle handle should be covered with nonslip material for a good grip. Some players also use rosin or proprietary "sure-grip" sprays.

**ball**
NPA rules specify an official brand of ball: the Pennsy Official National Paddleball ("Pennsy Purple"), made by General Tire-Pennsylvania Athletic Products, Akron, Ohio. When dropped from 6 feet it should rebound about 3½ feet. APA/USPbA rules require a rubber ball measuring $1\frac{7}{8}$ inches in diameter (with $\frac{1}{32}$ inch tolerance) and weighing $2\frac{3}{10}$ ounces (with $\frac{1}{5}$ ounce tolerance). When dropped from 70 inches (at 68° Fahrenheit) it should rebound 44 to 52 inches.

**clothes**
Usual dress for paddleball is shirt and shorts, and sports shoes (sneakers). For playing outdoors in cold weather, a sweat suit is needed. Tournament dress must be white or light-colored. Useful accessories include head and wrist sweatbands. Gloves, and knee and elbow pads of soft material, are also allowed. For safety, eyeguards (or shatterproof prescription lenses) are very important, and protective helmets or padded hats are also often used.

All rules for four-wall paddleball are the same as for four-wall racquetball—except as specifically noted here.

**the service**
In paddleball, a "fault" is called an "illegal service," and an "out" is called a "serve out." But the actual rules are exactly the same as for racquetball, except for the following.
a) It is not in itself a serve out if the server happens to bounce the ball outside the serving zone when serving (he simply attempts the bounce again).
But it is a serve out if the server bounces the ball anywhere more than twice before serving it, or if the ball happens to hit the side wall when it is bounced by the server.
b) It is not given as a serve out if the server wets the ball (although the general rules require paddle and ball to be kept dry).
c) The service is taken again (i.e., what racquetball calls a "dead ball"), if the rebound passes so close to the server as to obstruct his opponent's stroke (as well as if it obstructs his view).

**playing the point**
The rules are exactly as for racquetball, except that:
the receiving lines are not always marked;
when receiving service, a player has to remain 5 feet behind the short line only until the ball is struck by the server;
a good return is called a "volley";
and it is an illegal return if the player does not have the safety thong of his paddle around his wrist.
If a receiver plays a service before it has bounced, no part of his body may cross the short line.

**ball out of court**
Unlike racquetball, if the ball goes out of court (before bouncing twice on the floor) the last player to hit it loses the rally.

**hinders**
In paddleball, a "dead ball hinder" is called an "unintentional hinder," and an "available hinder" is called an "intentional hinder." But the actual rules are as for racquetball, except that:
it is also an unintentional hinder in paddleball if there is any unintentional interference or crowding—even if the opponent still reached and/or struck the ball;
and it is also an intentional hinder if there is any intentional blocking of an opponent's movement by moving into his path;
but it is judged an unintentional rather than an intentional hinder if a player moves and is hit by the ball his opponent has just played, before it reaches the front wall (i.e., the point is replayed).
In general, paddleball rules warn that a player must give his opponent a fair chance to see, reach, and/or strike the ball from any part of the court, and to play the ball to any wall. (However, in competition play a paddleball player may not call any hinders—not even contact on backswing.)

**incidents**
Rules for a ball hitting a player, and for other incidents, are as in racquetball—except that the point is not replayed if a player loses any equipment.

**winning**
If the score in a match reaches one game all, the third game is played out in full; there is no 11-point tiebreaker.

**officials**
The referee's decision is always final. But he has no point penalty to impose (only loss-of-match, for refusal to abide by his decision).

**interruptions**
a) rest periods. Rules are the same as IRA racquetball rules, but with only 2 minutes between the first and second games.
b) time outs. A side is allowed only two per game, and there is no extra time out for faulty equipment.
c) injury. As for racquetball.
d) deliberate delaying. A side loses the service or a point for any deliberate delaying.

**doubles service**
All rules are exactly as for racquetball, except that:
the server's partner must have his back actually against the wall, in the service box;
and it is only an out if the served ball hits him when he is out of the box.

**doubles returns**
It is still a good return if both partners happen to strike at and hit the ball simultaneously.

The following rules for the one-wall game have been agreed by the American Paddleball Association and the United States Paddleball Association. Doubles is the usual game in one-wall paddleball, but singles matches are also played. So in these rules the "sides" referred to can be singles players or doubles partnerships.

**the service**
It is a good service if -
the server bounces the ball once on the floor, inside the serving zone (**1**)
and hits it on the rebound (**2**)
so it goes to the front wall without touching the floor (**3**)
and then rebounds to touch in court behind the short line (**4**).
(In singles there are further limitations: see "singles service.")

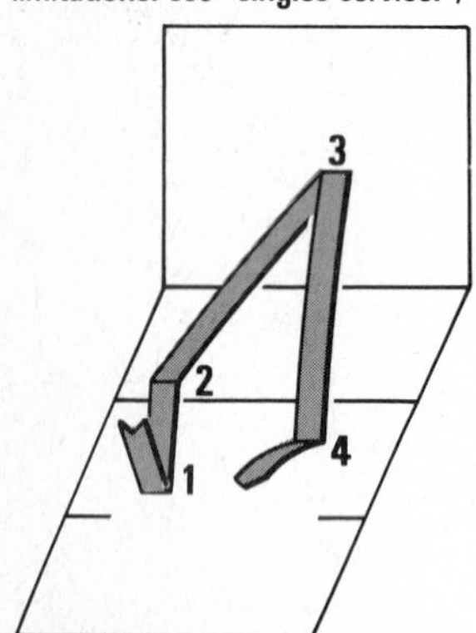


**serving position**
The server may stand anywhere in the serving zone, but must have both feet in the zone. As he serves, his paddle may pass over the short line or side lines, but not go back over the service line (i.e., the imaginary line between the service markers).
Once he has served, he may move beyond the short or side lines; but he may not go back over the service line until the receiving side has played the ball.

**server's partner**
In doubles, while the service is being made, the server's partner must stand outside one side line, between the short line and the service marker, and must not leave this position until the served ball has passed him on its way back from the front wall.

**defective services**
There are two types of defective service: faults, and outs.
a) If a player makes a "fault" service, he must attempt the service again. If he serves two faults in succession, the service passes to his opponent (or, in doubles, to the next player in the serving order).
b) If a player makes an "out" service, the service passes immediately.

**outs**
It is an out service if:
the server serves out of turn;
or he misses the ball;
or he hits it twice in serving;
or the ball hits the floor before it hits the front wall;
or it comes back from the front wall to go out of court across the side lines before bouncing;
or the server (or his partner in doubles) crosses the service line before the receiving side has played the ball.
Note that a service can become an out service even if it has already become a fault.

**faults**
It is a fault if:
the server crosses the short or side lines as he serves (it is not a fault if just his paddle crosses them);
or his paddle crosses the service line as he serves;
or he makes more than three practice bounces before serving;
or he hits the ball before it has bounced on the floor;
or he hits it after it has bounced twice on the floor;
or (in doubles) the server's partner does not stand in the correct position during the service, or leaves it before the served ball has passed him on the rebound;
or the served ball passes between the legs of the server or his partner;
or it comes back from the front wall to touch the floor in front of the short lines;
or it comes back from the front wall to go out of court beyond the long line (between the extensions of the side lines) before bouncing.
Note that the last is a fault even if the receiving side tries to volley the ball and misses it; but if it is played before it bounces, it is a good service.

**first service**
At the start of the match, a coin is tossed, and the side that wins the toss has the choice of serving or receiving first in the first game (and again in the third game, if there is one). The other side has the choice whether to serve or receive first in the second game.

**losing the service**
A player's turn of service ends if:
he makes an out service;
or he makes two fault services in succession;
or during a rally his side fails to keep the ball in play with a good return;
or his side makes any other action that loses it the rally.
In singles, when one player loses the service, it passes to his opponent. In doubles, it passes to the next player in the serving order.

**the rally**
Once the ball has been served correctly, the opposing sides hit it alternately, until one side fails to make a good return. If it is the serving side that eventually does this, no point is scored, but the service passes to the opposing side (or, in doubles, to the next player in the serving order). If it is the receiving side that fails to make the good return, the serving side scores one point, and the same player serves again for the next point. Only the serving side can score points.

**calling the scores**
After each point, the score is called: e.g., "13-19." (The score of the side making the next service is given first, and the next server makes the call if there is no scorer or other official.)

**receiving service**
Once the rally is under way, players may play from anywhere in the court, except as limited by the safety rules. But to receive service, the receiving side must stand behind the service line (whether in or out of court); and the receiver who plays the return must hit the ball and complete his follow-through without his body or his paddle crossing the service line.
If either of these rules is broken, the serving side wins one point.

**good returns**
For a good return, a player must -
hit the ball before it has bounced twice on the floor (**1**)
so it goes back to the front wall without touching the floor (**2**)
and then comes back to land in court (**3**).
It does not matter if the ball has not bounced when he hits it.
Note that if a player tries to play the ball but misses, both he and his partner may go on trying to hit it, until it has touched the floor twice. Also note that a player is allowed to switch his paddle from one hand to the other.

**losing the rally**
The offending side loses the rally if:
on its turn, a side fails to play the ball before it has bounced twice;
or a player hits the ball twice in trying to return it;
or (in doubles) a player and his partner hit the ball in succession;
or a player hits the ball so it touches the ground out of court over the side lines or long line – either on its way to the front wall, or coming back from the front wall before bouncing in court;
or the ball hits the floor on its way to the front wall;
or it hits the junction of front wall and floor, striking both simultaneously.
A side also loses the rally in some cases of safety infringement, obstruction, body contact, and contact between ball and player.
Loss of the rally may also be given as a penalty for some offenses.

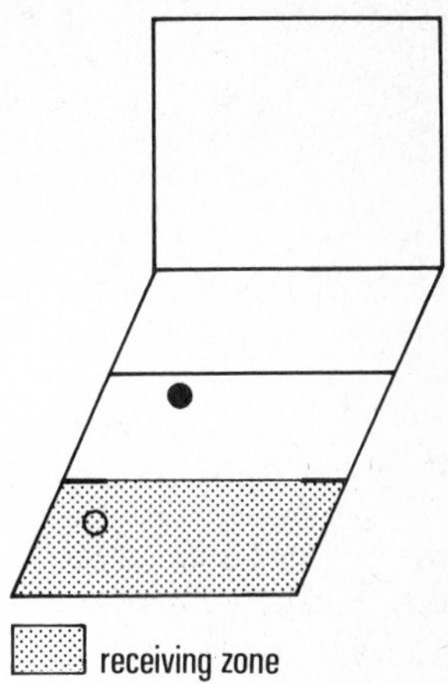


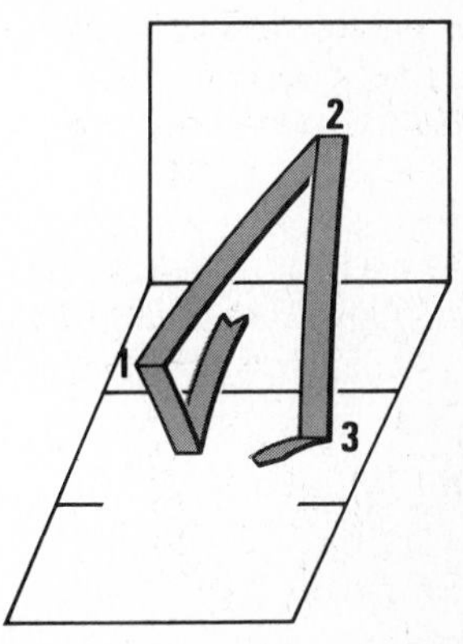

**singles service**

In singles, the server must indicate before his service which side of his serving position the service will return.

This is done by imagining that the court is divided into three segments (**a**). The segment running through the server's position is called the automatic fault area. The larger of the two remaining areas is called the major service area, the smaller the minor service area. If the server is going to serve into the minor service area, he simply points to it before serving. If he is going to serve to the major area, he makes no gesture.

It is a fault if:

the ball comes back to bounce in the automatic fault area;

or the server points to the minor area, and then the ball comes back to bounce in the major area;

or the server does not point to a service area, and then the ball comes back to bounce in the minor area.

The width of the automatic fault area is the width of the extreme right and left foot positions of the server. If he moves during his service action, all the area between his starting and finishing positions is included (**b**).

If the server's position (or movement) creates two equal service areas, both count as minor areas (**c**). So, for his service to be good, he must have pointed to one of these and served to it.

If the automatic fault area lies against one of the side lines (**d**), there is no minor service area.

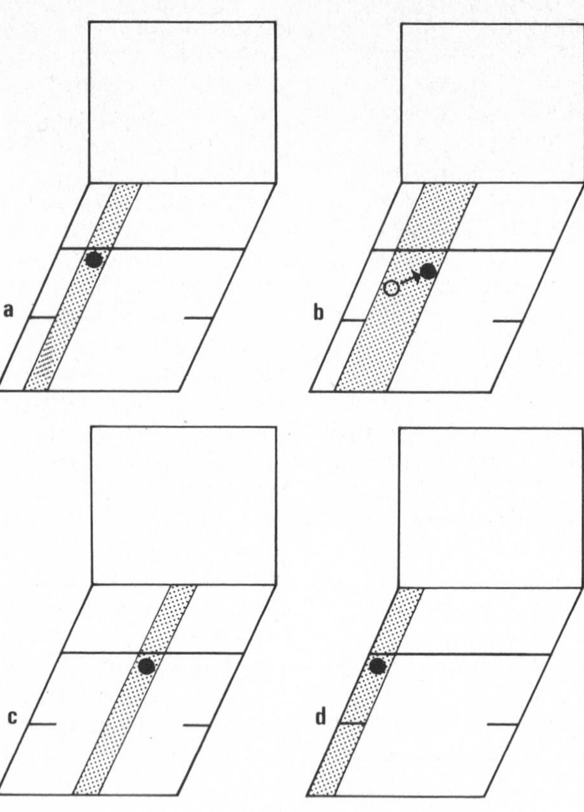


**doubles serving order**

Each side decides its serving order at the beginning of each game, and must keep to that order throughout the game.

Both players of a side normally have a turn of service, in order, before the service passes to the other side. But at the start of a game only the first server, of the side serving first, has a turn of service before his side loses the service.

For example, suppose a and b are playing x and y, and a and b have the right to the first service in the game that is about to start. So a and b decide which of them will serve first – they choose a, for example; and x and y decide which of them will serve first – they choose x, for example. Then in the game each player serves until he loses the service, in the order: a, x, y, a, b, x, y, a, b, x, y, etc.

**winning**
Each game is won by the first side to score 21 points – except that, if the scores are separated by only one point, play continues until one side has a two-point lead. A match consists of a previously agreed number of games (usually three), and is won by a side as soon as it wins more than half that number.

**officials**
The officials for competition play are referee, scorer, and linesmen. The linesmen call outs and faults. The referee governs the game, and can penalize certain offenses.

**blocks**
A "block" means that the point is replayed (though any service fault still stands). There are three types of block.
a) safety block. A player must claim this by calling "block" and not playing the ball. It must have been his side's turn to play the ball, and he must have been in a position to play it. For the circumstances in which it should be called, see "safety." Play stops, and the referee then rules on the call. If he agrees with it, the point is replayed. If not, the calling side loses the rally.
b) unintentional block. For the circumstances in which this should be called, see "obstruction." It is called like the safety block, but the player must continue to play the ball if he can, and play stops only if the referee indicates that he agrees by calling "stop." If he stays silent, play continues.
c) other blocks. In some other situations a block is called automatically by the referee.

**safety**
If a player thinks there is a danger of his paddle striking an opponent, he must call "block" and not play the ball. The referee may also stop play if he thinks there is this danger. If a player does not call a block in a danger situation, he may be penalized. He is also penalized if he does hit his opponent in playing the ball, unless the referee rules that the player did not have a reasonable view of his opponent, or that the opponent moved into the area of the swing. (In the last case, if it was deliberate, the opponent may be penalized.)
If there is unintentional contact on a backswing, the referee calls a block. If there is contact on a follow-through, after hitting the ball, the referee judges from the circumstances whether to stop play and whether to impose a penalty.

**body contact**
If a player pushes or pushes off an opponent (intentionally or unintentionally), his side loses the rally.

**obstruction**
a) interference with movement. It is an unintentional block if a player of the side that has just played the ball moves in a way that interferes with an opponent's ability to move or chance to play the ball. (But the opponent need not claim the block if he thinks the movement has also put the obstructor's side at a disadvantage.)
b) ball passing between opponent's legs. This is a block only if the player calling it otherwise had a reasonable chance to play the ball.
c) obstruction of opponent in pursuit of ball. If an opponent moving backward in pursuit of the ball is unintentionally obstructed, it is a block. Any deliberate obstruction of any movement to the ball means loss of the rally.
d) taking position. A side loses the rally if one member moves alongside or in front of an opponent while the other is playing the ball.
e) "cutting down wall." If a player deliberately moves so as to block or partly block an opponent's chance of playing the ball to the wall, his side loses the rally.
f) vision block. If an opponent's static position impedes a player's view of the ball it is not a block. But if an opponent's movement impedes a player's view, it is a block.

**ball hitting player**

a) If the ball hits an opponent on its way to the front wall, it is a block and the point is replayed – provided the referee judges that it would have been a good return. (If he rules otherwise, the side that played the ball loses the rally.)

b) If a player is hit by a ball his own side has just played, his side loses the rally (even if a block has been called.)

c) If a player deliberately stops the ball reaching the front wall, his side loses the rally.

d) If the ball comes back past both players of the side that should be returning it – so they clearly have no chance of doing so – and then hits an opponent after bouncing in court, the opponent's side still wins the rally. If it hits the opponent before bouncing in court, the referee rules whether it would have bounced in court. If it would, his side again wins the rally; if not, it was a bad return by his side, and they lose the rally.

e) If, in playing the ball, a player hits it with his playing hand below the wrist, it is not an offense.

**interruptions**

A side must be ready to serve or receive within 10 seconds of the announcement of the score after the last point. The only approved interruptions are as follows.

a) rest periods. Five minutes are allowed between the first and second games of a match, and 10 minutes between second and third. Also a side winning a semifinal may choose to rest for one hour before playing in the final.

b) time outs. During a game, when the ball is not in play, a side may at any time ask for a "time out" – to dry hands, wipe glasses, adjust clothing or equipment, etc. Each time out must not last more than one minute, and a side may not have more than three in any one game.

c) injury. If a player is injured by an opponent, and the opponent is disqualified as a result, the injured player's side wins the match. But if he is unable to start the next match on time, his side loses that match (except that in doubles his partner may start playing alone, until the injured player recovers). If a player is injured (or unable to go on playing due to some other result of an opponent's action), and the referee rules that the opponent should not be disqualified, then the injured player's side is allowed up to 5 minutes' injury time out. But his side loses the match if he is not ready to play at the end of this, or not ready to start the next game or match on time (except that again, in doubles his partner may start playing alone, until the injured player recovers).

d) other interruptions. If play is interrupted during a rally for reasons outside players' control, the rally is void and the point is served for again (but any preceding fault still stands).

**offenses and penalties**

Offenses include:
unsportsmanlike conduct;
leaving court without the referee's permission;
failing to report for play within 15 minutes of the scheduled time;
using more than minimum conversation during play;
deliberate delaying;
and deliberately hitting or throwing the ball out of the playing area so it is lost.

Penalties include: loss of the rally, and a warning; loss of the match; and removal from the competition.

---

**NPA three-wall / one-wall rules**

The NPA also publishes rules for three-wall and one-wall paddleball. These are exactly the same as NPA four-wall rules (p. 151), with just the following exceptions or modifications.

a) serving zone. This is the area between the short line and the service lines.

b) good service. The ball must come back to touch the floor in court behind the short line. (In the three-wall game, it may touch a side wall on the way back.)

c) illegal services. It is also an illegal service if:
the ball comes back to bounce beyond the end line, between the extensions of the side lines; or (in three-wall) the ball hits both side walls before touching the floor.

d) serve outs. It is also a serve out if the ball comes back to pass over a side wall or side line without having bounced once on the floor.

e) server's partner. He must stand outside the service line, between short line and service marker. It is an illegal service if he leaves this position before the served ball passes the short line.

f) receiving position. The receiver(s) must stand behind the service line until the ball passes the short line.

### grip

Several grips are used in one-wall paddleball. The most common is the Eastern grip, which is exactly the same as the racquetball forehand grip (p.105). But a good grip for beginners is the choke grip shown: note the position of the forefinger. Neither of these grips is changed for the backhand, in paddleball: the wrist turns to adjust the paddle's angle.

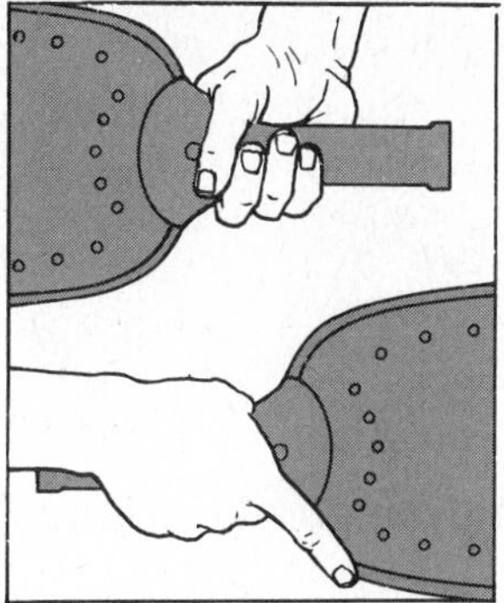

### four-wall skills

The skills for the four-wall game are almost exactly as for racquetball: please study pp. 105-111. The main difference is that, due to a less lively ball, ceiling balls and around-the-wall balls are not played. Instead, the lob shot is important – arcing slowly back to graze the side wall deep on the opponent's backhand, before dropping into the back corner.

### forehand stroke

Many shots have to be rushed. From your ready position (p.18), just pivot the paddle back at waist height, leaving your feet square to the front wall (**1**). On the stroke (**2**), let the paddle lead your arm, as you pivot back. Meet the ball just in front of you as your weight comes forward, and follow through across your body (**3**).

From the back court there is time for a full-blooded swing (**a**). Also for extra power you can cock your wrist on the backswing and snap it on impact (**b**). But for this you need the Eastern grip; with the choke grip the wrist should be kept locked. Finally, switching hands (**c**) gives you forehand shots on your backhand side (note: this is not allowed in the four-wall game).

### backhand stroke

The action here is similar, but: your backswing takes the paddle higher, and there is usually time for you to slide your left foot back for a less square stance (**1**); your elbow leads into the stroke, and your arm should straighten only just before impact (**2**); and the follow-through carries high to your forehand side (**3**).

**overhead service**
This is the most effective service. Throw the ball down for a high rebound, as paddle and body weight swing back (**1**). Then let the paddle tip over into the backscratcher position (**2**), before you uncoil to meet the ball at full stretch (**3**). Aim about three-quarters of the way up the wall, for a rebound to the back court.

**underarm service**
This is used mainly in singles. Toss the ball away from you for a low rebound (**1**), and move after it with a cross-step as you backswing (**2**), before stepping into the stroke (**3**). Bend low to meet the ball near your front leg, snapping your wrist for the impact. Follow through high to your left shoulder. Alternatively, serve sidearm from a static stance.

**volleying**
About half of all paddleball shots are volleys, so a good ready stance is vital. On backhand and forehand shots, use the basic short stroke. On shots that come straight at you, try to get sideways to the wall (**a**); but if there is no time, keep a square stance and take the ball on the backhand in front of you, with an open paddle angle (**b**). On half volleys, reach low for the ball (**c**).

lob

**other strokes**
For the lob (left), use the basic stroke, but with open paddle (**1**) and upward follow-through (**2**). If rushed, simply place the angled paddle in the ball's path. For overhead lobs and drives (right), do not just reach above your head: swing back (**1**), then up (**2**). Angle the paddle for the shot you want. But for an overhead smash, use an action like the service.

overhead

These subject guides are meant to be more useful to you than a normal index. Rules are dealt with on this page, skills on the next. The key letters tell you which sport is referred to:
(t) tennis
(b) badminton
(is) International squash
(as) North American Squash
(r) racquetball
(pt) paddle tennis
(tt) table tennis
(plt) platform tennis
(p) paddleball
(i) basics common to most of these games.
Note: (p1) refers to one-wall paddleball, and (p4) to the four-wall game.

**RULES**

## SKILLS

(For the skills of four-wall paddleball, please see note on p. 157.)